Losing Control

D1646077

Praise for *Losing Control*

'In this short, profoundly serious but immensely readable book Paul Rogers challenges a great number of widely held, comfortable, assumptions. His analysis can also be challenged and his conclusions debated, but what he has to say should not be ignored. Many officials will disagree with him; it would be strange if they did not. The book, however, is a "must-read" for anyone caught up in international security from the dabbling amateur, through erudite academics, to committed policy-makers. Paul Rogers is one of those dangerous people who can change your mind; at the least he will stimulate your thinking.' Former Director, Rear Admiral Richard Cobbold CB FRAeS, Royal United Services Institute for Defence Studies

'The current security paradigm is essentially one of an elite global community of around one billion people, mainly but not only located in western states, maintaining control of a global system that works continually to their advantage. *Losing Control* argues that attempts to maintain this unjust world order in the interests of that minority elite are unsustainable and will, instead, increase the risk of instability and conflict. It calls for a radical re-thinking of western perceptions of security that embraces a willingness to address the core issues of global insecurity.' *Peace Studies News*

'*Losing Control* combines a glimpse behind the security screens with sharp analysis of the real global insecurities – growing inequality and unsustainability.' *The New Internationalist*

'Rogers' thesis should worry many politicians and strategists: for its key point is that the principal causes of future insecurity and conflict for everybody are a) the widening gap between rich and poor in the world, and b) the environmental crisis, most notably climate change... *Losing Control* suggests that a very wide range of organisations, from the Zapatista National Liberation Army in Mexico to the Tamil Tigers in Sri Lanka... are products of unfulfilled expectations all over the developing world. It makes very little difference if each organisation has its own exclusive ideology, or is chronically riven with internecine squabbling. What matters is the pattern of wholesale revolt against the hegemony of the rich world which the emergence of these organisations represents, and which was dramatised on TV at Seattle, Prague and Nice.' *The Tablet*

'Analysing global security, the book argues that the current Western security posture is one of elite societies maintaining their power in an increasingly divided and environmentally constrained world.' *Oxfam Review of Journals*

'*Losing Control* makes a convincing case for a new – and more compassionate – concept of security.' *Peace News*

'This book combines enthusiasm for the details of military technology and strategy with a radical view of militarism, the US and world politics. The argument spans the Cold War and post-Cold War years, and the basic point is that the rich global core of capitalism cannot remain secure if a large periphery remains impoverished and excluded.' *International Affairs*

'If you only read one book on global foreign policy this year, do read this one. And ask your local public library to buy a copy and put it on display.' *Green Socialist*

'No security policy adviser worth their salt can afford to be without this book.' Dr Scilla Elworthy, Founder, Oxford Research Group

Paul Rogers

Losing Control

Global Security in the Twenty-first Century

Third edition

PLUTO  PRESS

First published 2001
Third edition published 2010 by Pluto Press
345 Archway Road, London N6 5AA and
175 Fifth Avenue, New York, NY 10010

www.plutobooks.com

British Library Cataloguing in Publication Data
A catalogue record for this book is available from the British Library

ISBN   978 0 7453 2938 3   Hardback
ISBN   978 0 7453 2937 6   Paperback

Library of Congress Cataloging in Publication Data applied for

This book is printed on paper suitable for recycling and made from fully managed and sustained forest sources. Logging, pulping and manufacturing processes are expected to conform to the environmental standards of the country of origin.

10   9   8   7   6   5   4   3   2   1

Designed and produced for Pluto Press by
Chase Publishing Services Ltd, 33 Livonia Road, Sidmouth, EX10 9JB England
Typeset from disk by Stanford DTP Services, Northampton, England

To Zoë Frances

... it was a dangerous world and we knew exactly who the 'they' were. It was us versus them and we knew exactly who them was. Today we're not so sure who the 'they' are, but we know they're there.

George W. Bush
January 2000

Contents

Introduction to the First Edition

It has been a delight to work at Bradford University's Department of Peace Studies for the past 20 years, not least because of the hundreds of people who have come to study there from all over the world, many of whom have first-hand experience of the disastrous effects of war and are personally committed to the peaceful resolution of conflict. This book is the product, in part, of innumerable discussions and arguments with past and present students.

Similarly, there have been many opportunities to share views with development and peace activists at meetings in many parts of Britain and abroad, often organised by local UNA, Quaker, WDM, Oxfam or CND groups. Some of these ideas have also been explored at meetings of the Development Studies Association and the British International Studies Association, at several defence colleges in Britain, Belgium and Germany, at conferences in Bangladesh, Iran, India, Morocco and South Africa, and with successive groups of students at the Universitat Jaume I at Castellon in Spain. In all cases, though, the responsibility for the end result must be entirely my own.

Some parts of the book have arisen from other pieces of work. Chapter 2, on the lessons of the Cold War, has been developed from a chapter in *Deconstructing and Reconstructing the Cold War*, edited by Alan Dobson, that was originally written for a seminar involving staff and students of the Politics Department at the University of Wales, Swansea. Chapter 3 has been condensed and updated from a research report produced for the British American Security Information Council in 1996, in which the co-authors were Simon Whitby and Stephen Young.

The material on economic targeting by paramilitary groups stems from a detailed study of the strategy of the Provisional IRA published from the Department of Peace Studies in 1996. That study was greatly aided by discussions with James O'Connell, Michael Mullan, Michael Page, Redmond Mullins, Malcolm Dando and Simon Whitby. Jenny Pearce was helpful in providing me with material on developments in Latin America.

More generally, I am indebted to Malcolm Dando, co-author of *A Violent Peace* (1992), one of our earlier attempts to get to grips with post-Cold War trends in international security, and to Geoff and Kath Tansey, co-editors of *A World Divided* (1994). Malcolm Dando and his associates, Graham Pearson, Simon Whitby and Jez Littlewood, have done extraordinary work on the problems of biological weapons and their control, and my knowledge of the Iraqi BW programme and its wider implications stems directly from their work.

I owe a special debt to Simon Whitby, who helped me as a research assistant when I was Head of Department at Peace Studies for several years in the mid-1990s, helping to dig out all kinds of resources and ideas, and able to track down the most obscure topics. I also owe a debt to Roger van Zwanenberg and the staff at Pluto Press for taking the risk of publishing a book which, whatever else it is, does not follow the current mainstream in the study of international security. Finally, I would like to thank all my fellow members of staff in Peace Studies – collectively the most committed, stimulating and knowledgeable group of academics I have ever met.

Paul Rogers
March 2000

Introduction to the Second Edition

One of the main arguments discussed in the first edition of this book was that wealthy industrialised states had an innate vulnerability to paramilitary action against their centres of power and influence. A number of examples were discussed to illustrate this contention, including the use of economic targeting by Provisional IRA paramilitaries during the early and mid-1990s in Britain, and actions against US interests, both in the Middle East and in the United States itself. In particular, the book examined the bombing of the World Trade Center in New York in 1993, and discussed the likely consequences had the attack succeeded.

Partly in response to such vulnerabilities, it was suggested that the belief that Western states could maintain control of a fractious and unstable international system would eventually prove to be wrong, and that, ultimately, it would be necessary to put far greater emphasis on responding to the root causes of potential future conflict. These, it was argued, included the rapidly increasing socio-economic divide between a wealthy elite of around 1 billion people, and a marginalised but increasingly knowledgeable majority of 5 billion people. They also included the effects of environmental constraints, especially in relation to the potential for resource conflict and the effects of climate change.

In this second edition of *Losing Control*, the arguments and analysis are presented as before but extended to cover the traumatic events of 2001 and their aftermath. The first edition had ended on a hopeful note – that it would be possible for the Western security paradigm to be reconsidered in order to address the fundamental problems likely to lead to a more insecure and volatile world. At the time of writing, it would seem that the atrocities of 11 September are having the opposite effect.

As we move well into 2002, some six months after the attacks in New York and Washington, the actions of the United States indicate an utterly firm commitment to regaining, and then maintaining, control. This will probably involve a series of military responses that go well beyond attempting to dismantle the al-Qaida network that is believed to be responsible for the attacks. In parallel with the war in Afghanistan, a network of bases has been established across Central Asia, US troops are aiding counter-insurgency operations in the Philippines, and there is to be a substantial increase in aid to the Colombian government in its actions against leftist insurgents.

There are indications of possible counter-terrorist action in Somalia and Yemen, and even of substantial military action against the Saddam Hussein regime in Iraq. The US defence budget is set to rise rapidly in the coming years, President Bush talks of an 'axis of evil' encompassing Iran and well as Iraq and North Korea. At the same time, issues of international development and global environmental management recede rapidly into the background.

This approach, so typical of the existing security paradigm, is causing increasing concern among politicians in Europe, and is almost totally at variance with opinion in the 'majority world' of the South. Even so, it appears that, in the United States, the effect of the attacks last September has been to massively re-inforce old ideas of security, to the extent that any alternatives are not remotely worthy of consideration.

This is a core issue in any analysis of trends in international security over the next decade or more, and one small attempt to address these issues is the second edition of this book. The text, as originally published two years ago, is therefore updated with an extensive additional chapter that seeks to discuss and analyse the early effects and significance of the US response to 11 September.

In doing so, I have been greatly helped by discussions and arguments with staff and students in the Peace Studies Department at Bradford University, especially in the form of a series of open meetings that have taken place in recent months. In addition, I have had the very valuable discipline, over the past six months, of writing a weekly analysis of the developing 'war on terror' for the Open Democracy website. I have also had the good fortune to take part in meetings in Germany, the United States, and Costa Rica, although I take sole responsibility for the views expressed here.

One of the most frequently asked questions in recent months is: did the world really change on 11 September 2001? One answer, developed from the analysis in the first edition of this book, is that those traumatic events served primarily to accelerate trends that were already under way, trends that do truly represent a change in the world order. That this change remains unrecognised, and that we persist in the old paradigm, is one of the most fundamental issues that faces us. The sooner this is recognised, the better for all of us.

Paul Rogers
March 2002

Introduction to the Third Edition

When the first edition of *Losing Control* was written at the end of the 1990s, many questions were being raised over the negative consequences of globalisation, and there was a slowly increasing interest in climate change and other problems of environmental limitations on human activity. The Cold War era was long gone and the main security issues related to conflicts in the Balkans, the Caucasus and the Great Lakes region of Central Africa. There was some interest in the phenomenon of irregular or asymmetric warfare but there was a confidence among western security analysts that the military power of the United States and its closest allies would be sufficient to maintain order in a rather fragile and unpredictable world.

Losing Control argued that this was a deeply flawed outlook and that a combination of a deepening global socio-economic divide and environmental constraints would result in conflicts that could not be controlled by traditional military approaches. Industrial societies were vulnerable to irregular warfare as technical and other advances made it easier for 'the weak to take up arms against the strong' (p. 61).

That analysis proved appallingly accurate just 18 months later, with the 9/11 attacks in New York and Washington. The destruction of the World Trade Center killed thousands, but the attack on the Pentagon was even more significant – a group of paramilitaries armed only with parcel knives were able to strike the military headquarters of the world's most powerful state. A second edition of *Losing Control* therefore added a chapter, written early in 2002, that sought to bring the analysis up to date while attempting to predict the course of action as the 'war on terror' took shape. It concluded that the immediate effect of 9/11 was to harden the 'control paradigm' which was rooted in the belief that military force was the necessary response, not least because it was essential to regain control of the New American Century.

The chapter was deeply critical of this approach and argued that it risked the onset of a never-ending war, extending beyond Afghanistan to Iraq. The one possibility might be that as the futility was demonstrated there might be an opportunity to challenge the discredited but dominant security paradigm. What happened in the next decade would 'prove pivotal in determining the degree of international instability that could prevail for much of the new century' (p. 150). In the event, the United States and its coalition partners did indeed embark on that world-wide 'war on terror' in a determination to regain control, an exercise that has proved just as futile as predicted, with the war now moving towards its second decade.

This new edition looks back on the past decade and adds two further chapters. The first examines the wars in Afghanistan and Iran and the increasing violence in western Pakistan. It argues that the war on terror has been hugely costly in human terms and has been deeply counter-productive for the United States and its closest coalition partners. Because of this failure, there is now an opportunity to dispute the basic premise of the control paradigm and promote, with some vigour, many of the alternative approaches to international security proposed when *Losing Control* was first written.

The second chapter goes back to the original analysis and updates it. Over the past ten years, the wealth/poverty divide has widened, and environmental constraints have become far more widely recognised – indeed the issue of climate change has risen up the security agenda with quite remarkable speed. Furthermore, the sudden and severe economic downturn that started in 2007 helps to confirm the argument that the globalised free market is deeply flawed. Thus, this new edition reinforces the argument that the world's elite cannot maintain control and that a far more emancipatory and sustainable approach to global security has to be developed. The first decade of the twenty-first century may have been a lost opportunity, but the manner in which it has demonstrated the futility of 'old thinking' at least makes it possible that the second decade could hold the prospect of real progress.

Paul Rogers
June 2009

Abbreviations

ABL	Airborne Laser
ABMT	Anti-Ballistic Missile Treaty
ACC	Air Combat Command
ALCM	Air-Launched Cruise Missile
ATACMS	Army Tactical Missile System
BTWC	Biological and Toxin Weapons Convention
CAL	Capital Account Liberalisation
CALCM	Conventional Air-Launched Cruise Missile
CENTCOM	Central Command
CND	Campaign for Nuclear Disarmament
CPA	Coalition Provisional Authority
CTBT	Comprehensive Test Ban Treaty
CWC	Chemical Weapons Convention
DEATAC	Directed Energy Applications for Tactical Air Combat
DfID	Department for International Development
EU	European Union
FCO	Foreign and Commonwealth Office
GSD	Global Social Democracy
IBC	Iraq Body Count
ICBM	Intercontinental Ballistic Missile
ILO	International Labour Office
IMF	International Monetary Fund
INF	Intermediate Nuclear Force
IPPC	Intergovernmental Panel on Climate Change
LOW	Launch on Warning
LTTE	Liberation Tigers of Tamil Elam
LUA	Launch under Attack
MAI	Multilateral Agreement on Investment
MDGs	Millennium Development Goals
MIRV	Multiple Independently-targetable Re-entry Vehicle
M-X	Missile-experimental
NAFTA	North American Free Trade Area
NATO	North Atlantic Treaty Organisation

NPT	Non-Proliferation Treaty
OECD	Organisation for Economic Cooperation and Development
OPEC	Organisation of Petroleum Exporting Countries
OSCE	Organisation for Security and Co-operation in Europe
PACAF	Pacific Air Force
RoK	Republic of Korea
SAC	Strategic Air Command
SALT	Strategic Arms Limitation Treaty
SAS	Special Air Service
SBL	Space-Based Laser
SDI	Strategic Defence Initiative
SEAL	Sea-Air-Land
SHAPE	Supreme Headquarters, Allied Powers Europe
SIOP	Single Integrated Operational Plan
SLBM	Submarine-Launched Ballistic Missile
START	Strategic Arms Reduction Treaty
THAAD	Theatre High-Altitude Area Defence
TMD	Theatre Missile Defence
TNC	Trans-National Corporation
TNF	Theatre Nuclear Forces
UAV	Unmanned Aerial Vehicle
UCAV	Unmanned Combat Aerial Vehicle
UNA	United Nations Association
UNCTAD	United Nations Conference on Trade and Development
UNSCOM	United Nations Special Commission on Iraq
USAF	United States Air Force
USSOCOM	United States Special Operations Command
WCMD	Wind-Corrected Munitions Dispenser
WTO	World Trade Organisation
ZNLA	Zapatista National Liberation Army

1

A Violent Peace

A few years ago a conference took place in Dhaka on the links between environmental degradation and poverty, organised by a Bangladeshi NGO and financed by the World Bank. It brought together experts from many parts of the world and, as is usually the case with such meetings, it was held in an international hotel. This particular well-appointed hotel had been built in a secluded part of the city a few years before, but the explosive growth of Dhaka meant that it was now surrounded by a large shanty town crowded with people who had come in from the countryside in search of work.

The poverty was extreme, with little fresh water, open sewers, rats everywhere and many of the squatter huts liable to repeated flooding during the monsoons. In the midst of this was the hotel, with its carefully tended tropical gardens, large swimming pool, sun-loungers, sauna and fitness centre. The whole complex was surrounded by a high fence and barbed wire, with just one entrance, protected by armed guards. Conference delegates came in from the airport in taxis or hotel bus, stayed there for the duration of the conference, earnestly discussing poverty, and then departed.

No disrespect is intended towards the World Bank, at least on this occasion. The Bangladeshi organisers did their best to bring the conference down to earth, with some hard-hitting papers from local researchers who worked among the shanty dwellers. Moreover, several of the participants from Bangladesh and overseas argued forcibly and effectively that the problems of poverty within the country stemmed far more from its debt burden and perennial trade difficulties than from internal corruption and mismanagement, serious though that was. After all, East Bengal in the eighteenth century had been one of the most successful economies in Asia, before the East India Company got to work on it. There was certainly no little irony in discussing poverty in such surroundings, but the circumstances of that hotel could be repeated throughout the world.

During the past 30 years, intercontinental business travel and tourism has increased at a remarkable rate. Many people think nothing of moving from Rio to Cape Town or from Delhi to Bangkok on business, or visiting the game parks of Zimbabwe, Tanzania and South Africa or the beaches of Goa, Thailand, Kenya and the Gambia. In their travels they live in an almost perpetual cocoon, carefully protected from the real lives of the great majority of the people around them. Tourists will stay in high-rise hotels on spectacular sea-fronts and will travel by coach out to the mountains and game parks. They may well visit the expensive and fashionable down-town shops. These may be only a few blocks from the hotel, but they will not walk there after dark – indeed they will not be encouraged to walk anywhere after dark. They will certainly not see the massive shanty towns that are a feature of so many cities across the world.

The world's elite, numbering many hundreds of millions, is mobile as never before yet travels the world in a perpetual mirage, constantly protected and made comfortable, happily unaware of the real world. Not that such poverty is restricted to the countries of the South. In the last 20 years especially, the rich-poor divide has grown alarmingly in many Northern states, with large districts of many cities just as dangerous as most of Johannesburg, Nairobi or Lagos. Nor is this enduring rich-poor divide restricted to the circumstances of business travellers and tourists – it is demonstrated even more dramatically by the life-styles of the elites. Take, for example, the case of Heritage Park which follows.[1]

Closing the castle gates

South Africa, like many countries that have particularly deep divisions of wealth and poverty, has a serious crime problem, especially in the major cities and townships. Many actions of the government may be directed towards improving the basic conditions of the marginalised majority, but it is proving to be an enormous task. Meanwhile, the richer elites of the country, mainly but not all white, take personal security seriously. Many live in gated communities or apartments protected by security guards, deserting the cities for suburban security at the end of each working day.

It is a pattern increasingly common in many parts of the world, but one development in South Africa is perhaps taking this to its logical conclusion. Heritage Park is to be built close to the exclusive Cape settlement of Somerset West, and will be an almost completely self-contained community of the wealthy, surrounded and protected by a formidable electrified fence. When completed, within a decade, the 500-acre site will contain about 2,000 attractive high-cost homes surrounding a 50-acre central park with lakes, forest and bird sanctuary. Waterways, jogging tracks, a horse trail, children's playground, recreation ground, sports field and sports hall will all be within the perimeter fence, as will a church and even a village green. The community will also have shops, schools, restaurants, a hotel, a theatre, a small business park and light industries.

Entry into Heritage Park will be by permit through one of four security entrances, and it will have its own police force of 40 people primarily to provide protection from outside. Crime is not expected to be a serious problem within the fence, which will be screened by trees and shrubs to make it difficult to see from the inside, though residents can expect fine views of the distant mountains. Heritage Park will be open to all, white, black or coloured, provided they can afford to live there, although the acknowledged reality is that most are expected to be white. Given the availability of education, employment and recreation facilities, it is expected that most residents will spend the great majority of their time within the fence, rarely having to go outside.

Although Heritage Park is proving popular with potential residents, one problem remains. Over 1,000 squatters live alongside the site and legal restrictions mean that they cannot be moved. The developers believe that this problem can be turned to an advantage. They plan to provide the squatters with cheap housing, just outside the electrified perimeter fence. They expect that some will find work inside the fence as shop assistants or maids, entering Heritage Park by day but returning home at night.

Heritage Park is an advanced example of a way of living that has become progressively more common throughout the world. In one sense it is nothing new, in that the richest and most powerful people throughout history have commonly found it necessary to pay particular attention to their own security and that of their possessions. What is more common is the manner in which the security of the richer sectors of society has become such a major phenomenon throughout the world, but especially in those many places where the wealth-poverty divide is particularly marked.

An even more extreme example is found in São Paulo in Brazil, where the richest citizens have taken to the sky for their own safety:

> Carjackings, kidnappings of executives and roadside robberies have become a part of the risks of daily life for anyone perceived to have money. So the demand for private helicopters in São Paulo has turned the city into one of the most vibrant markets for helicopter dealers.[2]

What a difference a day makes

As the castle gates close, almost literally, around the protected residents of Heritage Park, so the richer states of the world try to close their gates to the seekers of a better life, a process which, for politicians, is greatly aided in many countries by the tabloid press. Occasionally, the effects are bizarre. In the early morning of 6 February 2000, an internal flight of the Afghanistan airline Ariana was hi-jacked and the crew was forced to fly it to Tashkent in Uzbekistan. From there it went on to Aktyubinsk in Kazakhstan before flying to Moscow. A few passengers were released before the plane headed west, landing at Stansted Airport in Britain at 2 a.m. the following day with 164 people on board, 21 hours after it had left Kabul.

The next day, 8 February, the British tabloid press gave the hi-jack the full treatment, concentrating on the ordeal of the passengers, already imprisoned in the plane for 48 hours, and the presence at Stansted of crack paramilitary units from the SAS, ready to storm the plane and free the hostages. The assumption was that these terrorists were seeking some concession from the Taliban leaders in Kabul in exchange for the lives of the frightened passengers.

A day later, the tabloid view had changed dramatically as it became clear that the hi-jackers were seeking asylum in Britain. Now 'Stansted' became 'Scamsted' as they were portrayed as scroungers seeking to sponge on Britain's welfare state. Worse was to follow when the tired passengers were finally released and housed for a couple of days in an airport hotel, with many of them hoping to be allowed to stay. Now they, too, were scroungers, being accommodated at tax-payers' expense in a luxury hotel while seeking an easy entry into 'soft touch' Britain. Almost immediately, the ever-vigilant Home Secretary announced that he would personally vet every application.

Keeping the violent peace – the Secret Squirrels

Heritage Park and its many equivalents across the world represent the need of elites to protect their lifestyles and the Afghan airline hi-jack is just one example of hardening attitudes as wealthy states close down on immigration, but this is also a process that operates at the global level. Elite states and alliances also have to protect their interests in a security paradigm that has changed dramatically since the ending of the Cold War. For 45 years, the West had one primary security concern, the con- frontation with the Soviet bloc. It was straightforward, easy to understand and very simple – 'them versus us'. Now, the world is a much more uncertain place, with diverse threats to western well-being, so that the function of the western military is one of 'keeping the violent peace', being able to project military force anywhere in the world where western interests are affected.

A near classic example of this was the response to the sudden and unexpected threat to oil supplies that started with the Iraqi invasion of Kuwait in 1990 and ended when the Iraqi forces were defeated and forced out of Kuwait a few months later in Operation Desert Storm. In the process, there was one particular event that featured in the war but did not even get into the public domain for several years. It concerns an operation by a little-known US Air Force unit deploying new missiles known colloquially as the 'Secret Squirrels' after a cartoon character. In its own way, the story of this unit is as much a metaphor for the future as is Heritage Park.

Operation Desert Storm commenced on the evening of 16 January 1991, with sustained air attacks on targets in many parts of Iraq. In Western Europe, the early indications of the attack became apparent very late in the evening as CNN and other TV networks interrupted programmes to bring the first news of the air raids. According to all available public sources, the air raids on Iraq were all launched from bases in the region, especially Saudi Arabia, Bahrain and other western Gulf states, and from aircraft carriers and missile ships in the Persian Gulf and the Red Sea.

This was not quite true. More than 15 hours before the raids on Baghdad commenced, a flight of seven B-52G long-range bombers took off from Barksdale Air Force Base in Louisiana on what was to become the longest air raid in history. Over the course of a day and a half, the planes flew out over the Eastern United States, over the North Atlantic, Southern Europe, the Mediterranean and Egypt, and into air space over western Saudi Arabia. At no time did they cross into Iraqi air space. Instead, they launched a total of 35 air-launched cruise missiles at eight targets in Iraq, including power plants at Mosul in the north, and a telephone exchange at Basra in the south. Having completed their task, the planes turned round and flew back to the United States. The entire operation involved a 35-hour 14,000-mile flight supported by multiple air-to-air refuellings involving tanker aircraft operating out of air bases in Spain and the Azores.[3]

There were three remarkable features to this air raid. The first was the length (the first truly global demonstration of air power in time of war), the second was the weapons used to carry it out. Unlike the Tomahawk cruise missile used by the US Navy throughout the Gulf War, the US Air Force's air-launched cruise missile had originally been deployed only in a nuclear-armed form, yet here it was being used to deliver a high-explosive warhead. Third, the raid was entirely experimental – the same targets could have been attacked with cruise missiles launched from ships close to Iraq.

There was no immediate military requirement to stage the hugely expensive operation from bases in the United States, except, of course, to demonstrate the capacity of the US Air Force to project military power on a global scale. While this stemmed partly from a rivalry with the US Navy and its carrier-based air power, it also arose out of the experience of the air force in the previous decade. It is a story worth recounting, not least because of what it tells us about the way in which military thinking is adapting to the post-Cold War world.

The process starts in the early 1970s, nearly 20 years before the Gulf War, with a series of developments in military technology. The most significant of these concerned progress made in miniaturised power plants and guidance systems. Over a number of years in the early 1970s, small, high performance turbofan jet engines were developed by the Williams Company in the US. These weighed only 145lb, yet were able to power small pilot-less aircraft – cruise missiles – ten times that weight. So efficient were these engines that they could use on-board fuel to propel missiles armed with nuclear warheads for more than a thousand miles.

Over the same period, using newly developed computer technology combined with satellite-generated maps and accurate terrain-measuring radar, guidance specialists developed systems that could guide these new cruise missiles throughout their flight, enabling them to land within fifty feet of their intended targets.

By the late 1970s, substantial contracts had been let for a new class of cruise missiles for use by the US Air Force and the US Navy. They were all broadly similar in form, 20 feet long and with stubby eight-foot wings. The US Navy bought thousands of the missiles, naming them the Tomahawk Sea-Launched Cruise Missile or SLCM. Some were nuclear-armed but most were fitted with conventional high-explosive warheads intended for use either against ships or against targets on land. Hundreds of these land attack missiles were fired during the Gulf War.

The US Air Force restricted itself to nuclear-armed cruise missiles, but they were produced in two rather different forms. The best-known, at least in Europe, were the ground-launched cruise missiles (GLCMs) produced by General Dynamics. Over 500 were built and they formed a substantial part of the nuclear re-arming of the United States forces in Western Europe in the early 1980s, leading to a wave of anti-nuclear protests before eventually being withdrawn after the 1987 Intermediate Nuclear Force Treaty.

A much lesser known version was the air-launched cruise missile (ALCM) produced by Boeing and built in very large numbers, also in the 1980s. The idea was to be able to launch the ALCM from a strategic bomber flying outside the heavily defended air space of the Soviet Union. The missile would then fly at very low level towards its target, making detection by radar very difficult. The missile carried a thermonuclear warhead with a destructive force of 200 kilotons, about 15 times the power of the Hiroshima bomb. Such was the momentum of the nuclear arms race in the early 1980s that the Reagan administration ordered 1,700 of these missiles. Deployments started in December 1982 and each B-52 could carry up to 20 missiles, six under each wing and another eight in an internal bomb bay.

By the late 1980s it was already becoming apparent to the more far-sighted planners in the US Air Force that the Cold War was starting to wind down and that a new era was unfolding in which there might be larger numbers of small-scale conflicts. Thousands of nuclear-armed missiles and bombers were not necessarily the most appropriate weapons for such a disorderly world, and there might therefore be a renewed demand for long-range conventional bombing. This created an immediate worry – the risk of aircrew being shot down and held prisoner as in Vietnam – so some planners began to look at the possibility of developing a conventionally-armed version of the ALCM. Using this, a plane could approach a regional conflict and attack targets with 'stand-off' weapons, without putting the crew at risk.

One of the overall worries for the US Air Force was that its role in projecting military power might diminish, and might even be taken over by its bitter rivals, the US Navy, with its aircraft carriers and sea-launched cruise missiles. After all, interventions in the early 1980s in Lebanon and Grenada had mainly involved the Navy, the Marines and, to an extent, the Army. Future threats looked likely to include sudden regional crises that could break out many thousands of miles from the United States, especially in the Middle East or South East Asia. For the Air Force to get 'a piece of the action', it would normally have to find a way of forward-basing its aircraft within range of the conflict, whereas the more flexible Navy, with its large nuclear-powered aircraft carriers, had a considerable advantage. The Navy therefore stood a much better chance of maintaining its budget at a time of defence cuts.

All of these potential problems were brought home to the USAF by the disaster of the raid on Libya in April 1986, intended to punish the 'rogue state' of Colonel Gaddafi. This was a joint operation between the Air Force and the Navy, with the latter flying its strike aircraft against Libya from aircraft carriers only a few hundred miles away in the Mediterranean. The Air Force, though, had to use F-111 bombers operating from bases in Britain, as Southern European allies such as Italy were unwilling to let the USAF conduct this controversial operation from bases in their countries.

Worse still, although the British government under Margaret Thatcher was more than willing to let British bases be used, the Spanish and French governments refused even to let the bombers over-fly their territories. As a consequence, the aircraft had to fly an extraordinary 'round-the-houses' route out over the Bay of Biscay and the Eastern Atlantic, through the Straits of Gibraltar and across the Western Mediterranean, using multiple air-to-air refuellings. Crew fatigue in the cramped cockpits was high, bombs were mistakenly dropped on civilian areas, killing and injuring scores of people, and one plane was lost with its crew.

After the Libya raid, the Air Force planners sought to find a way to provide the much larger strategic bombers such as the B-52, designed specifically for long-range operations, with the ability to project conventional air power world-wide. But their role was to deliver nuclear weapons and the ALCMs were one of the main ways of doing this. What was clearly required was a change of policy and a re-equipment process to give the Air Force 'global reach' with conventional weapons.

As a result, a highly secret programme was started to convert nuclear-armed ALCMs into conventional missiles. The nuclear warhead was stripped out and replaced with a 1,000lb blast fragmentation warhead, and the guidance system was updated with a global positioning satellite receiver. The result was the conventional ALCM or CALCM, known by the bomber crews as the Secret Squirrel.

By the end of the 1980s the process was complete and a small number of crews were trained in the new system. With the ending of the Cold War, the US Air Force waited for an opportunity to prove its new weapon, and that came on the opening day of Desert Storm. It was not relevant that the targets could have been attacked much more easily with the Navy's ship-launched missiles a few hundred miles from Iraq; the point was that it demonstrated the ability of the US Air Force to hit targets almost anywhere in the world with impunity. In short, it provided one instrument for keeping the violent peace in the uncertain world that has replaced the Cold War era.

Winning or losing control

This short book is an attempt to discuss that uncertain world of the early decades of the twenty-first century and how the world's most powerful elite states will seek to maintain control. It begins with a review of the Cold War years, pointing to several features of that era which have substantial implications for the future. The Cold War was immensely wasteful of human and material resources, especially when compared with the problems of poverty and underdevelopment that persisted for the whole period. It was also a period that saw the development of a remarkable range of military technologies, many of them now proliferating across the world – a Cold War legacy that is likely to have a profound impact on the effects of conflict.

The Cold War was also a period of intense nuclear confrontation. To a detached observer, the excesses of the nuclear arms race are almost unbelievable, yet two apparently sane alliances embarked on an arms race in which extraordinarily dangerous postures became the order of the day. Some of the nuclear accidents and crises of this era were acknowledged at the time, but others are only just beginning to see the light of day as the archives are opened up and some of the participants talk with a freedom that would have been impossible at the time.

There was a succession of anti-nuclear movements, especially in the 1960s and 1980s, but these have withered, at least until recently, as it has become received wisdom that the age of nuclear danger is over. In Chapter 3, devoted to 'nuclear futures', the recent developments within the nuclear powers are reviewed and current trends are assessed. Leading on directly from the experience of the Cold War, the conclusion has to be reached that the nuclear age is far from over, merely in a state of transition. The massive Cold War nuclear arsenals and the risk of a world-wide 'central nuclear exchange' may be diminished, but the utility of nuclear weapons remains a key component of the defence strategies of the declared nuclear powers, as well as Israel. Moreover, the development of biological and chemical weapons and the proliferation of ballistic missiles is seen to represent a means by which weaker states can challenge the power of the stronger, a challenge that may require a nuclear response.

While nuclear and other weapons of mass destruction will be major features of the coming decades, the main methods by which the world's powerful states, especially the United States, seek to maintain their control of international security are through the appropriate use of conventional forces. Threats are seen to stem from a possible revival of a belligerent Russia, or of an increasingly powerful China, together with the activities of 'rogue states' and terrorists and even of ideological or religious movements, especially militant Islam. Chapter 4 explores the way in which the western military are making the transition to post-Cold War forces that can keep the lid on threats to western security. Global reach, rapid deployment forces, counter-insurgency and missile defences all have their role to play, and there is a persistent emphasis on control from a distance, especially if it can involve a minimum of risk. The death toll for coalition forces in the Gulf War in 1991 was in the low hundreds (many of them through friendly fire), compared with tens of thousands of Iraqis killed. In Kosovo, none of the NATO military lost their lives in combat, yet the Serbian economy was wrecked and several thousand Serbs were killed, including over 1,000 civilians.

Stretching on from the current era of cruise missiles and stealth bombers will come the deployment of pilot-less aircraft, small unmanned aerial vehicles (UAVs) that can roam and deploy weapons at will, together with cyber-war and other techniques intended to disable an enemy's command and control systems and wreck an economy. Beyond this will come a further military revolution, still in its very early stages, that will lead to directed energy weapons – lasers, particle beams and their relatives, that will achieve remarkable accuracy and speed and will also be well-nigh invulnerable to conventional defences.

The overall effect of these developments in weapons, postures and strategies, will be to provide convincing arguments that the world's elite states can indeed maintain their security, but the next two chapters suggest that this is fundamentally wrong. It is argued that the core parameters of international conflict in the coming decades are the growing rich-poor divide and the increasing problem of environmental constraints on human development. Furthermore, western strategies for controlling a polarised and environmentally constrained world do not take into account the fundamental vulnerabilities of modern urban-industrial states to asymmetric warfare, not least the development of 'force equalisers' such as biological weapons. Attempting to keep the lid on insecurity – 'liddism' – without addressing the core reasons for dissent, will not work. It is more likely to make western elite societies more vulnerable, a trend already beginning to be recognised by some military analysts.

In the concluding chapter, it is suggested that some quite fundamental rethinking of our attitudes to security is necessary, that countering socioeconomic divisions and embracing sustainable development are actually core requirements for stable international security. In one sense this is nothing new and has been a common argument in writings on environmental and development issues for a couple of decades, such as the Brandt and Bruntland reports. What is different is the need to link this to thinking on international security so that the prevailing paradigm of a western elite maintaining its security, if need be by military means, is recognised as not just unsustainable but actually self-defeating. There are many impressive arguments that a polarised and constrained world is not acceptable on the grounds of morality and justice. The argument of this book, drawing mainly on a security perspective, is that, in practice, it cannot and will not work. An alternative security paradigm is required.

Learning from the Cold War

The Cold War lasted for 45 years until 1990 and, since its ending, two broad views of the confrontation have emerged. The first, held by most of the strategic studies community, is that the Cold War ended with a clear and unequivocal victory for the United States and its NATO allies, with the Soviet bloc collapsing first into the Commonwealth of Independent States and a number of independent Eastern European countries, and subsequently into an even looser alliance, with the Russian Federation itself under threat of decline, if not disintegration through rebellions in Chechnya and elsewhere.

A core part of this analysis is the belief that the Cold War's nuclear confrontation was an essential part of the process. Nuclear weapons kept the peace, and did so without there being any real risk of nuclear war. Thus nuclear deterrence provided an essential stability within which the much greater free market economic success of the western liberal democracies could ultimately lead to the downfall of a rigid and authoritarian centrally-planned economic ideology. Central to this process was the way in which the Soviet Union and its Warsaw Pact allies were forced into crippling defence budgets in a desperate attempt to maintain military parity with NATO.

This view of the Cold War, seeing it as a clear victory for the western alliance stemming from a necessary and essentially safe process of maintaining very large military forces, leads to a post-Cold War paradigm in which military security remains the ultimate guarantee of western well-being. The world may be much more uncertain and volatile in the early twenty-first century, and this may well demand different kinds of military force. In essence, though, adequate and appropriate military forces saw the western alliance safely through the Cold War, and suitably organised forces will serve a similar purpose in the future.

There is a very different way of looking at the Cold War, an analysis that suggests that it is a thoroughly inappropriate model for ensuring future security, and that the Cold War period was highly dangerous and inordinately wasteful.[1] Furthermore, it has resulted in a momentum in the development of a range of military technologies that has lasted well beyond the end of the Cold War itself and may ensure that future conflicts could be devastating for individual states and dangerous for international security as a whole. This chapter explores this alternative view, contrasting defence spending and the consumption of talent with key indicators of social expenditure as well as some of the after-effects of the Cold War as military technologies spread across the world.

It looks, in particular, at the dangers of the nuclear confrontation itself, not just the development of nuclear war-fighting ideas but also the false alarms and crises and the numerous nuclear accidents, some involving the loss of nuclear weapons. Much of the information was in the public domain during the Cold War, if not widely known, but some of it has only come to light more recently. Put together, they indicate a degree of danger during many of the Cold War years which turns out to be fully supportive of the much-derided warnings of anti-nuclear campaigners and peace researchers, so often dismissed as scare-mongering at the time.

The general public perception of the Cold War nuclear era in the west was of a persistent threat from the Soviet bloc that had to be matched by the United States and its NATO allies. In particular, there was an enduring acceptance of the need for a balance of terror, with mutually assured destruction ensuring a stable confrontation. An examination of the history of the nuclear arms race suggests otherwise, with a picture emerging of an action-reaction arms race as each side tried to gain an advantage over the other. Added to this was the persistent fear, on both sides, of a surprise attack. Much of the nuclear targeting and planning was about preparing for worst-case scenarios, pervaded by a 'get your retaliation in first' mentality.

Above all, the public perception that nuclear weapons were solely weapons of last resort, was frankly false – the declaratory statements of the superpowers that supported this view were simply not matched either by targeting policy or by the very weapons that were developed and deployed. Although the Cold War might now be over, at least in its extreme form, the United States, Russia and the middle ranking nuclear powers such as Britain and France all retain nuclear forces, show no signs whatsoever of rejecting their nuclear postures, and see uses for nuclear armaments in the decades to come. For this reason, if for no other, it is worth discussing the broad features of the Cold War nuclear arms race and of current knowledge about the crises and accidents of that era.

Origins and early development of the nuclear arms race

Nuclear weapons were originally developed as a result of the collaborative Manhattan Project in the United States, with the first atomic device tested on 16 July 1945 and atom bombs dropped on Hiroshima and

Nagasaki on 6 and 9 August that year. The bombs were small by the standards of the later years of the Cold War. Both yielded less than 20 kilotons (equivalent to 20,000 tons of high explosive), but they destroyed two cities and killed over 150,000 people. As well as being a massive research and development effort, the Manhattan Project included an immediate production capability, and had Japan not surrendered in August 1945 as many as ten more atom bombs could have been produced within six months. Even with the ending of the war, one source estimates that the US already had six nuclear weapons by the end of the year.[2]

Immediately after the end of the Second World War, the United States began to build up a substantial nuclear weapons industry and progress was so rapid that it had an arsenal of 50 atom bombs within three years. By 1948, tensions with the Soviet Union were rising as the Cold War took root, and the Soviet Union was putting massive resources into a crash programme to counter the US nuclear monopoly, seen as a fundamental threat to the Soviet state.[3] In a further complication, the McMahon Energy Act was passed in the United States, one of its provisions being the ending of nuclear co-operation with wartime allies such as Britain. This was a key factor in encouraging Britain, still under the illusion that it was a superpower, to start its own atom bomb programme.

In the immediate post-war years there were limited efforts to bring nuclear weapons under international control within the fledgling UN system, with the US-inspired Baruch Plan and its Soviet counterpart, the Gromyko Plan, both failing to make progress. Instead, the Soviets made rapid progress in their own nuclear programme, exploding an atom bomb in 1949, several years earlier than western analysts had expected.

By the early 1950s, a full-scale nuclear arms race was in progress between the US and the USSR. With Europe divided, Berlin a source of tension and the Korean War causing some 3 million deaths, each side sought to produce substantial arsenals of atom bombs and planes or missiles to carry them, and to develop the immensely more destructive thermonuclear or fusion bomb. The United States tested a device in 1952 with the USSR following a year later; both states went on to develop largely thermonuclear arsenals in the following decade.

The arms race had many other facets, one of which was that each country had historic technological advantages that the other sought to match. During the Second World War, the United States had fought long-range conflicts in Europe and the Pacific and had, as a consequence, substantial experience of building long-range bombers. The Soviet Union, in contrast, had a relatively weak air force but a powerful army with substantial experience in artillery rockets. As a result, the US concentrated on developing nuclear-armed bombers while the Soviets also went for missiles, but each saw the need to match the other in their particular area of expertise.

By the mid-1950s, the United States and the Soviet Union were engaged in a full-scale nuclear arms race comprising very powerful nuclear weapons delivered initially by bombers. Concern over their vulnerability to air defences led to intensive programmes to develop ballistic missiles, initially with medium range missiles based in Europe, and an attempted Soviet basing in Cuba that resulted in the 1962 crisis.

In 1957, the Soviet Union tested an SS-6 long-range intercontinental ballistic missile (ICBM) and also launched the first satellite, Sputnik. Both events caused consternation in the United States, but it was actually the US that deployed the first ICBM two years later. Indeed, a feature of the whole of the Cold War was the deployment of large but relatively crude missiles by the Soviet Union, contrasting with smaller, more reliable and accurate weapons by the United States.

As well as a wholesale and immensely costly arms race under way between the superpowers, others were following suit. The sheer cost and technological commitment involved could be staggering. After the decision of the Attlee government to develop the atom bomb, Britain invested considerable resources in a crash programme, testing its first atom bomb in 1952 and a fusion bomb five years later. Even as these programmes were under way, the fragmented British aircraft industry was competing to develop bombers and, in an extraordinary period in the 1950s, Britain was buying three different nuclear bombers (the Valiant, Vulcan and Victor V-bombers), was developing the air-launched Blue Steel cruise missile and was even trying to develop a medium range ballistic missile, the Blue Streak, and a supersonic tactical bomber, the TSR-2, both later cancelled.[4]

All this was in addition to a wide range of conventional weapons programmes as well as maintaining 800,000 people in the armed forces. Only after Suez did British defence policy begin to 'cut its cloth', but British defence spending and its commitment to a range of intensely costly weapons systems was to continue to absorb money and talent throughout the Cold War and beyond as the country persisted in attempts to 'punch above its weight'.[5]

The French and Chinese were also actively pursuing a nuclear option during the 1950s. The French succeeded in their first test in 1960 and the Chinese followed in 1964. Israel started developing its own programme, with French aid, in the 1960s and probably had a limited capability by the end of the decade, India tested a device in 1974 and South African and Pakistani programmes followed shortly afterwards.

The nuclear arms race – acceleration or control?

With the benefit of hindsight, the acceleration of the nuclear arms race in the 1960s seems extraordinary. Hiroshima and Nagasaki had shown that just two small crude atom bombs could each destroy a large modern city, yet the superpowers were already building first hundreds and then thousands of much more powerful bombs. Each side was locked into a mutually reinforcing competition in which it perceived itself faced with an implacable opponent determined to gain a strategic advantage.

Table 1: Superpower Nuclear Stockpiles[6]

Year	United States	Soviet Union
1945	6	0
1950	370	5
1955	3,050	200
1960	20,400	1,600
1965	32,100	6,100
1970	26,500	11,650
1975	27,200	19,400
1980	23,900	30,100
1985	23,500	39,200
1990	21,800	37,000
1995	14,100	27,000

Note: All figures rounded. From 1990 onwards, figures include warheads put into storage, with the great majority of Russian nuclear forces no longer deployed but not dismantled. If the nuclear weapons of Britain, France and China are included, the peak year for global nuclear arsenals was 1986 with just under 70,000 nuclear warheads available.

During the late 1950s, both superpowers developed extremely powerful weapons, with the largest of the free-fall bombs and missile warheads having destructive yields of 10 to 25 megatons (up to 25 million tons of high explosive equivalent). Used against cities, these would be utterly devastating – a 25 megaton warhead detonated at an altitude of 100,000 feet would cause near total devastation over an area of 500 square miles and would start serious fires over an area of 2,000 square miles. A single warhead exploded over London or New York would destroy the entire city and its suburbs, killing many millions of people.

By the early 1960s both the Americans and the Soviets had ICBMs armed with thermonuclear warheads. The early missiles were based on land, were liquid-fuelled and were slow to prepare for launching, making them vulnerable to surprise attack. If a missile took several hours to prepare for launching, but had a flight-time of less than thirty minutes, there was a vulnerability which led on readily to a 'use them or lose them' outlook that was to permeate strategic thinking and nuclear planning for the rest of the Cold War.

More immediately, other solutions to this problem of missile vulnerability were sought. One was to develop ICBMs with storable solid fuels that could be kept at more or less instant readiness for launch. A second was to place them in heavily protected underground silos which could survive almost anything short of a direct nuclear strike. The third was to develop submarine-launched ballistic missiles (SLBMs) which could be fired from large nuclear-powered submarines when submerged and which were, in theory, impossible to detect and destroy.[7]

Both the United States and the Soviet Union went on to develop so-called 'triads' of strategic nuclear forces based on ICBMs, SLBMs and heavy bombers, with the Soviet Union placing most emphasis on ICBMs. For each leg of the triad, there was offensive and defensive competition. Thus each side tried to develop superior missiles and planes, with constant competition and interminable warnings, especially from industry and their armed forces, that the other side was getting ahead. Similarly, there was intensive competition to develop anti-aircraft defences, anti-submarine warfare and even anti-missile missiles.

During the course of the 1960s there were some efforts to develop methods for controlling the nuclear arms race, prompted partly by public opposition to nuclear weapons, partly by the dangers exposed by the Cuban missile crisis in 1962 and partly by some advisers and politicians, including many in non-nuclear countries, who were genuinely concerned with the costs and the dangers of the East-West confrontation. A Limited Test Ban Treaty was agreed in 1963 and the first Strategic Arms Limitation Treaty (SALT I) was negotiated later in the decade, though this could do no more than set substantial upper limits on the numbers of missiles and bombers to be deployed. The first of the nuclear-free zone treaties were also concluded, one covering Latin America and another trying to prevent deployments in outer space.

Perhaps more significant was the Non-Proliferation Treaty that sought to place firm limits on the proliferation of nuclear weapons to new states. While supported by many non-nuclear states, it was controversial from the start. Some states, such as India, saw it as a means of maintaining a nuclear *status quo* for a few powerful states while preventing others from gaining similar power. Within the treaty there was a provision for existing nuclear states to sign and ratify it, but they were required to embark on nuclear disarmament. As the treaty put it:

> Each of the Parties to the Treaty undertakes to pursue negotiations in good faith on effective measures relating to cessation of the nuclear arms race at an early date and to nuclear disarmament, and on a treaty on general and complete disarmament under strict and effective international control.[8]

By the time the Treaty was signed in 1968 and entered into force in 1970, production lines for several types of strategic nuclear weapon were operating intensively in the United States and the Soviet Union, and total nuclear arsenals, strategic and tactical, were numbered in the tens of thousands. Much of this stemmed from a perceived need to have very large forces to ensure the survival of some part of the nuclear arsenal in time of war, but the extent of the arsenals amounted to a remarkable degree of 'overkill'. Given that the destruction of a handful of cities and industrial centres could devastate the economies of the United States or the Soviet Union, there was already a developing air of unreality, but this was to be carried to extremes with two new strategic developments under way by the early 1970s.

The first was the development of multiple warheads on each missile, a number of smaller warheads giving a wider 'spread' over a larger target and ensuring greater destruction. These multiple re-entry vehicles were then superseded by multiple independently-targetable re-entry vehicles (MIRVs) in which each warhead could be directed at a different target. The US Poseidon SLBM was an example of a MIRVed missile – carrying ten warheads (14 over a reduced range), it could direct them at targets spread over an area of more than 20,000 square miles.

In one of the greatest ironies of the whole Cold War era, this MIRVing of missiles coincided with the second round of the SALT negotiations from 1972 to 1979, which set out to put upper limits on the number of warheads for each superpower. Over this precise period, as the arms controllers were trying to set limits, the armourers were pushing ahead with warhead production and MIRVed missiles – during the seven years of the talks, the US increased its strategic warheads from 5,700 to 9,000 and the Soviets from 2,100 to 5,000.

In parallel with this MIRVing was a remarkable increase in warhead accuracy. Early missiles were able to deliver large single warheads to within one or two miles of their target, but major improvements in guidance made it theoretically possible for warheads to be accurate enough to destroy missiles in hardened underground silos. By 1980, the United States had a missile, the Minuteman III, which had an accuracy of 600 feet CEP (circular error probable – a 50 per cent chance of a warhead landing within this distance of the target). The Soviets followed suit – although their warheads were less accurate, they compensated for this by having much more massive missiles carrying more destructive warheads.[9]

Highly accurate missiles carrying multiple warheads could theoreti- cally 'disarm' an opponent's land-based missiles while leaving the attacker with many missiles in reserve. Developments in anti-submarine warfare and air defences also suggested that other legs of the strategic triad might have some vulnerability, and the notion of a 'disarming first strike' acquired impetus, leading to the development of hair-trigger responses such as launch-on-warning. In such a scenario, a proportion of a state's nuclear arsenal could be launched in a pre-programmed sequence when warning of an incoming attack had been received but before missiles hit their targets. A variant was launch-under-attack, in which retaliation would be delayed until the first detonations of an incoming salvo of missiles, but both strategies had deeply worrying aspects because of the possible effects of false alarms.

By the early 1980s the United States had over 10,000 strategic nuclear warheads and the Soviet Union about 8,700; missile and bomber programmes then in progress indicated that the two states would have well over 30,000 strategic warheads by the early 1990s. In the eventuality, the peak was reached in the late 1980s and improving relations, the ending of the Cold War and the negotiations on a new set of Strategic Arms Reduction Treaties (START) began to have an effect, both on total strategic arsenals and also on the most destabilising strategic weapons, the accurate multi-warhead missiles.

In terms of numbers of weapons and sheer destructive power, the Cold War nuclear arms race was characterised, at the strategic level, by an absurd degree of overkill, far greater than could have been warranted by even the greatest commitment to mutually assured destruction. In the public mind, the nuclear aspects of the Cold War were all about such a balance of terror. In reality, the targeting policies of both the United States and the Soviet Union were much more about being prepared to fight a nuclear war and emerge victorious. This orientation towards nuclear war-fighting was true of strategic forces for much of the Cold War, as it was also for tactical nuclear weapons where both NATO and the Warsaw Pact maintained policies of first use of nuclear weapons.

Strategic nuclear postures and war-fighting

If the public perception of nuclear weapons was to see them as ultimate deterrents, then the declaratory nuclear weapons postures of the superpowers systematically endorsed this perception. The difficulty was that declaratory policies and actual deployment policies were never the same, even as governments tended to promote the idea of mutually assured destruction in the public mind. This contrasted with military thinking, as demonstrated powerfully by an exchange between Senator Tower and General Jones, then Chairman of the US Joint Chiefs of Staff, at a Senate hearing in 1979:

> *Senator Tower*: General Jones, what is your opinion of the theory of mutual assured destruction?
> *General Jones*: I think it is a very dangerous strategy. It is not the strategy we are implementing today within the military but it is a dangerous strategy...
> *Senator Tower*: Your professional military judgement is that it is a dangerous strategy and it is not the one we should follow?

General Jones: I do not subscribe to the idea that we ever had it as our basic strategy. I have been involved with strategic forces since the early 1950s. We have always targeted military targets. There has been a lot of discussion...about different strategies. We followed orders, but basically, the strategy stayed the same in the implementation of targeting.

Senator Tower: Unfortunately I am not sure that your opinion was always shared by your civilian superiors.

General Jones: I agree that there have been some, including some in government, who have felt that all we require is a mutual assured destruction capability. I am separating that from our targeting instructions in the field...[10]

There is now ample evidence from the literature on nuclear targeting that both the Soviet Union and the United States targeted their opponent's nuclear forces. General Jones simply did not accept that the basic US strategy had ever been based just on deterrence through the threat of retaliation. Even as far back as the 1950s there are indications that US nuclear planners recognised the advantages to be gained from a first strike with nuclear weapons at a time of crisis, an outlook illustrated by a briefing from the then head of Strategic Air Command, General Curtis le May:

Q: How do SAC's plans fit with the stated national policy that the US will never strike the first blow?

A: I have heard this stated many times and it sounds very fine. However, it is not in keeping with United States history... I want to make it clear that I am not advocating a preventive war; however, I believe that if the US is pushed into a corner far enough we would not hesitate to strike first...[11]

From the late 1950s, the United States produced a series of integrated strategic nuclear targeting plans, designed to bring together the targeting undertaken by the three legs of the triad, the ICBM, SLBM and bomber forces. These were (and are) known as the Single Integrated Operational Plans (SIOPs) and, with the rapid expansion of strategic arsenals, reached their peak in the early 1980s at the height of the Cold War.

By 1982, Desmond Ball, a leading analyst of nuclear strategy, could write of SIOP-5: 'As a result of these developments, the US target plans for strategic nuclear war are now extremely comprehensive. The current version of SIOP-5 includes more than 40,000 potential target installations, as compared to about 25,000 in 1974.'[12]

According to Ball, SIOP-5 had targets in four broad categories. *Soviet nuclear forces* included ICBM and intermediate range missiles, their launch facilities and command centres, nuclear weapons storage sites, airfields with nuclear-capable aircraft and ballistic missile submarine bases. There were approximately 2,000 targets in this category. *Conventional military forces* included barracks, naval bases, supply depots and conventional airfields and comprised 20,000 targets. *The Military and Political Leadership* included command bunkers, key communications and intelligence facilities and ran to around 3,000 targets. Finally, *economic and industrial targets* included war-supporting industries such as munitions and weapons factories, transport and energy facilities and industries that might contribute to economic recovery after a nuclear war, such as coal, steel and cement production facilities. This economic and industrial base included about 15,000 targets.

Furthermore, targeting plans such as SIOP-5 involved a number of levels of nuclear war-fighting, ranging from limited use of strategic nuclear weapons for specified actions through to all-out nuclear war – a central nuclear exchange. Thus, *regional nuclear options* might involve the destruction of leading elements of an attacking force, a form of strategic nuclear targeting that was very similar to NATO's policy for using tactical nuclear weapons in Europe. *Limited nuclear options* might involve a more substantial use of nuclear weapons leading to the selective destruction of fixed enemy military or industrial targets. This might amount to an attack falling short of general destruction but might induce a negotiated end to nuclear war-fighting short of a central nuclear exchange.

SIOP-5 included *major attack options* meaning the substantial use of strategic nuclear forces against a wide range of Soviet targets, but it also included a series of possibilities termed *selective attack options*. Some of this gives a clear idea of the tendency to nuclear war-fighting. They included the targeting of Soviet facilities adjacent to allied states, one example up until the end of the 1970s being the destruction of Soviet military facilities such as army bases and airfields close to Iran, then an ally of the United States.[13] Another selective option, in the event of a war involving China against the Soviet Union, would have been destroying Soviet military forces close to China, an option known colloquially as 'kicking the back door in'.[14]

According to Ball, within each of these groups of options, there was a wide range of further plans, including 'with-holds' – targets not attacked – such as population centres and national command and control systems. Specifically avoiding the destruction of population centres *per se* ran in the face of the declaratory policy of mutually assured destruction, although any major attack on military and political targets would have led to mass civilian casualties. Avoiding the destruction of command and control systems made it more possible, at least to the nuclear planners, to envisage a nuclear war being controlled, with a negotiated end to the conflict. It is clear that SIOP-5 and the deployment policy which it embraced was firmly based on the idea that nuclear wars could be fought without assured destruction – that victory was possible.

Furthermore, the idea of first strike was certainly embraced in the 1980s, just as General le May had indicated in the 1950s. As Ball comments: 'Special categories of targets have also been delineated for pre-emptive attacks against the Soviet Union and for launch-on-warning (LOW) or launch under attack (LUA) scenarios in the event of unequivocal warning of Soviet attack.'[15]

By the early 1980s, another element was intruding into nuclear strategy, the Strategic Defence Initiative (SDI – popularly called 'Star Wars') and its Soviet equivalent. There had been limited deployment of anti-missile defences in the previous two decades, but mutual agreement embodied in the Anti-Ballistic Missile Treaty had limited this to help prevent a further escalation of offensive forces. SDI made superficial sense in that it appeared to suggest that a state could be fully defended from incoming ballistic missiles. It was politically popular with the Reagan administration and also with defence manufacturers who could see the possibilities of substantially expanded research and development budgets, but expert opinion was, from the start, dubious that any missile defence system could be so effective as to provide full protection from thousands of warheads. The much more troubling aspect of SDI was the idea that it might be employed in conjunction with highly accurate MIRVed missiles. While an SDI system could not protect against an all-out missile attack, it might offer significant protection against a residual nuclear attack coming from a state that had lost the great majority of its nuclear forces to a disarming first strike.[16]

Tactical nuclear weapons and first use

Reviewing the development and deployment of strategic nuclear weapons overall, it is evident that an enduring feature has been a commitment to nuclear war-fighting. Although far less is known of Soviet targeting policy, the available evidence, coupled with the nature and extent of the strategic systems developed during the Cold War, indicates that the Soviet outlook had many similar features.[17] This was also the case with the development of tactical nuclear weapons, where NATO has maintained a long-time policy of flexible response, an anodyne term that embraces first use.

Although the early nuclear weapons were essentially strategic – intended for use against the core assets of an opposing state, the development of nuclear weapons intended for tactical use within particular war zones was an early feature of the East-West nuclear confrontation. By the late 1950s both the United States and the Soviet Union were developing relatively low-yield free-fall bombs as well as early forms of nuclear-capable artillery. Over the next 25 years, a remarkable array of tactical nuclear weapons was developed and deployed, covering almost every type of military posture.

As well as free-fall bombs, short-range battlefield missiles were developed along with nuclear-tipped anti-aircraft missiles and several types of nuclear artillery and mortars. Nuclear land mines known as atomic demolition munitions were developed that could be emplaced to destroy major bridges or tunnels or even block mountain passes. At sea, submarines were equipped with nuclear-tipped torpedoes, surface ships carried anti-submarine nuclear depth bombs which could be delivered by missile or helicopter and aircraft carriers could fly off strike aircraft carrying several kinds of nuclear bomb. There were even air-to-air missiles such as the US Genie, that were nuclear-armed.[18]

By the 1980s there were around 20,000 tactical nuclear weapons deployed by the United States and the Soviet Union, based in more than 15 countries and on warships and submarines throughout the world. In the great majority of cases, the presumption was that if such weapons were used, they would not necessarily involve an escalation to an all-out nuclear war. In other words, nuclear war-fighting could be controlled. In Europe, perhaps the most tense region of the Cold War nuclear confrontation, both alliances had policies of the first use of nuclear weapons in response to conventional attack.

For NATO in the 1950s, prior to the Soviet Union having developed a large arsenal of nuclear weapons, the posture was codified in a military document MC14/2, colloquially termed the 'trip-wire' posture. Any Soviet attack against NATO would be met with a massive nuclear retaliation, including the use of US strategic nuclear forces, and this assumed that the US could destroy the Soviet Union's nuclear forces and its wider military potential without suffering unacceptable damage itself.

By the early 1960s the Soviet Union was developing many classes of tactical and strategic nuclear weapons, making it less vulnerable to a US nuclear attack. In such circumstances, MC14/2 became far less acceptable to western military planners who consequently sought to develop a more flexible nuclear posture for NATO. This became known as flexible response and involved the ability to respond to Soviet military actions with a wide range of military forces, but also with the provision that nuclear weapons could be used first in such a way as to force the Soviet Union to halt any aggression and withdraw. Once again, there was the belief that a nuclear war could be fought and won.[19]

The new flexible response doctrine was progressively accepted by NATO member states in 1967 and 1968 and was codified in MC14/3 entitled *Overall Strategic Concept for the Defence of the NATO Area*. It was a posture with one particular advantage for the United States in that it might avoid nuclear weapons being used against its own territory. A US Army colonel expressed this rather candidly at the time, writing that the strategy: 'recognizes the need for a capability to cope with situations short of general nuclear war and undertakes to maintain a forward posture designed to keep such situations as far away from the United States as possible.'[20]

Flexible response was to remain in operation for most of the last 25 years of the Cold War, including periods of considerable tension in the early 1980s. Operational plans for nuclear use were (and are) developed by the Nuclear Activities Branch of the Supreme Headquarters, Allied Powers in Europe (SHAPE) near Mons in Belgium, operating in conjunction with the US Joint Strategic Target Planning Staff responsible for the SIOP strategic nuclear posture from its base in Omaha, Nebraska.

By the early 1970s, flexible response was well established under the Nuclear Operations Plan which embraced two levels of the use of tactical nuclear weapons against Soviet forces, selective options and general response. Selective options involved a variety of plans, many of them assuming first use of nuclear weapons against Warsaw Pact conventional forces. At the lowest level, these could include up to five small air-burst nuclear detonations intended as warning shots to demonstrate NATO's intent.

At a rather higher level of use were the so-called pre-packaged options involving up to 100 nuclear weapons, the US Army Field Manual at the time defining a package thus:

> a group of nuclear weapons of specific yields for use in a specific area and within a limited time to support a specific tactical goal... Each package must contain nuclear weapons sufficient to alter the tactical situation decisively and to accomplish the mission.[21]

While these different levels of selective use were thought to be possible ways of winning a nuclear war, the possibility remained that this would fail, and a more general nuclear exchange would result. This was the second level of use of tactical nuclear weapons and was termed a general nuclear response in which NATO nuclear forces in Europe would be used on a massive scale along with US strategic forces.

Thus, by the end of the 1970s, NATO had developed a flexible response strategy which involved detailed planning for the selective first use of nuclear weapons in the belief that a limited nuclear war could be won. This was followed, in the early 1980s, by two further developments that made the strategy even more risky.

Since the formulation of MC14/3, the West Germans had been unhappy at the prospect of short range nuclear weapons being used, since this would involve huge civilian casualties among their own people. They therefore argued within NATO nuclear planning circles that first use should involve the immediate selection of targets within the Soviet Union. This required highly accurate ballistic missiles with a very short flight time yet with a range sufficient to destroy key targets such as command centres within the Soviet Union. The terminally-guided Pershing 2 missile was the first to have this capability and was deployed in West Germany from late 1983. It was one of a new generation of mobile 'theatre nuclear forces' (TNF) that caused considerable concern in the Soviet Union which did not have a similarly accurate missile.[22]

In addition to the deployment of missiles such as the Pershing 2, there was also evidence that NATO was moving towards a policy of early first use of nuclear weapons, one indication of this coming eventually from a remarkably candid interview given by the NATO supreme commander, General Bernard Rogers, who said that his orders were:

> Before you lose the cohesiveness of the alliance – that is, before you are subject to (conventional Soviet military) penetration on a fairly broad scale – you *will* request, not you may, but you *will* request the use of nuclear weapons...[23]

In presenting its nuclear policy to the public, much of the NATO argument was based on the idea of countering overwhelming Soviet conventional forces with nuclear weapons. With the benefit of hindsight, and observing the rapid collapse of Soviet conventional strength at the end of the Cold War, it is arguable whether the massive but largely conscript armies of the Warsaw Pact would have presented the threat to NATO that was so often supposed. Furthermore, there is evidence that first use was more about an overall concept of winning a war than just compensating for any perceived conventional imbalance. This was demonstrated in a revealing presentation of NATO nuclear policy by the UK government:

> The fundamental objective of maintaining the capability for selective sub-strategic use of theatre weapons is political – to demonstrate in advance that NATO has the capability and will to use nuclear weapons in a deliberate, politically controlled way with the objective of restoring deterrence by inducing the aggressor to make the decision to terminate his aggression and withdraw. The role of TNF is not to compensate for any imbalance in conventional forces. The achievement of conventional parity could have very positive conse-quences for the Alliance's strategy of deterrence. But it would not, of itself, obviate the need for theatre nuclear forces.[24]

United States strategic policy, together with NATO nuclear policy, were both mirrored by the policies of the Soviet Union. Although the US tended to maintain a technical lead, especially in such crucial areas as missile accuracy, the Soviet Union established a massive nuclear weapons industry, producing numbers of nuclear warheads which, as became clear after the end of the Cold War, even exceeded the apparently inflated western intelligence estimates of the Cold War years. Moreover, Soviet strategic weapons were often much more powerful than their US counterparts, somewhat compensating for US technical superiority.

For much of the Cold War era, the Soviet Union insisted that it had a policy of no first use of nuclear weapons. In more recent years, there is ample evidence that this would not have not been the policy in practice. If an East-West crisis had spilled over into a war, then Soviet policy in Europe would have been to escalate rapidly, including the early use of nuclear weapons. Quite possibly this was because of the Soviet awareness of NATO's technical superiority, especially the deployment of highly accurate missiles capable of destroying Soviet command and communications systems.[25]

Overall, there was a dynamic of two superpowers entrenched in a nuclear arms race where the first use of nuclear weapons was considered a rational part of military planning and where strategic nuclear developments were so destabilising that tactics such as launch-on-warning were considered necessary developments. Underlying this was a belief that a nuclear war could be fought and won.

Anti-nuclear campaigners and a few peace researchers and conflict analysts questioned such policies at the time, but they were roundly criticised as pro-Soviet defeatists, even when they pointed to the risks of nuclear accidents and crisis instability. Since the ending of the Cold War, however, their views have begun to resonate with those of some senior retired military and even a few former nuclear planners who are now able to recognise the extent of the dangers faced during the Cold War, dangers exemplified both by the experience of actual nuclear accidents and also of crises which now appear to have been far more dangerous than was publicly acknowledged at the time.

Nuclear accidents

During the Cold War years there were more than 40 accidents involving nuclear weapons or military nuclear reactors, some of which resulted in radioactive contamination and others in the loss of nuclear weapons. In addition, the United States, the Soviet Union and Britain all experienced major problems with their nuclear weapons industries. In Britain, for example, a serious fire occurred at the Windscale plutonium production plant in 1957, when one of the reactor piles caught fire and burned for three days, releasing radioactive iodine and polonium into the atmosphere. Close to half a million gallons of milk from dairy farms in the area were withdrawn from consumption and poured into local rivers and the Irish Sea. In the United States, there were protracted problems with nuclear weapons plants at Hanford River and Rocky Flats, and US intelligence reports indicated major problems of radioactive contamination in the Soviet Union stemming from production accidents.

The record on nuclear weapons accidents is far from complete, especially in the case of the Soviet Union where information relates almost entirely to naval accidents in international waters, but what is already known indicates a series of problems stretching over four decades or more.[26]

One of the earliest accidents involved a B-47 bomber on an overseas flight in March 1956, probably to a US base in Europe, that was lost with its crew and two nuclear capsules and never found. Later that year, another B-47 crashed into a nuclear weapons storage igloo at RAF Lakenheath in Suffolk, killing the four crew members. The plane was unarmed but the fire that followed enveloped the store, which contained three B6 nuclear bombs. The bombs were burnt and damaged although, fortunately, the high explosive elements did not detonate. Another B-47 jettisoned a nuclear bomb over the Atlantic coast of Georgia after a mid-air accident 18 months later. The bomb was not recovered.

During the 1960s the United States maintained a large force of B-52 strategic bombers, and two were involved in serious accidents within four days in January 1966. At Palomares in Spain a B-52 collided with a tanker aircraft. One of its four nuclear weapons was recovered from land, and another after a 15-week search at sea, but the high explosive components of the other two detonated, leading to substantial radioactive contamination. Over 1,400 tons of soil and vegetation had later to be moved to a safe storage site in Texas. In the second accident a B-52 crashed while seven miles out from Thule Air Force Base in Greenland. All four H-bombs were destroyed in the crash and 1.5 million gallons of ice, snow and water had to be removed in the decontamination operation.

Much more recently, in June 1995, a B-52 practising for an air show at Fairchild Air Force Base near Spokane, Washington, crashed within 50 feet of a nuclear weapons storage bunker. Witnesses reported that the pilot appeared to throw the plane into a turn to avoid striking the weapons storage area. The pilot was one of the four crew members killed in the crash.[27]

Both the United States and the Soviet Union suffered a series of nuclear submarine accidents during the Cold War, some involving the loss of nuclear weapons. In April 1970, for example, a Soviet *November*-class twin-reactor submarine sank about 170 miles south-west of Land's End after a reactor fire. This class of boat was known to carry tactical nuclear weapons and western attempts at salvage were hindered by a Soviet naval vessel which took up station over the wreck for many months.

There were several serious incidents involving submarine bases. In 1966 a radiation leak is reported to have occurred in a nuclear-powered submarine near Polyarny, close to the Northern Fleet submarine base. According to some reports, members of the repair team may have died of radiation sickness. Early in 1970, another incident took place when a large explosion wrecked part of the Gorki submarine yards leading to radioactive contamination of the Volga River and its Black Sea estuary.

More recently, during the 1980s, the Soviet Union experienced a further series of submarine accidents, the most serious being the loss of a *Yankee*-class ballistic missile submarine in the Atlantic in October 1986. The 8,000-ton submarine carried 16 SS-N-6 ballistic missiles, each probably equipped with two 500 kiloton nuclear warheads rather than the earlier one-megaton warheads which originally equipped this missile. The submarine experienced a fire and the explosion of the propellant of one of the missiles, killing three crew and blasting a hole through the side of the submarine's hull. The fire was eventually extinguished two days later and an attempt was made to take the submarine in tow. This failed and the boat was lost with all its 32 nuclear warheads still on board.

Among the most serious of the US submarine accidents was the loss of the *USS Scorpion* with all of her crew, 450 miles south-west of the Azores on 21 May 1968. This followed an accident believed to have been caused by the explosion of an accidentally armed non-nuclear torpedo, but the submarine is also known to have been armed with nuclear-tipped anti-submarine weapons, probably the UUM-44A SUBROC weapon which carried the W55 warhead with a 1–5 kiloton yield.

Perhaps the most remarkable nuclear weapon accident of the Cold War years took place on 19 September 1980 and involved a Titan II ICBM, a liquid-fuelled missile carrying a massive 9-megaton W53 thermonuclear warhead in a Mark 6 re-entry vehicle. During routine maintenance of the missile a mechanic dropped a wrench down a silo which hit the side of the missile and ruptured a fuel tank. Release of the propellant led to a large explosion several hours later that killed two men. The force of the explosion ejected the re-entry vehicle with its thermonuclear warhead from the silo and threw it 200 feet. Although not reported in the press at the time, it was later confirmed that there had been contamination of the site.

A near-farcical event took place four years later at a Minuteman III ICBM silo at Warren Air Force Base near Cheyenne, Wyoming, when a computer system appeared to indicate that the missile was about to launch itself. Air Force officials promptly parked an armoured car on top of the silo door so that the missile would be irreparably damaged if it started to launch. Officials later insisted that there was no risk of an accidental launch but could not explain why it was necessary to take this unusual precaution.[28]

Although many of the nuclear accidents took place in locations away from immediate zones of tension, there were exceptions. One example, which did not specifically involve a nuclear weapon, is salient for other reasons. On 25 May 1982, an RAF Phantom interceptor in North

Germany accidentally fired a Sidewinder air-to-air missile which locked on to an RAF Jaguar nuclear-capable strike aircraft that was within range. The missile severely damaged the plane which then crashed, although the pilot ejected safely. That such an accident could happen caused grave concern, the more so as it took place at a time of considerable tension. At the time, Britain was involved in a bitter war with Argentina over the control of the Falkland/Malvinas islands, a major crisis was developing between Israel, Lebanon and Syria, and East-West tensions were rising, not least because of the impending deployment of cruise and Pershing missiles in Western Europe.

The experience of Cold War crises

As far as is known, none of the numerous accidents with nuclear weapons during the Cold War caused the detonation of a nuclear weapon, and protagonists of nuclear strategy cite this as an indication of the extent of the safety measures in place. At the same time, it is likely that a number of the known incidents, and possibly some incidents which are still classified, may have been more dangerous than has so far become apparent. There are indications of this in the writings of some analysts with intimate knowledge of events of the period. One of the leading US strategists of the Reagan era was Fred Iklé, a strong supporter of a vigorous US military posture at the time. He has recently felt able to indicate his concerns about the problems of that era by writing about the potential dangers of future nuclear proliferation:

> ...despite the several accidents and mistakes that could have sparked a large-scale nuclear war (and whose horrid details are still largely shrouded in secrecy), the superpowers always stopped just short of the abyss. At each of these fateful moments, the world escaped nuclear holocaust – seemingly by accident.[29]

During the Cold War there were a number of crises or false alarms, the seriousness of which is now clear, three of them dating back to the earliest years of the Cold War. The Korean War, from 1950 to 1953, was officially a UN operation, although the leadership was American and the great majority of the forces ranged against the North Koreans and Chinese were American and South Korean. The US gave consideration to both the tactical and strategic use of nuclear weapons – tactical against troop concentrations and transit routes, and strategic against troop assembly areas and industrials targets both in North Korea and China.[30]

President Truman contemplated the risk of an escalation to a nuclear war involving the Soviet Union, writing in his journal in January 1952 that 'It means that Moscow, St. Petersburg, Vladivostok, Peking,

Shanghai, Port Arthur, Dairen, Odessa, Stalingrad, and every manufac-turing plant in China and the Soviet Union will be eliminated.'[31] Unlike the head of the forces in Korea, General MacArthur, Truman was ultimately against the use of nuclear weapons, partly because of the risk of escalation to war with the Soviet Union involving Soviet action against European targets, but also because it was a UN operation and would involve, in MacArthur's estimation, up to 50 of the limited stock of 400 nuclear weapons available in the early part of the war.[32]

The Korean War ended in stalemate in 1953, but the Indo-China war between the French and the Viet-Minh was entering its final phase in early 1954, with the French facing a potentially catastrophic defeat as their strategic fortress town of Dien Bien Phu came under attack. The French requested US aid and Operation Vulture was planned, which would involve conventional and then nuclear strikes by US bombers against Viet Minh positions around Dien Bien Phu. According to Polmar, President Eisenhower and the majority of the Chiefs of Staff were in favour of Operation Vulture, but there were divisions in Washington, and the British were also opposed. A key factor was the reluctance of the French to accept US direction of the war, and the plan was not implemented. Dien Bien Phu fell to the Viet Minh early in May 1954.[33]

Later that year, a crisis developed over the status of the offshore islands of Quemoy and Matsu, controlled by the nationalist Chinese government on Taiwan but close to the coast of mainland China. Again, use of tactical nuclear weapons was considered by the United States in the event of a Chinese invasion of the islands, but the crisis was resolved early in 1955 without the Chinese taking that action.

Nearly a decade later, possibly the most serious crisis of the Cold War developed. In the summer and early autumn of 1962 the Soviet Union began to deploy medium-range ballistic missiles to Cuba, capable of reaching a wide range of targets in the United States. Part of the motive was to counter the US ability to hit Soviet targets with Thor and Jupiter missiles based in Britain and Turkey, partly it was to counter the perceived strategic threat from US ICBMs, especially the new solid-fuelled Minuteman missiles that were just starting to be deployed. When the US became aware of the Soviet move in October 1962, it considered it to be a grave threat to US security, and a naval quarantine was ordered to prevent further Soviet shipments to Cuba.

As the crisis deepened, the US began to organise for a possible air assault against Cuba followed by an invasion which would involve 180,000 troops. US intelligence reported that there were only 10,000 Soviet troops in Cuba and that they did not have tactical nuclear weapons. In both respects the assessments were wrong – the Soviet Union had 43,000 troops on the island alongside more than 250,000 Cuban troops. Furthermore, the Soviet Union already had 90 tactical nuclear warheads in Cuba, and as the crisis reached its peak, warheads were moved from storage sites to positions close to their delivery systems in anticipation of an invasion.

The US Secretary of Defense at the time, Robert McNamara, has recently reviewed these events:

> Clearly, there was a high risk that, in the face of a US attack – which many in the US government, military and civilian alike, were prepared to recommend to President Kennedy – the Soviet forces in Cuba would have decided to use their nuclear weapons rather than lose them. We need not speculate about what would have happened in that event. We can predict the results with certainty. Although a US invasion force would not have been equipped with tactical nuclear warheads – the President and I had specifically prohibited that – no one should believe that had American troops been attacked with such weapons, the US would have refrained from a nuclear response. And where would it have ended? In utter disaster, not just for the Soviet Union, Cuba and the United States but for all nations across the globe that would have suffered from the fall-out of the nuclear exchange. [34]

One of the most worrying aspects of the Cuban Missile Crisis concerns the behaviour of some sectors of the US military at the time. As the crisis developed, Strategic Air Command secretly placed nuclear warheads on nine of the ten test ICBMs being held at Vandenberg Air Force Base in California. This was a procedure to give them an additional supply of ICBMs that were just coming into service. Vandenberg was the main base for testing these new missiles and a tenth missile, which was unarmed, was launched on a scheduled test flight. This launch apparently took no account of the likely effect on Soviet intelligence if it had become aware of the arming of the other missiles. [35]

At one point in the crisis, the North American Air Defence command system received data indicating that a missile had been launched from Cuba and was about to hit the city of Tampa in Florida. In reality, a test tape had been fed into the computer system. Perhaps the most remarkable event took place at Malmstrom Air Force Base in Montana at the height of the crisis. Minuteman missiles were being installed at the base and air force technicians broke the safety rules and jerry-rigged some missiles so that they could, *in extremis*, launch them themselves without receiving orders to do so. [36]

Eleven years after the Cuban Missile Crisis, the Yom Kippur/Ramadan war between Israel, Egypt and Syria was an occasion when both tactical and strategic nuclear weapons could have become involved. By 1973, Israel had a small number of Jericho ramp-launched surface-to-surface missiles fitted with 20-kiloton nuclear warheads. Early in the conflict, when Israel was hard pressed by the Egyptian attack through the Bar Lev line across the Suez Canal and by the Syrian attack across the Golan

Heights, there was huge concern that Israel's own territory might be occupied by Arab forces.

In three days of urgent activity, Jericho missile warheads were prepared for possible use at the Dimona nuclear weapons plant near Beersheba. The United States learnt of this, obtaining confirmation by a reconnaissance flight of an SR-71 Blackbird spy-plane. There is also some evidence that the Soviet Union was prepared to provide Egypt with a balancing force of nuclear warheads for its Scud missiles – a freighter with such warheads aboard is reported to have left the Nikolaev Naval Base at Odessa on the Black Sea.[37]

In the event, Israel succeeded in holding Egyptian and Syrian forces by conventional means, and within two weeks of the start of the conflict was threatening the Egyptian Third Army with defeat, aided, in part, by substantial logistical support from the United States. In these circumstances there were fears that the Soviet Union might intervene to prevent an Egyptian defeat, precipitating a major regional war. As part of its response, the United States moved its nuclear forces to an unusually high state of alert around the world, from DefCon 5 (Defense Condition 5, normal peace-time operations) to DefCon 3. In doing so, the United States neglected to inform its allies for several hours, including states such as Britain which was host to substantial US nuclear forces.[38] Again, further escalation was avoided, not least as Washington put pressure on Israel to accept a cease-fire short of a potentially unstable victory over Egypt.

Potential for nuclear use also applied to other states. Britain deployed nuclear-capable V-bombers to Malaysia in the early 1960s at the time of confrontation with Indonesia over Borneo. Twenty years later, in 1982, tactical nuclear weapons were deployed on Task Force ships during the Falklands War, and a Polaris strategic missile submarine was deployed away from its normal area of patrol in the North Atlantic to bring it within range of Argentina.[39]

One of the most indicative crises of the Cold War happened in Europe in the autumn of 1983 and did not enter the public domain until several years later. From 1979 through to 1983, East/West relations deteriorated markedly. In part, this was in response to the Soviet invasion of Afghanistan, but it is also related to the election of the hawkish Reagan and Thatcher governments in Washington and London, and the development of a range of new nuclear weapons systems including the US Trident, Pershing 2 and cruise missiles and the Soviet SS-20 and SS-24 missiles.

According to the Soviet defector, Oleg Gordievsky, the near-moribund Soviet leadership, led by the ageing Brezhnev, had expected the incoming Reagan administration of 1981 to tone down its vigorously anti-Soviet rhetoric once in office, emulating his Republican predecessor, Richard Nixon. In the event, the reverse happened as the US nuclear modernisation programme accelerated, bringing in more accurate ballistic missiles as well as open discussions about countervailing (war-winning) strategies.

One Soviet response, code-named RYAN, required operatives in western countries to watch out for possible preparations for war, a process started in November 1981 and still in progress two years later. By the autumn of 1983 Brezhnev had died and his successor, Andropov, was already terminally ill, Reagan was fully engaged in 'evil empire' rhetoric, was fully committed to the new Strategic Defence Initiative and deployment of the highly accurate Pershing 2 missiles was just starting in West Germany. To make matters worse, a civilian Korean Airlines Boeing 747 was shot down by a Soviet fighter when it strayed into Soviet airspace in the Far East.

Early in November 1983, NATO commenced a set of highly secret exercises to test the release plans for nuclear warheads, *Able Archer* being the first such exercise to follow the deployment of the Pershing 2 missiles.[40] Warsaw Pact surveillance systems monitored this process and NATO systems, in turn, monitored Warsaw Pact activity. According to one account, it quickly became apparent that NATO was 'listening in' to a gathering crisis:

> Instead of the normal monitoring to be expected from across the Iron Curtain, a sharp increase was registered in both volume and urgency of the Eastern Bloc traffic. The incredible seemed to be happening, namely that the Warsaw Pact suspected it might really be facing nuclear attack at any moment.[41]

Documents later released from Warsaw Pact military committees in East Germany later confirmed this view: 'On November 9, KGB stations in Europe were warned that American bases had been put on alert. The KGB suspected that a NATO exercise, Able Archer, could be a full-scale nuclear assault.'[42]

As NATO officials became aware of the unexpected effect of *Able Archer*, significant changes were made to such exercises and the whole process of testing nuclear tactics was modified to avoid any such misinterpretations happening again.

A crisis out of nowhere

Perhaps one of the most remarkable examples of a sudden and entirely unpredictable crisis occurred several years after the end of the Cold War. Early on the morning of 25 January 1995 a Norwegian–US research team launched a large four-stage Black Brant XII rocket as part of a long-term programme to study the Northern Lights. The rocket was launched from an island off the north coast of Norway, an area that had been very sensitive during the Cold War, given that it was close to a possible launch zone for US submarine-launched ballistic missiles aimed at targets in the former Soviet Union.[43]

To avoid false alarms, such experiments were notified in advance to the relevant Russian authorities, and the Norwegian Foreign Ministry had sent a letter to them reporting an impending launch of a research rocket in late January or early February, depending on weather conditions. Probably as a result of the chaotic state of the Russian bureaucracy at the time, this message had not been received by Russian radar crews. Moreover, the Black Brant XII rocket was much larger than previous experiments and its four stages resembled the multiple stages of a US submarine-launched Trident missile.

The Trident D5 missile carries six substantial thermonuclear warheads and, to the radar operators, it was not possible to dismiss the idea that it might be part of a surprise attack on Russia. Within minutes the alert had reached the highest levels in Russia and, possibly for the first time, President Yeltsin's 'nuclear briefcase' was activated. It would have been possible for a Trident missile launched from off the Norwegian coast to have delivered its warheads over Moscow within 20 minutes, giving Yeltsin very little time to decide whether to launch a retaliatory strike. In the event, the early warning system was able to detect, within those 20 minutes, that the Black Brant rocket was not heading for Russian territory and the alert status was reduced.[44]

The idea that such a crisis could develop in a matter of minutes 'out of the blue' may seem far-fetched, but there are two features of this incident that offer a degree of explanation. The first is that if a surprise nuclear attack on the Soviet Union, or its successor state, Russia, had ever been contemplated, then it would almost certainly have started with submarines launching ballistic missiles from Arctic seas towards the command and control centres in Moscow, with some of the warheads fused to detonate at high altitudes to produce a massive electro-magnetic pulse (EMP) to disrupt electronic equipment in and around the capital.

Another explanation for this sudden and dangerous alert lay with an event in 1987 when a young German, Mathias Rust, flew a light aircraft right across Russia to Moscow and landed in Red Square. Rust's ability to evade detection by Soviet air defences had had a profound effect, making operatives highly sensitive to the need to avoid getting caught out. Thus, at several levels up the ladder of command, officers decided to play safe and pass on the alert rather than check in detail before doing so.

When they first detected the research rocket, the radar operators could be blamed for causing a false alarm by passing on details of the launch, but they were concerned that the rocket might just have been part of a missile attack, and passed on responsibility to a higher level. The general on duty adopted a similar stance, not least because of the slight possibility that the missile might be equipped with an EMP warhead intended for Moscow as a prelude to a more general attack.[45]

Once the warning of the rocket's trajectory had been passed on to the Russian command and control system, Kazbek, predetermined procedures came into operation, ending with alerts in the three nuclear briefcases held by the Russian President, Defence Minister and Chief of Staff. With the command and control system now operating in combat mode, the trajectory of the rocket was monitored as Yeltsin and his colleagues conferred. Only when it was concluded that the rocket was not a threat was the alert terminated, the whole episode lasting just a few minutes.

Resourcing the Cold War

The 45 year period of the Cold War was an era of uniquely high military expenditure outside of a world war. The peak was reached in the late 1980s, at a global level of well over $1 trillion dollars at 2000 prices, with the great majority of the expenditure being within the industrialised countries of the North. At the peak of the Cold War, public spending on the military even exceeded public spending on health or education. At 1987 prices, expenditure on the military was $926 billion, of which 84 per cent was spent in the developed world, the overwhelming majority of it by the NATO and Warsaw Pact alliances. In that same year, world public expenditure on health was $794 billion and on education it was $904 billion. Put another way, spending by NATO and the Warsaw Pact on the military was $745 billion, whereas public spending on health and education in the whole of the developing world was less than one-fifth of this at $143 billion.[46]

Perhaps a more graphic contrast is demonstrated by referring to one particular global problem – food supply. In the early 1970s, the world experienced a sudden and unexpected down-turn in food production, with the effects being serious food shortages in many third world countries. At its peak the world food crisis in 1974 put some 40 million people at risk of famine in 22 countries across Asia, Africa and Latin America. One major UN response was the 1974 World Food Congress in Rome and, partially as a result of that conference, emergency steps were taken to meet the immediate shortages.

The conference went further than this, setting out a 10-year programme of public support for tropical agricultural development designed to improve self-reliance in food production across the Third World and prevent further crises. The support necessary for such a programme involved a three-fold increase in spending on agricultural development to $5 billion a year for the ten years (at 1974 prices). This amounted to approximately 2 per cent of world military spending at that time. In the eventuality, there were modest increases in agricultural development funding that came nowhere near meeting the demands, and further famines and food shortages were experienced in the 1980s and 1990s.[47]

There are innumerable other examples that can be drawn from the financing of the Cold War confrontation, and there is a frequent counter-argument that if the military spending had not been so high, there was no guarantee that social expenditure would have been improved. While this may be true, the fact remains that the Cold War was an extraordinary diversion of resources to what, in other respects, was a systematically dangerous confrontation.

This diversion of resources extends also to research expenditure. Supporting data is available for the whole of the Cold War period, but it is appropriate to take the year 1982, when the final stages of the Cold War were under way but before the peak commitments of the mid-1980s. In that year, US government-funded research and development on the military was $22 billion, compared with $11.3 billion for all government-funded civil research. The contrasts between military and health research are even more extreme – taking the United States and the European community together, and providing a per capita measure, military research spending was four times that of health research spending.

Proxy wars

Although NATO and the Warsaw Pact never engaged in direct military conflict, the whole of the Cold War period was marked by proxy wars, fought in most regions of the world, in which major conflicts were fuelled by Cold War tensions, were enhanced by massive arms commitments from the superpower alliances and were immensely costly in human terms.

Many of the conflicts in Central America, Southern Africa, the Horn of Africa, Indo-China, Korea and Afghanistan had direct or indirect superpower involvement. 100,000 people died in El Salvador and nearly as many in Nicaragua, 750,000 died in Angola, 1 million in Mozambique and over 900,000 in the Horn of Africa. In Asia the losses were even greater – 1.5 million in Afghanistan, 2.3 million in Vietnam and 3 million in Korea. While the Soviet Union and the United States had troops directly involved in some of these wars, not least Afghanistan and Vietnam, the overwhelming majority of the casualties were local people, mostly civilians. Indirectly, the proxy wars of the Cold War era were responsible for the deaths of at least 10 million people.[48]

Proliferation of weapons

The Cold War era was also a period of rapid developments in military technology, with many of these developments proliferating then, and since, across the world. In the decade since the end of the Cold War, as much of the conventional military equipment has been scaled down, a result has been a 'cascading' of light arms into zones of conflict or even of civil unrest. This has been especially marked in South Asia and Africa, with semiautomatic rifles and other light arms available on the grey and black markets for a fraction of their original cost.

The Cold War was also marked by the development and proliferation of nuclear, chemical and biological weapons of mass destruction, ballistic missiles, area-impact munitions and anti-personnel landmines. Nuclear proliferation was, to an extent, under some control in the latter part of the Cold War. There was even some limited progress as Brazil and Argentina abandoned their nuclear ambitions, South Africa gave up its small arsenal, and Ukraine, Belarus and Kazakstan returned the Soviet nuclear arsenals to Russia. More recently though, Indian and Pakistani nuclear ambitions have accelerated and Iraq was clearly involved in substantial nuclear ambitions.

There is a similar picture for chemical and biological weapons. The United States and the Soviet Union had massive chemical arsenals by the late 1980s, certainly over 50,000 tons each. They, and France, began a progressive disarmament in the 1990s, but states such as Egypt, Israel, Iran, Iraq, Libya, North Korea and Syria were still involved, although Iraq's chemical warfare programme was heavily limited by the activities of the UN Special Commission (UNSCOM).

The United States and the Soviet Union were heavily involved in biological weapons research, development and stockpiling in the early Cold War years. Along with Britain, France and many other countries, they were then committed to the Biological and Toxin Weapons Convention after 1972, although there is now abundant evidence that the Soviets continued with a covert programme, not least because they did not believe that the US, with its impressive expertise in genetic engineering and biotechnology, had abandoned its own programme. In the 1990s there were repeated assessments from western intelligence agencies that a significant number of states were maintaining active offensive biological warfare programmes, especially in the Middle East and East Asia.

For the past 20 years or more, there has been a strong public perception that missiles and bombs are getting steadily more accurate, and are now able to destroy targets without causing other damage. While this has indeed been a trend, although with many serious errors in recent wars in the Balkans and Middle East, it has been accompanied by another far less well-known development, that of area-impact munitions. The crude napalm of the Korean and Vietnam Wars has long since been overtaken by far more sophisticated devices. Among these are fuel-air explosives, cluster munitions and multiple-launch rocket systems. Cluster bombs typically distribute hundreds of 'bomblets', each exploding into hundreds or even thousands of high velocity shrapnel fragments. A standard British cluster bomb produces nearly 300,000 shrapnel shards over an acre and a half, shredding anything exposed to it. Some fuel-air explosive arrays can be detonated to give an explosive effect as damaging as a small tactical nuclear weapon and a single salvo of a modern multiple-launch rocket system can destroy a small town in less than a minute.[49]

These kinds of weapons were developed in the 1960s and 1970s, initially by the US and the Soviet Union, but they are now produced by a dozen or more countries and are becoming more commonly used in war. Their effect is to make any major conventional conflict much more devastating, especially when used against unprotected civilians.

Lessons to learn

While this chapter has looked at the history of the Cold War years, and especially the nuclear confrontation, there are conclusions to be drawn that have plenty of relevance for the future. The first is that the sheer intensity of the nuclear arms race was almost unbelievable. Rational politicians, military leaders, planners and strategists were willing parties to a process of overkill that reached the level of a farce. They, or most of them, were also caught up in targeting strategies that went far beyond the declaratory policy of deterrence through the fear of mutually assured destruction, and embraced nuclear war-fighting at both tactical and strategic levels.[50]

This necessarily embraced issues of first use, damage limitation and 'getting your retaliation in first', a process which incorporated highly accurate long-range multiple warhead missiles and ballistic missile defence programmes such as SDI. In particular, the existence of desta-bilising first strike weapons greatly increased the risk of instability at a time of crisis, yet the paradigm or mind-set was so firmly entrenched that there were very few people in the entire system who were able to break out of it.

Furthermore, for much of the Cold War, proponents of nuclear strategy were at pains to point out that there were numerous safeguards built into nuclear systems and that crisis management, too, was robust and stable. Here again, practical experience suggests otherwise, with more and more information coming to light both about nuclear accidents and the dangers of a number of major crises. If such problems can occur in a relatively stable, though massive, confrontation, then such behaviour can also be expected in much less stable and complicated instances of international insecurity in the future.

The Cold War was also a long period of military innovation, much of it permeating the world in the aftermath of the Cold War. It was an extraordinary waste of human and economic resources and it consumed some of the most impressive research talent of most industrial countries for two generations. Powerful modern states led by intelligent leaders and advised by experienced strategists failed to break out of a rigid confrontation for nearly half a century. For each 'side', its own perceptions of its own security needs made it impossible to break out from a narrow view and recognise the overall wastage and dangers of the confrontation. If that paradigm can exist for a substantial part of the world for so long, then similarly simplistic paradigms can be assembled for explaining and controlling the disorderly world that has replaced the Cold War era.

Nuclear Futures

During the 45 years of the Cold War nuclear confrontation, there were two periods of intensive anti-nuclear campaigning in western countries. The first lasted from 1959 to 1963. It developed initially in response to widespread concerns about the health effects of the atmospheric testing of nuclear weapons, but was given a substantial added boost as large numbers of powerful thermonuclear weapons were deployed and as the first ICBMs joined the long-range bombers in the forces of the United States and the Soviet Union.

After the Cuban Missile Crisis of the autumn of 1962, relations between the United States and the Soviet Union began to improve. In the so-called 'Kennedy experiment', President Kennedy initiated a series of moves, starting with a moratorium on nuclear tests in the atmosphere, aimed at curbing the nuclear confrontation, the Soviet Union under Krushchev reciprocated, and a process of confidence-building measures was set in motion that lasted until Kennedy's assassination. The direct result was a treaty involving the United States, the Soviet Union and the United Kingdom that banned all further atmospheric testing. This was completed in 1963 and further treaties were agreed later in the decade, not least the Non-Proliferation Treaty.

As East-West strategic relations improved, the United States became embroiled in the Vietnam War, with substantial domestic implications, and with the anti-war movement stretching over much of the rest of the decade, there was little further anti-nuclear activity in North America or Europe.

At the end of the 1970s, with new Cold War tensions erupting in the wake of the Soviet intervention in Afghanistan, the Iranian Revolution and the development of many new nuclear weapons, a new surge of anti-nuclear campaigning emerged that was to last through to the mid-1980s and finally died down as the Cold War came to an end. From around 1989 onwards, there was a belief that a post-Cold War world could usher in a new world order, a concept dealt a rapid blow by the

Gulf War, the collapse of Yugoslavia into war and civil disruption in many parts of the old Soviet Union.

During the course of the 1990s, the nuclear issue retreated from the arena of public concern, with only occasional flurries coinciding with such events as the French nuclear testing in the Pacific and the World Court ruling on nuclear weapons. The perception was that with the nuclear arms race between the United States and Russia now out of the way, the dangers of nuclear war had passed. This perception was damaged right at the end of the twentieth century with the flurry of nuclear tests by India and Pakistan and the failure of the US Senate to ratify the Comprehensive Test Ban Treaty.[1]

The aim of this chapter is to explore the extent of the nuclear developments of the 1990s and to examine the trends that appear to be emerging for the next 20 years or so. The core question to answer is whether there has been a move towards nuclear disengagement that could take us towards a nuclear-free world, or whether there is, in reality, a transition under way that results in a continuing if quantitatively different commitment to a nuclear future.

Trends in the 1990s

The ending of the Cold War coincided with the all-time peak in world nuclear stockpiles at close to 70,000 nuclear warheads in the late 1980s.[2] Progress in withdrawing warheads was slow at first, but more rapid towards the end of the 1990s, with a halving of total arsenals by the end of the century. In the early 1990s, the United States and the Soviet Union (and its successor, Russia) negotiated the first Strategic Arms Reduction Treaty (START I) that limited strategic arsenals to a maximum of 6,000 warheads each, down from a figure of well over 10,000 each. This was followed by START II negotiations aiming at ceilings of 3,500, but this treaty has not been formally implemented. Britain, France and China all made modest cuts in the nuclear forces but were not party to the START process.

During the course of the 1980s, Argentina and Brazil had given up their nuclear ambitions and US pressure on Taiwan and South Korea appeared to have led them to curtail their own plans. In the early 1990s Ukraine, Belarus and Kazakhstan returned Soviet-era nuclear weapons to Russia and South Africa dismantled its small nuclear arsenal.

There were three specific negative developments and one area of overall concern. First, the inspectors of the UN Special Commission on Iraq were able to demonstrate early in the decade that Iraq had developed a substantial nuclear weapons programme in the previous decade, using multiple routes to produce weapons-grade uranium, and would have had a nuclear capability by the mid-1990s. Second, North Korea remained a state with a siege mentality and an apparent nuclear commitment, US efforts to control this through bilateral agreement being thoroughly uncertain. Third, the continuing tensions between India and Pakistan over Kashmir were made more serious by Indian and Pakistani nuclear test programmes and commitments to nuclear forces at the end of the decade.

The area of overall concern was an abundance of evidence that, despite progress in some areas, the core nuclear powers were intent on maintaining nuclear forces indefinitely. Moreover, all five declared nuclear powers now see clearly defined uses for nuclear weapons in the coming decades – the risk of all-out nuclear war may be diminished, but 'small nuclear wars in far-off places' may become steadily more likely. Nuclear futures are therefore usefully explored by examining recent and current developments in the declared nuclear states as well as trends in proliferation.

US nuclear developments

Recent US experience with nuclear weapons and strategy divides into three phases, all of which give useful indicators of future trends and all of which relate closely to changes in domestic politics, especially the political make-up of Congress. All three have taken place against a background of substantial cuts in overall nuclear warhead stocks, especially of tactical nuclear weapons, and the shutting down of most of the nuclear weapons production facilities, although much of the latter was due more to safety concerns than redundancy.

The first phase was during the final two years of the Bush administration, 1990–92, in the wake of the collapse of the Soviet Union and the experience of the Gulf War. It was essentially a process of looking for new tasks for existing nuclear forces, usually a combination of fears of a resurgent Russia and of perceived Third World threats against US interests. This was reflected, late in 1991, in the publication of a leaked draft of the Strategic Deterrence Study undertaken for US Strategic Air Command (also known as the Reed Report).[3] Its terms of reference stated the belief that 'the growing wealth of petro-nations and newly hegemonic powers is available to bullies and crazies, if they gain control, to wreak havoc on world tranquillity'.

The study itself called for a new nuclear targeting strategy that would include the ability to assemble 'a Nuclear Expeditionary Force...primarily for use against China or Third World targets'.[4] There were indications that such a capability for what was called 'adaptive targeting' existed by 1992.[5] Along with such developments, there were also indications of new nuclear weapons research and development programmes aimed at producing weapons appropriate to new tasks. These included small nuclear warheads that might be fitted to missiles intended to destroy missiles armed with biological warheads, others for attacking deep underground bunkers, as well as electromagnetic pulse (EMP) warheads for disabling electronic equipment. A seminal article in *Strategic Review* in the autumn of 1991 by two Los Alamos researchers had advocated these kinds of systems for use primarily against regional threats from Third World 'rogue' states.[6]

Also at the tail-end of the Bush administration, a vigorous counter-proliferation initiative began to gain momentum, aimed primarily at potential nuclear weapon states but taking in the proliferation of missiles and chemical and biological weapons. It included substantial emphasis on theatre missile defenses (TMD), stemming partly from the Gulf War experience, but also a reflection of the increasing disdain in many circles for the 1972 Anti-Ballistic Missile Treaty and the belief that it limited US abilities to develop defences against 'rogue' states.

This phase of nuclear thinking and planning was very much a part of a much more general right-wing agenda. The Soviet Union was diminishing as a threat, but this was not the time for the United States to drop its guard. In seeking to maintain international stability in American interests, it was essential to have diverse military capabilities at all levels, including nuclear forces. Any idea of moving away from a comprehensive nuclear capability and towards a nuclear-free world was anathema.

There was a pronounced change in the political climate after the Clinton administration took office early in 1993. It brought in a number of people from the Washington arms control community, giving the community more influence than it had had since the start of the Carter administration in the late 1970s. In this atmosphere, some opinion-formers began to suggest that a nuclear-free world was both necessary and desirable. Representative Les Aspin, then Chair of the House Armed Services Committee and later Secretary of Defense, said 'a world without nuclear weapons would actually be better. Nuclear weapons are still the big equalizer but now the United States is not the equalizer but the equalizee.'[7]

Such ideas were endorsed by several retired generals and defence officials, not least the former Chair of the Joint Chiefs of Staff, General Colin Powell, and Robert McNamara, Kennedy's Secretary of Defense.[8] Much of the motivation was similar to that of Aspin – a proliferating world would be difficult to control, whereas a nuclear-free world would be relatively safe for the United States with its formidable conventional forces, but opinion in Congress was sufficiently strong to curb a number of budget proposals for research and development of new nuclear weapons.

Even so, some analysts suspected that work continued in classified or 'black' programmes and that the Stockpile Stewardship Program, an anodyne term for ensuring the safety of the nuclear arsenal, included a capability to design and produce new warheads. Other aspects of this changed climate of opinion looked more positive. At the Department of Energy, responsible for producing nuclear weapons, the Secretary, Hazel O'Leary, initiated a programme of declassifying thousands of documents relating to the history of the nuclear weapons programme. Even when Clinton's September 1994 Nuclear Posture Review made clear the administration's continuing commitment to nuclear weapons, its presentation and outlook was noticeably less hawkish than that of the Bush administration.[9]

Already, though, the debate was entering a third phase, aided hugely by the Republican gains in Congress in the November 1994 mid-term elections leading to a majority view that was antagonistic to arms control and favoured increased funding for new nuclear projects. Among the early casualties was the Arms Control and Disarmament Agency which lost its independence and was swallowed up by the State Department. Congress also cut funding for the Nunn-Lugar Co-operative Threat Reduction Program that aids disarmament and non-proliferation efforts in Russia, and there was vigorous support for a national missile defence scheme and opposition to the ABM Treaty.

Although much of the motivation initially concerned the risk of a resurgent Russia and the perceived need to counter Chinese capabilities, this was rapidly augmented by the need to counter 'rogue' states such as Iraq, Iran, Libya and North Korea and their potential for developing chemical and biological weapons, let alone nuclear weapons. As a report from the Defense Secretary put it in April 1996:

> We received a wake-up call with Saddam Hussein's use of Scud missiles during Operation Desert Storm and new information on his ambitious nuclear, biological, and chemical weapons programs. The proliferation of these horrific weapons presents a grave and urgent risk to the United States and our citizens, allies and troops abroad. Reducing this risk is an absolute priority for the United States.[10]

In testifying in Congress, the Defense Secretary confirmed that nuclear weapons could be used in response to a chemical attack: 'The whole range would be considered.. We have conventional weapons, also advanced conventional weapons – precision-guided munitions, Tomahawk land-attack missiles – and then we have nuclear weapons.'[11]

Such a posture contradicted US negative security assurances (NSAs) dating back to 1978 that said that the US would not use nuclear weapons in response to a non-nuclear attack unless the attacker was linked to a nuclear-weapons state. When questioned whether these assurances apply to attacks using chemical or biological weapons, officials have been very cautious not to make clear NSA commitments. For example:

The US position on the non-use of nuclear weapons is a broad formulation and is not intended to delineate specific US responses to hypothetical aggression against the United States and its allies, such as attacks by chemical and biological weapons... [12]

The future US nuclear posture

The whole of the 1990s is best characterised by an enduring commitment to a nuclear posture embracing smaller but highly versatile nuclear forces, with a range of new roles, especially in the Third World, adding to traditional concerns about Russia and China. Against this, there has been a lively and active debate on an alternative view – the desirability of radically scaling down nuclear arsenals. Though this view held sway in the first couple of years of the Clinton administration, it has been in retreat in the later years of the decade and current prospects are for the vigorous pro-nuclear lobby to prevail.

Such an analysis is supported by two developments in the closing years of the 1990s, both of which have considerable implications for the future. The first is the failure of the US Senate to ratify the Comprehensive Test Ban Treaty. The CTBT was completed in 1996 after years of exhaustive negotiation. Although it did no more than ban nuclear tests, allowing countries to continue with computer simulations and non-nuclear component testing, it was hailed as a breakthrough, not least because it included some quite stringent verification procedures.

Although the US, Russia, Britain, France and China all signed the treaty, entry into force requires ratification by them and another 39 states deemed nuclear capable. By the end of 1999, 26 of these 44 states, including Britain and France, had ratified the treaty, but many key states had not done so, including India, Pakistan, Russia, China and Israel. A number of the states that had not ratified were waiting to see if the United States would do so, and this failure is therefore a very substantial setback for the treaty – indeed the cornerstone treaty in efforts to curb the development and proliferation of nuclear weapons has suffered a serious reversal. Clinton administration officials declared that the US would abide by the treaty, and there is a possibility that political pressures in the US may reverse the vote within two or three years, but there is no disguising that serious damage was done to prospects for nuclear arms control in 1999.

The second feature of US nuclear policy has attracted far less attention than the loss of the CTBT: the commitment to modernising and upgrading its nuclear weapons. This takes two forms, one being the ability to design and test new nuclear weapons and the other being the actual process of producing new weapons. Both of these run directly against the spirit of the CTBT but there is ample evidence that both processes are under way.

Research and development of novel warhead designs requires either explosive nuclear tests (which would have been ruled out by the CTBT) or advanced simulation techniques. Although there is continuing pressure from some right-wing circles for a resumption of testing, this is not likely in the near future. But there has been considerable investment in computer simulation and other forms of non-explosive testing, certainly far in advance of that of any other country.[13]

At first sight, the greater problem for the US is that, with or without new warhead design, it apparently lacks facilities to produce new warheads as almost all production facilities have been shut down, partly because of safety problems that have dogged the entire programme for several decades. However, one plant remains available, the four-acre TA-55 complex at the Los Alamos National Laboratory in New Mexico. Within this complex is Plutonium Facility 4 (PF-4),[14] the main purposes of which are to study weapons ageing processes and to dismantle the 'pits' or cores of plutonium-based nuclear weapons. But it also has the capacity to produce new pits, and may already be doing so:

"We don't know how many pits might be required – a lot depends on final START treaty provisions – but Los Alamos could probably do 50 pits a year," as part of an integrated research and development, enhanced surveillance and limited remanufacturing program, a LANL official said. "In any event, we need to keep that capability intact here by doing at least some small number of pits every year."[15]

Thus the Stockpile Stewardship Program includes a capability to produce nuclear weapons, and this is in addition to a programme to modify existing warheads for new functions.[16] In September 1995 there were reports that a two-year programme was being started to modify the B61 free-fall nuclear bomb to enable it to take on a new earth-penetrating role. This would enable it to target underground command bunkers or CBW facilities that were too well protected to be damaged by conventionally-armed bombs. Progress was rapid and, by the end of 1996, the US Air Force had an emergency capability of some 50 nuclear bombs, with full operational certification coming 15 months later.[17]

The official government view is that the B61-11 is not a 'new' nuclear bomb, merely a modification, in that existing bombs have been upgraded. In a strict technical sense this is true, but the modification is so substantial that the weapon can take on entirely new roles. In the past, it would have been possible for US forces to destroy deeply buried and heavily protected targets, but only by using massive megaton-range nuclear weapons that would have produced huge amounts of radioactive fall-out. The new bomb can burrow up to 50 feet before it detonates, producing an earthquake effect with a small explosive force. The B61–11 is reported to have an explosive yield that can be varied from 0.3 kilotons to 300 kilotons. It is therefore highly flexible and fits in firmly with the idea that small but very accurate nuclear weapons might be used in limited conflicts.[18]

Another nuclear weapon, one of the most numerous in the whole stockpile, is also being modified. The W76 warhead is fitted to most of the Trident submarine-launched ballistic missiles, is carried in a Mk4 re-entry vehicle and is designed to explode above a target. It is therefore intended for use against ports, airfields, army bases, industrial centres and the like, but is not effective against hardened targets. To overcome this, a new fusing system is being developed that will enable the warhead to be detonated at ground level, having a greater effect against a much wider range of targets. There are also reports that the warhead itself may be remanufactured to improve these capabilities.[19]

The standard warhead on the M-X ICBM, the most modern in the US inventory, is also reported to be subject to modifications to increase its capabilities, as is the B-83 megaton-range bomb carried by the B-2 bomber. There are also plans to develop a new ballistic missile submarine and missile system, to undertake further modifications to the B61 nuclear bomb and to undertake research into high-power radio frequency (HPRF) warheads.[20] In short, what appears at first sight to be a stewardship programme that has the function of preserving existing nuclear forces, actually masks a sustained programme of research and development of new nuclear weapons. On present trends, US nuclear weapons will be maintained and modernised and new weapons will be developed. The motivation arises, in part, from the risk of nuclear confrontation with existing or new nuclear powers but also because of the development of other weapons of mass destruction, especially biological weapons. Although there has been a vigorous debate about the validity of moving towards a nuclear-free world, this is having little or no effect on a US nuclear posture that sees nuclear weapons as an essential component of long-term security.[21]

The Russian nuclear programme

After the end of the Cold War, Russian nuclear force levels dropped dramatically, though in most cases nuclear weapons were put into storage rather than dismantled. Even so, production of ballistic missile submarines was stopped, many were withdrawn from service and the numbers on patrol dropped to a handful. No more strategic bombers were produced and only one ICBM, the SS-25, remained in limited production. Most land-based tactical nuclear weapons were withdrawn to storage, and all naval tactical nuclear weapons were withdrawn by early 1993.[22]

All of these developments were within the context of an extraordinary decline in the capabilities of Russian military forces overall. In part, this was because of the collapse of the old Soviet Union, the fragmenting of the republics and the failure of the Commonwealth of Independent States to retain any unity or purpose, but even more significant was the decay of the Russian economy as the rush to a particularly extreme brand of free-market capitalism resulted in a rapidly widening wealth-poverty divide, the impoverishment of a large minority of the Russian population and a substantial decline in government revenues.

In the current context, the extent of this change is reflected in the changes in defence spending compared with that of the United States. At the end of the Cold War, in 1989, the Soviet Union's defence budget was estimated at $120 billion, compared with a US defence budget of $290 billion (both at 1989 prices). The Soviet budget may well have been an underestimate, possibly excluding significant items such as military space programmes, the war in Afghanistan and even nuclear programmes. By 1999, the United States budget was estimated at $276 billion, whereas the Russian budget was just $31 billion (at 1999 prices). Even allowing for inflation, the US defence budget shrank somewhat during the 1990s, but the Russian budget collapsed.[23]

Furthermore, Russia was trying to maintain very large numbers of increasingly obsolete forces, had very little money for research and development or training and was able to purchase hardly any equipment. The state of readiness of the Russian armed forces by the end of the decade was abysmal, and one of the key reasons for Russian failure during the first Chechen War (1994–96) was that its forces were grossly incompetent, with strike aircraft having to be flown by test pilots and instructors, the only air force personnel who had even been able to maintain a minimum number of flying hours to ensure competence.

With this chaotic decline in its economy and the status of its armed forces, nuclear weapons are seen to provide a much cheaper military option in the event of security threats to Russia.[24] This is also indicated by the abandonment of the no-first use policy of the former Soviet Union.[25] It could be claimed that the earlier policy was little more than political rhetoric, but the change does indicate an increased reliance on nuclear forces in the face of the disarray in conventional forces. Indeed, there is a clear trend toward seeing nuclear weapons as a ready answer to foreign threats.

More generally, nuclear forces are seen as almost the only way of maintaining any semblance of military superpower status, especially in the face of NATO's perceived eastern encroachment into Russia's traditional sphere of influence. These trends, in combination, help to explain Russia's continuing commitment to maintaining core strategic and tactical nuclear forces, including modernising some systems. In April 1999, shortly after NATO started its air campaign against Serbia, a special meeting of the Russian Security Council took place. Following this, the then Secretary, Vladimir Putin, announced that there would be new investment in strategic and tactical nuclear weapons, including a further programme of sub-critical tests intended to ensure the safety of existing systems.[26]

The new programme has two components – the speeding up of the production of new weapons and the extension of the service life of existing systems. By the end of 1999, 20 new SS-27 ICBMs had become operational, the service life of *Delta-III* ballistic missile submarines was extended by six years and the development of a new *Dolgoruky*-class submarine would continue.[27] There were also indications of a new tactical multipurpose battlefield missile, first reported to be under development in 1996. Furthermore, a new nuclear command and control architecture is emerging in Russia, including a major underground centre at Kosvinsky Mountain in the Urals. Future plans include two possible responses to any deployment by the United States of a national missile defence system – the equipping of the SS-27 with multiple warheads and the production of a new air-launched cruise missile.

All of the current Russian nuclear developments are being undertaken at a time of extreme financial stringency and this serves to indicate just how important they are believed to be. They may appeal most strongly to the weakened military and the extreme nationalists but the appeal is certainly not restricted to these groups. The nuclear option is seen as one of the few sources of military power and status available to an otherwise impoverished state. Although much of the overall nuclear weapons infrastructure is in disarray, it would seem that a rigorous process of selective maintenance of nuclear systems is under way, ensuring that a core nuclear force involving strategic and tactical weapons is available. The end result is likely to be a nuclear weapons posture comprising core strategic forces seeking to counterbalance western and Chinese forces, together with a range of tactical forces suited to limited nuclear crises which might well involve first use against non-nuclear-armed states. According to Roman Popkovich, Chair of the Defence Committee of the Duma:

> Russia's new military doctrine should include a provision stating that if the threat of the use of general-purpose forces of any state against Russia considerably exceeds the ability of the national general-purpose forces to defend Russia, it shall have the right to deliver a pre-emptive nuclear strike, rather than only a reply or a retaliation strike.[28]

Britain, France and NATO

Several developments in Britain during the 1990s served to give the impression that Britain had embarked on a substantial programme of nuclear disarmament that amounted to a fundamental change in its nuclear posture. There certainly was a process of partial de-nuclearisation, but whether that amounted to a real change in posture was much more debatable.

During the Cold War years, Britain had diverse nuclear forces and was also a base for numerous US deployments. At the height of the Cold War tensions of the early 1980s, Britain maintained a force of four Polaris submarines and a mixed fleet of around 200 Tornado, Jaguar, Vulcan and Buccaneer nuclear strike aircraft, all carrying British-made nuclear warheads. The Royal Navy maintained Sea Harrier nuclear-capable strike aircraft and scores of helicopters that could deliver nuclear depth bombs. The RAF deployed Nimrod anti-submarine aircraft that could deliver American nuclear depth bombs, and British Army units were equipped with nuclear-capable 155mm and 203mm howitzers and Lance battlefield missiles, all intended to use US nuclear shells or warheads. Britain was also used by the United States as a base for ballistic missile submarines, nuclear-capable strike aircraft and cruise missiles.

By the mid-1990s, all of the US systems except a small number of nuclear bombs had been withdrawn, as had the US warheads for use by British forces. Furthermore, all of the British tactical nuclear weapons had been withdrawn, with the exception of a small number intended for Tornado strike aircraft. This process was conducted under the Conservative administration of John Major, prompting the ironic notion that it was a singularly unilateralist government – while Russia was also withdrawing many nuclear forces, none of the changes in Britain, apart from the removal of cruise missiles, was covered by arms control treaties.

The Labour Government after 1997 took some further modest steps. It speeded up the removal of the last of the tactical nuclear bombs, introduced a greater degree of transparency concerning the level of nuclear forces, eased the alert status of the Trident missile submarine force and stated a commitment to maintain loadings of nuclear forces on Trident submarines at substantially below the design capability. Even so, while the withdrawal of the last of the tactical nuclear bombs meant that Trident became the sole British nuclear weapon system, it had, in the process, been developed into a highly versatile system, capable of being deployed in 'sub-strategic' (tactical) and strategic roles.

To take on the sub-strategic role previously undertaken by bombers, a proportion of the missiles on a Trident submarine, perhaps 6 out of 16, will be equipped with small single warheads with a destructive power of about 5 to 10 kilotons, compared with the standard Trident warhead of about 100 kilotons. As well as being available for independent use by Britain, these sub-strategic Trident missile warheads will also be available to NATO.

There are interesting nuances in the history of British nuclear attitudes that are particularly relevant in the coming decades. Although most aspects of British nuclear strategy have related to the Cold War and NATO contexts, a significant subsidiary thread has been the perceived value of nuclear weapons to counterbalance relative weaknesses in conventional forces, not just in relation to the Soviet Union during the Cold War era, but also in regional confrontations outside the NATO area.

Tactical and strategic nuclear weapons were deployed during the Falklands War of 1982 and Britain had a regional nuclear capability, and indicated a willingness to consider nuclear use, during the Gulf War of 1991 (as it apparently had during the much earlier Indonesian confrontation in the early 1960s).[29] This should not come as any great surprise, since it forms part of a continuum in military thinking about nuclear weapons that has parallels in the United States, the Soviet Union, post-Soviet Russia and France, as well as being clearly represented in NATO's planning for early first use of nuclear weapons.

Britain reserves the right to deploy Trident independently of NATO. According to one of the more detailed assessments of the range of options for sub-strategic Trident warheads:

At what might be called the 'upper end' of the usage spectrum, they could be used in a conflict involving large-scale forces (including British ground and air forces), such as the 1990–91 Gulf War, to reply to an enemy nuclear strike. Secondly, they could be used in a similar setting, but to reply to enemy use of weapons of mass destruction, such as bacteriological or chemical weapons, for which Britain possesses no like-for-like retaliatory capability. Thirdly, they could be used in a demonstrative role: i.e. aimed at a non-critical uninhabited area, with the message that if the country concerned continued on its present course of action, nuclear weapons would be aimed at a high-priority target. Finally, there is the punitive role, where a country has committed an act, despite specific warnings to do so would incur a nuclear strike.[30]

It is worth noting that three of the four circumstances envisaged would involve the first use of nuclear weapons by Britain, but such scenarios resemble aspects of United States and Russian nuclear targeting and strategy at present and for the forseeable future. Britain's Trident missile system is due to remain in service for the first quarter of the twenty-first century and it is seen as a versatile nuclear system capable of operating in diverse conflict environments. The idea of withdrawing Trident, and with it Britain's commitment to nuclear forces, is not currently on the UK political agenda.

The position in France is broadly similar to that in Britain, except that French nuclear thinking also involves the need to retain a distinct detachment from the United States. There has long been a debate in France between a broadly centre and leftist view of nuclear strategy focusing on minimal deterrence, an avoidance of limited options and a concentration on policies to promote non-proliferation, contrasted with a more right-wing Gaullist view which:

emphasises the defence of French and allied interests through robust and flexible military capabilities – both offensive and defensive. This includes the development of nuclear forces capable of being used, if necessary, with control and discrimination, particularly in confrontation with countries of 'the South' that may be armed with nuclear, chemical or biological weapons.[31]

Chirac's Presidential election victory in 1995 ensured a pre-eminence of this view, as demonstrated by the subsequent decision to resume a nuclear testing programme intended to complete the development of two warheads and ensure a simulation capability in the event of a Comprehensive Test Ban Treaty. The French nuclear tests were internationally controversial and caused substantial opposition within France, but, even so, the fundamental French commitment to having its own nuclear forces remained domestically popular.

As with Britain, a number of French nuclear weapons systems were withdrawn during the 1990s, including a small force of 18 land-based medium-range nuclear missiles and the Hades tactical nuclear missile, but a new class of ballistic missile submarines is being deployed, and air-launched nuclear missiles will be updated and will remain in service with the new Rafale strike aircraft.

French nuclear strategy has four elements, all of them likely to be relevant for some years to come. The first is the long-held view that France cannot rely on the United States for a nuclear umbrella in a disorderly world and must therefore have its own forces. This view is well-nigh certain to persist. A second and more recent development, that does not contradict this, is that a number of opinion formers in France would like to see the development of some kind of European nuclear deterrent, in conjunction with Britain but not involving the United States. This outlook has received some support elsewhere in Europe, especially in Germany, but is bound up with the future of NATO nuclear policy and the possible development of a so-called European Defence identity.

A third element underlying French nuclear strategy is the recognition that France's conventional forces are such that it will rarely be able to respond to a major regional crisis on its own unless it can supplement its conventional forces with a nuclear capability. Finally, French nuclear strategy is particularly geared towards counter-proliferation. One analysis of the French view is that:

...the Rafale armed with a long-range stand-off missile would be well-suited to deter the growing number of countries in the developing world that have acquired, or are acquiring, nuclear, bacteriological and chemical weapons as well as ballistic missiles.[32]

This 'suitability' of such a combination stems from having a low-yield accurate nuclear system appropriate for precision attacks on military installations, a further move away from the more traditional French concentration on counter-city targeting.

NATO's nuclear posture underwent a number of changes during the 1990s, although these did not include any alteration to the basic policy of nuclear first-use. Its Strategic Concept of 1991 had accepted that the risk of a nuclear confrontation was much diminished and the great majority of all of the sub-strategic forces allocated to NATO by the United States were withdrawn during the course of the decade, leaving a few hundred air-delivered nuclear bombs and Britain's Trident commitment.

Towards the end of the decade, there were growing internal demands for NATO to engage in a thorough review of its nuclear posture, with the strongest demands coming from Canada and Germany. The NATO Summit in Washington in April 1999 was dominated by its involvement in the air war with Serbia, but a modified Strategic Concept was adopted which paid some attention to demands for a review. The alliance would maintain, 'at a minimum level consistent with the security environment, adequate sub-strategic forces based in Europe, which will provide an essential link with strategic nuclear forces, reinforcing the transatlantic link.'[33] This represented little change on the position eight years before, but a separate communiqué also reported that the alliance would be prepared 'to consider options for confidence and security building measures, verification, non-proliferation and arms control and disarmament.'[34]

Although this represented a modestly positive attitude towards denuclearisation, it did not seek to promote the idea of further withdrawals of NATO nuclear forces. Moreover, one of the key new missions for NATO, embodied in the 1999 Strategic Concept, was the control of the proliferation of weapons of mass destruction and their delivery. This formed part of planned 'improvements in NATO's capability to undertake new missions to respond to a broad spectrum of possible threats to Alliance common interests'.[35] Thus, NATO in the post-Cold War era has moved well beyond a concentrated concern with a threat from the Soviet Union to a much wider expression of security interests, certainly including perceived threats from proliferators affecting any part of the entire alliance, including the Middle East and East Asia.

Chinese nuclear policy

While the extent and development of China's nuclear forces remains largely shrouded in secrecy, and precise details of nuclear forces, reliability, accuracy and strategy are not readily available, it is clear that China is fully committed to retaining nuclear forces. Moreover, recent developments in Chinese nuclear thinking are potentially disturbing and demonstrate a firm commitment to nuclear forces that includes an increasing interest in flexible forces for nuclear war-fighting. There is also a deep concern over US plans for a national missile defence which might require China to substantially upgrade its long range missile forces.

China initially developed nuclear weapons in the 1950s and 1960s with Soviet aid, but, after the rift with Moscow, maintained an indigenous research, development and production capability. By the early 1980s, China had perhaps 300 nuclear weapons, and much of that decade was concerned with improving the quality of the systems, particularly in relation to reliability and survivability. The majority of the weapons were considered strategic, but this was in relation to the Soviet Union, considered to be the main threat at the time. Very few of the Chinese missiles could target the United States or Western Europe.[36]

There are three developments of the past decade that are particularly relevant to the future. The first is an unequivocal commitment to retaining nuclear forces. China may not oppose a comprehensive test ban, and it may support the START process, but its bottom line is a view of nuclear forces as an integral part of Chinese defence policy. In taking this view, China seems unwilling to recognise the effect this has on neighbours such as India.

The second development is evidence of a Chinese interest in developing a nuclear posture which, at the regional level, bears a similarity to NATO's flexible response. The Chinese are particularly concerned about Russia, where they believe there is potential for considerable instability coupled with the possibility of a strongly nationalist government. Such instability on the Chinese periphery is the context for changes in military thinking:

...strategists have been struggling to figure out how to link conventional and nuclear weapons with the operational requirements of potential high-tech local wars over resources and territory around the Chinese periphery. They are interested in how to integrate high technology weapons with 'long-distance striking power' so as to deter and, if necessary, deny an adversary victory in any conceivable conventional and nuclear military conflict.[37]

Finally, but no less important, is China's recent but substantial concern over American plans for theatre and national missile defences. There is strong opposition to any US proposal to facilitate ballistic missile defences in East Asia that might apply to Japan, South Korea and especially Taiwan, and also opposition to any longer-term plan for a US national missile shield:

> China's chief of arms control issued a new warning...that U.S. plans for a national missile defense system, even if intended to stop attacks from countries like North Korea and Iraq, would set off a global arms race and cause more countries to develop nuclear weapons.[38]

The particular concern was with US plans to seek an amendment to the Anti-Ballistic Missile Treaty to allow it to develop national missile defences. According to the Director of Arms Control at the Chinese foreign ministry, Sha Zukang, 'Amending it in search of national missile defense will tip the global balance, trigger a new arms race and jeopardize world and regional stability.'[39]

Allowing for rhetoric, this and other Chinese pronouncements at the end of 1999 indicated the concerns that China felt that its small long-range missile force might be countered by US anti-missile plans. There was probably a reluctance to engage in a substantial expansion of Chinese strategic missile forces, not least on grounds of cost, but recent reports suggest that China has the potential to do so. Two new ICBMs, the DF-31 and DF-41, are in early stages of development, and each might be capable of carrying multiple warheads. Each might ordinarily take some years to develop and deploy, but China is capable of accelerating such a process if required.[40]

In summary, China sees a continuing requirement for nuclear forces and has a determination to maintain adequate forces to satisfy its regional security requirements. Moreover, it is in a position to engage in substantial strategic nuclear developments, dependent on US decisions on a national missile defence programme.

Proliferation

This review of nuclear developments and attitudes by the five main nuclear powers indicates a solid commitment to maintaining nuclear forces, and much of this relates to the proliferation, not just of nuclear weapons, but of weapons of mass destruction as a whole. As suggested earlier, the 1990s saw some progress in nuclear disarmament in some former Soviet states and South Africa, added to progress in Latin America and East Asia in the previous decade. Even so, other developments have been far less positive, and adding concerns over chemical and biological weapons results in an analysis that indicates major problems for international security in the coming decades.

In the Middle East, Israel retains substantial nuclear forces, a factor frequently ignored in concerns over weapons proliferation among Arab states. Israel's nuclear forces are believed to comprise at least 100 warheads, including thermonuclear weapons and, quite probably, enhanced radiation (neutron) weapons. Delivery systems include nuclear-capable aircraft and the *Jericho 2* ballistic missile with a range of up to 1,200 miles. Israel may also have a chemical and biological weapons capability, whereas Syria has concentrated on chemical weapons, with delivery by missile or aircraft. Egypt has the technical potential to develop a wide range of chemical and biological weapons and almost certainly has an existing chemical weapons capability, and neighbouring Libya has had ambitions to develop weapons of mass destruction but, apart from some chemical weapons, the results may have been limited.

The Iraqi plans to develop nuclear, chemical and biological weapons in the 1980s were substantial. The extent of their capabilities, achieved within a decade, will be discussed in detail in Chapter 6, but they have had substantial regional implications, not least in encouraging Saudi Arabia to acquire ballistic missiles from China and allow substantial US forces to be based on its territory and stimulating Israel to invest heavily in ballistic missile defences.

Iran is situated next to one substantial nuclear power, Russia, another recent nuclear power, Pakistan, and a state with clear pretensions to have weapons of mass destruction, Iraq. In such circumstances it would be simplistic not to expect Iran to be seeking some kind of missile force equipped with weapons of mass destruction.[41]

In South Asia, the Indian and Pakistani nuclear tests in 1998 were both designed to prove a number of warhead designs. In the case of India, one assessment is that there are proven designs for a powerful two-stage thermonuclear weapon, a standard fission weapon in the 10–15 kiloton range and a smaller tactical nuclear weapon, probably in the 2–3 kiloton range. All of these weapons are plutonium-based, and India may have sufficient fissile material for around 50 warheads. Pakistan appears to have a single uranium-based fission weapon design, possibly incorporating a Chinese design, and may be able to produce around 12 weapons. With both states there is potential for the development of significant nuclear arsenals within five years involving free-fall bombs as well as warheads for ballistic missiles.[42] In the view of a British Foreign Office minister, Peter Hain, India and Pakistan were 'very close' to a nuclear exchange over Kashmir during the Summer of 1999, following incursions into an Indian-controlled part of the province.[43]

In East Asia, South Korean and Taiwanese nuclear weapons programmes appear to be on ice, and Japan, which could readily produce nuclear weapons, continues to hold back from doing so. The status of impoverished North Korea's nuclear ambitions remains open to question, but it should be remembered that the development of chemical and biological weapons by all major states in the region, including China, is feasible and may already have happened in some cases. Indeed, the proliferation of chemical, and especially biological, weapons, together with ballistic missiles in East Asia and the Middle East especially, is a feature of the concerns of the major existing nuclear powers, especially the United States and its NATO allies.

Nuclear futures

This chapter started with the comment that there had been two substantial periods of anti-nuclear concern in the West, in the early 1960s and early 1980s, but that general perceptions since the ending of the Cold War were that issues of nuclear instability and proliferation were of little concern, except when prompted by events such as the French nuclear tests in the mid-1990s and the more recent nuclear arms race in South Asia. The chapter has attempted only a brief analysis of the actual postures and policies of the existing nuclear powers, with an added note on the proliferation of other weapons of mass destruction, but even this shows that the 'nuclear future' is far less benign than is commonly believed.

As part of its intention to remain the world's most powerful state, the US is committed to maintaining and upgrading its nuclear forces and has developed a posture that retains a commitment to first-use against a variety of threats. It is concerned with Russian and Chinese nuclear capabilities and with the possibility of other states acquiring nuclear or other weapons of mass destruction. Furthermore, it is highly likely to develop some kind of national missile defence that, in turn, encourages Russia and China to upgrade their own forces. The damage to the Comprehensive Test Ban Treaty and the possible loss of the Anti-Ballistic Missile Treaty both indicate that prospects for arms control have diminished, and this includes a reduced likelihood of further cuts in strategic arsenals in the START process.

Russia, in turn, is actually embracing nuclear options to a greater extent than a decade ago, prompted partly by trends in the US but also by the collapse of its conventional forces. The disarray in much of Russia's nuclear industry is a concern for proliferation, and the instability of Russia, along with US trends, prompts China to enhance its own nuclear forces. Meanwhile, Britain and France have reduced their arsenals but remain committed to nuclear forces, with each country engaged in substantial modernisation programmes, as well as having their own concerns over the proliferation of weapons of mass destruction. In the Middle East and South Asia, nuclear stability is clearly lacking, and the combination of nuclear proliferation with that of chemical and biological weapons suggests a continuing danger that is likely to grow.

Perhaps the most worrying aspect is the trend towards useable nuclear weapons – the idea of 'small nuclear wars in far-off places'. Development of new nuclear weapons designed for specific functions in conflicts in the Third World, whether by the US, Britain or France, and the willingness of Russia and China to look to versions of flexible response are all indicators of this notion. Many analysts have argued that the most dangerous aspect of the Cold War was the long-held belief that a limited nuclear war could be fought and won. That mentality has endured beyond the end of the Cold War and is deeply embedded in the strategic thinking of the nuclear powers.

In looking ahead over the next twenty years or so, and concentrating for now on existing trends, we have to conclude that prospects for controlling nuclear weapons deteriorated in the final few years of the 1990s and there is no immediate sign of an improvement. The trends are, if anything, in the opposite direction. The widespread public perception that nuclear weapons are of diminishing concern is fundamentally wrong – the danger of an all-out nuclear war between two superpower alliances has diminished, but the prospects for a stable route to a world in which nuclear weapons are abolished or are even effectively controlled are, on present trends, minimal.

Taming the Jungle

A jungle full of snakes – the military view of a disorderly world

Shortly after the end of the Cold War, Bill Clinton was elected to the US Presidency in place of George Bush. Clinton proposed James Woolsey as the new Director of the CIA, and Woolsey was then questioned in Senate hearings on the changing threat environment facing the United States. He characterised it by saying that the US had slain the dragon (of the old Soviet Union) but now faced a jungle full of poisonous snakes.[1] Although this comment was made almost a decade ago, it remains an effective characterisation of US security attitudes, the near-universal view in security circles being that the United States is clearly the sole superpower, but its world-wide economic and political interests will be subject to diverse and unpredictable threats, not from a single superpower as in the Cold War era, but from a variety of states and sub-state actors, or to put it somewhat more crudely, rogue states and terrorists.

The 'Secret Squirrel' development, mentioned in Chapter 1, relates directly to this changed view and is a useful illustration for four quite different reasons. The first is that it demonstrates the frequently direct connections between old and new military postures in that a Cold War weapon was simply taken and converted to a form that was applicable to the new era. Second, it indicates the importance of inter-service rivalries, especially in an era of restricted defence spending when compared with the plentiful days of the Cold War era. [2] Third, it is indicative of a fundamental move towards 'global reach', the belief that permeates US military thinking as it defines its role of protecting US interests wherever they may be at risk. Finally, the cruise missile became the weapon of choice in the 1990s, and remains so, because of its ability to fulfil military functions without putting the lives of US service-people at risk. This was already a requirement at the time of the Libyan attack, but became much more significant after the disastrous loss of US troops in Somalia in 1993.

This chapter is concerned with military perceptions of the nature of conflict over the coming three decades. It concentrates primarily on the

United States, not least because it is the dominant military force in the world but also because its technological capabilities are so far advanced over most other states that they give a solid indication of longer-term trends. At the same time, some attention will be given to NATO allies, not least because of potential tensions between a US-dominated NATO and the possible development of some kind of European defence identity.

In looking ahead, the nuclear context needs to be recognised. As indicated in the previous chapter, all of the declared nuclear powers, including the newcomers of India and Pakistan, are clear in their determination to maintain a nuclear capability. There is abundant evidence that Russia is actually increasing its nuclear commitments, primarily because of the desperate need to maintain a semblance of great power status, coupled with the decay of its conventional forces. The United States is maintaining a formidable nuclear arsenal, and has already begun the process of developing nuclear weapons appropriate to a volatile world in which weapons of mass destruction, especially biological weapons, are proliferating.

The decade since the end of the Cold War has been characterised by the evolution of a world view within US security circles that is now reasonably clear-cut and is likely to remain relatively stable, at least on present trends, for the next decade or more. In this view, there are numerous areas of potential or actual conflict that may impinge on US security interests but are not central to them, there are two regions of enduring instability and there are two states that might conceivably threaten US ascendancy. Overlying all of these are two trends – the spread of ballistic missiles and weapons of mass destruction and the threat from international terrorism, with or without weapons of mass destruction. In addition, and less easy to analyse, are trends in illicit drug production and distribution and other aspects of trans-national criminal behaviour.[3]

Among the areas of sporadic conflict are the Balkans, parts of East and West Africa, isolated parts of the Caribbean and some areas within South East Asia, notably Indonesia. The US may intervene directly or may be part of an intervening coalition in some of these cases, especially where there may be a direct domestic interest, as with Haiti, or where US interests may be at risk.

Eastern Asia is seen as a source of potential conflict, primarily because North Korea remains independent and antagonistic, a veritable rogue state that develops and exports missile technology to unacceptable regimes, and has a long-standing interest in weapons of mass destruction. South-west Asia is the second region of danger, partly because Iraq and Iran are both viewed as rogue states, intent on regional hegemony, and partly because of continued US support for Israel. Behind the concern over stability in the Middle East lies a recognition of the singular importance of Persian Gulf oil and of the substantial US business interests in the region. Iraq, Iran, Libya and, to an extent, Syria, are also seen as states that seek to acquire missiles and weapons of mass destruction.

Two major states are seen as potential security problems for quite different reasons. Russia retains substantial nuclear forces even as its conventional forces wither almost to the point of collapse. The proliferation of armaments and the transfer of military technology from Russia is recognised as one of the few ways in which Russia can gain export earnings. This causes concern, but this is overshadowed by the unofficial export of knowledge in the fields of missile propulsion and guidance and the development of nuclear, chemical and especially biological weapons, as scientists and technologists seek work outside a collapsing Russian defence sector.[4]

In addition to instability and conflict in the Caucasus and parts of Central Asia, there is a longer-term fear that Russia may rebuild its military capabilities, perhaps under a strongly nationalist regime. Such a fear rarely recognises the significance of a near endemic Russian perception that NATO expansion and US commercial interests in the Caspian Basin are part of a strategic encroachment into Russia's historic sphere of influence.

China is recognised as a state that has substantial potential to develop from a regionally significant power to a potential superpower, albeit only beginning to match the superpowers of the Cold War era after some decades. Even so, the potential for China to play a leadership role from within the third world, presenting a possible focus of power to challenge US politico-economic superiority is recognised in some US military circles, with or without a continuing problem over Taiwan.

Suffusing these national and regional trends is a persistent concern with missile proliferation and with sub-state political violence directed at the US or its overseas interests. In part this comes from the experience of the Scud attacks in the Gulf War, in part from the Nairobi and Dar es Salaam embassy bombings in 1998 and other attacks on US interests.

The overall international security paradigm is thus reasonably clear-cut. The United States is the world's pre-eminent military power, it is not currently threatened by any state of even remotely similar power, yet it does face diverse threats to its own security and its wider economic and political interests. Even so, it has the capability to adapt its military forces to meet the new threats, and, in the final analysis, should be able, along with its allies, to maintain international security in such a way as to protect its interests and preserve its inherent power.

Within this overall security context, there are some significant features and nuances, and it is fair to say that some analysts take a more global view. There are two factors that are likely to have an effect on many of these potential security problems. The first is a remarkable determination by the US military to do almost anything to minimise casualties in foreign military operations. The 'body bag' syndrome has, in the past ten years and especially since the Somalia disaster, been taken to extraordinary lengths, not least in Kosovo and Serbia in the early months of 1999 when offensive operations were restricted to an altitude above 15,000 feet for most of the war.

The second feature is a recognition of the extent to which economic globalisation increases vulnerability to particular forms of political violence. As a report of the US Commission on National Security in the 21st Century put it:

> Many of the threats emerging in our future will differ significantly from those of the past, not only in their physical, but also in their psychological effects. Threats may inhere in assaults against an increasingly integrated and complex, but highly vulnerable, international economic infrastructure, whose operation lies beyond the control of any single body.[5]

Actions might involve elements of cyberwar – disruption of communications or computer systems controlling regional stock exchanges through hacking and viral infections, through to direct acts of violence against nodes of economic control.

Just occasionally, military analysts write from a more global standpoint, less concerned with narrow US perceptions of the manner in which world order may be controlled, more concerned with global trends. An example was an analysis by a former US submarine commander, Roger W. Barnett, that included most of the potential threats listed above but also mentioned:

- Widening economic differentials between the economic 'North' and 'South'.
- Inequitable distribution of world food supplies, and the dislocation of millions of people because of famine, war and natural disasters.
- Impact of high technology weapons and weapons of mass destruction on the ability – and thus the willingness – of the weak to take up arms against the strong.[6]

Although Barnett's analysis extended beyond the usual areas, his study was essentially concerned with promoting the value of the US Navy in being the most effective answer to regional problems affecting US security.

Even with these nuances to the security paradigm, the central problem remains – tailoring military forces for uncertain decades ahead. In their different ways, the main branches of the armed forces of the United States are all going about the business of being able to respond to unpredictable threats. The manner in which they, and some of their allies, are doing so provides a remarkably good indication of the future of international security as seen from the west.

Air power anywhere

The 'Secret Squirrel' ALCM air raid on Iraq is one good indication of the transition away from the US Air Force's Cold War outlook. During that era, the USAF contributed numerous missiles and strategic bombers to Strategic Air Command, maintained continental air defences and tactical air forces overseas and a capacity to undertake strategic conventional bombing, as demonstrated in Vietnam. There was an underlying belief, often disputed by analysts, that strategic air power could win wars. Although such an analysis was called into question by the Vietnam War, air force planners persisted with this view and many claimed vindication through the Gulf War of 1991.

The USAF was relatively quick to adapt to the post Cold War era, although it experienced severe cuts in personnel and equipment, dropping from 579,000 to 361,000 during the 1990s. Even so, it sought to maintain a full range of aircraft, seeking upgrades to existing types and new interceptors and strike aircraft, with an emphasis on stealthy features and precision-guided stand-off weapons.

During the early 1990s, and following on directly from the Gulf War, the USAF embraced the concept of global reach, seeking to establish a capability to attack targets anywhere in the world from the continental United States. This represented a considerable change from the Cold War years where there were bases run by or available to the air force around most of the periphery of the Soviet Union. For the future, such overseas basing could not be guaranteed, especially in the light of the Libyan experience in 1986, although a more recent experience has been even more traumatic.

Towards the end of 1998, one of the periodic crises with Iraq developed, leading eventually to an intense four-day bombing campaign, Operation Desert Fox, conducted mainly by the United States but with British involvement. A key aim of Desert Fox was to damage Iraqi air defences, command and control systems and weapons production facilities. For several years previously, USAF pilots had trained extensively for such operations, with many of the personnel, planes and equipment located in large and well-equipped bases in Saudi Arabia.

In the immediate run-up to Desert Fox, and to the consternation of the US authorities, the Saudi government refused to allow the USAF to use the bases for any offensive bombing of Iraq. To make matters worse, the Saudis even refused to allow the USAF to move the units to other bases in neighbouring countries from which they could operate. As a result, much of the Desert Fox operation involved cruise missiles and aircraft launched from US Navy ships. While not widely advertised at the time, this event went further in convincing the USAF that it had to maintain global reach.

In practice, this had already been developed over much of the decade, and in the middle of the 1990s, a series of operations was mounted to demonstrate this capacity. In 1993, there was a crisis in relations between the United States and North Korea over the latter's presumed nuclear weapons programme. The Pentagon determined on a show of force, described graphically, if not a little triumphantly, in *Air Force* magazine:

> The Air Force did something unusual with its B-1s last March. It sent a pair of bombers from Ellsworth AFB, South Dakota, via Guam, to the Republic of Korea, where they set down on an American air base within easy striking distance of a hostile neighbouring nation.
>
> The faraway, in-your-face deployment of the B-1s was part of an exercise Team Spirit, a muscular US/ROK combined-arms military exercise involving airforce units from Pacific Air Force (PACAF) and Air Combat Command (ACC). Among other things, it demonstrated to North Korea, now a likely nuclear threat, just how diverse and deadly US air power has become.
>
> By using B-1s in the exercise, including a third bomber out of Guam, the Air Force underlined the message delivered with a bang in the Persian Gulf War – that bombers armed with non-nuclear bombs and based in the continental United States are now the big guns in US global power.[7]

A Rand Corporation study released shortly after this episode supported this view of global air power:

> In future major regional conflicts, national and military leaders are likely to place a premium on US forces that can deploy rapidly over long distances, swiftly destroy invading armed forces as well as fixed assets, and engage the enemy effectively while placing minimal numbers of American service personnel in harm's way.[8]

A further demonstration of global reach was given the following year, following a pattern that has been repeated, with variations, on other occasions. In this case two B-52 bombers, each carrying over 50 bombs, flew out of Barksdale AFB in Louisiana, the same base used in the CALCM attack on Iraq in 1991. The bombs were dropped on a bombing range in Kuwait, and the planes then flew eastwards over the Indian Ocean, South East Asia and the Pacific and back to their base, an exercise lasting nearly two days and supported by five air-to-air refuellings.

A year later, B-1Bs carried out a similar operation, dropping practice bombs on ranges in Italy and Japan along the way.

By the end of the 1990s, the US Air Force had focused on two forms of global reach. One was the ability to use very long-range bombers, supported by tanker aircraft, to fly anywhere from the US.[9] The other was to re-organise the USAF into ten Air Expeditionary Wings, each comprising about 15,000 people with up to 200 aircraft including strike aircraft, interceptors, tankers, transports, reconnaissance and electronic countermeasures aircraft.[10] Two of these Wings are to be on deployment readiness at any one time, able to move rapidly to overseas bases when available. Thus, at the core of the USAF will be an ability either to conduct long-range strikes or to move entire forces to regional bases in response to crises.

Together with this basic structure come new generations of weapons and capabilities, some of these used against Iraq and Serbia. A range of stand-off missiles, including the original air-launched cruise missiles is available,[11] together with laser-guided bombs and earth-penetrating warheads, the latter intended for command bunkers, chemical and biological weapons stores and similar heavily protected 'high value' targets.[12] A substantial range of area-impact munitions, including cluster bombs and fuel-air explosives will be available for large targets, together with a new generation of highly specialised munitions. One such weapon, used in Serbia in 1999, dispersed large numbers of carbon fibre filaments to short-circuit electricity-switching stations and transformers. A variant of this, distributed by a new 'bomb' called the Wind Corrected Munitions Dispenser (WCMD) disperses thousands of microscopic fibres that form an almost invisible cloud that will get into a wide range of electronic and electrical devices, including personal computers, and short-circuit them.[13]

Such weapons, provided there is appropriate targeting, can be used alongside conventional munitions to do massive damage to the economy of a target state. In the air war against Serbia in the early months of 1999, it proved extremely difficult to detect and destroy Serbian military facilities, partly because of poor weather but mainly because of a restriction on operating below 15,000 feet (to protect aircrew) together with the Serb tactics of dispersal, camouflage and protection of their forces. During the course of the war, the US forces and their NATO allies moved progressively to target the Serbian economy as a whole. By attacking power plants, refineries, factories, transmission lines, roads, railways, bridges, tunnels and other aspects of the economy, the NATO forces did some $60 billion of damage to the Serb economy, reducing the already weakened state to the poorest country in Europe.[14]

From its current base of being able to deploy world-wide, to field a range of stand-off weapons and to use both precision-guided and area-impact munitions, the US Air Force believes it is the lead contender in the competition to ensure US ascendancy. In the coming decades, it sees four further trends. One is the further development of stealthy aircraft that are typically a generation ahead of any other aircraft available to potential opponents, as well as being resistant to air defences. A second is the further development of many different kinds of munitions, including small nuclear weapons, that can target all kinds of activities of states or paramilitary groups. Third is the development of many kinds of unmanned aerial vehicles (UAVs) for reconnaissance and combat, and finally there is the requirement to integrate all these forces, together with space-based surveillance, into an offensive capability available for any occasion.

Sea power

During the Kosovo War, Serbia was the fifth state to be targeted by cruise missiles during the mid and late 1990s, most of them being sea-launched Tomahawks. Others were Iraq, Afghanistan, Sudan and Bosnia, but the sea-launched cruise missiles represent just one part of an adaptation by the US Navy to the new era, an adaptation that has been made easier by many historic aspects of the development of US naval power.

Much of the modern US Navy and Marine Corps developed as a result of the Pacific War against Japan, with carrier-based air power and amphibious forces being central to the conflict. The navy and the marines developed many substantial Cold War roles, with the navy maintaining a significant part of the US strategic nuclear arsenals as well as extensive anti-submarine forces. The Maritime Strategy of the 1980s was essentially an aggressive posture directed against the Soviet Union that would use naval and marine corps forces to take a war to much of the Soviet periphery. As such, it was a major exercise in global reach, with carrier battle groups and marine expeditionary forces forming core aspects of the strategy.

A sub-set of aggressive containment was the pre-positioning of military supplies and the construction and development of bases in strategic locations. With the United States effectively dominant in NATO, two other areas were crucial: the East Asia/West Pacific region and South West Asia and the Middle East. For the latter, the Persian Gulf and its oil supplies were of fundamental importance, especially as the US had become a substantial net importer of oil from the mid-1970s.

To counter possible Soviet aggression towards the oil fields, the US first established the Joint Rapid Deployment Task Force at the end of the 1970s, and then elevated this into a full integrated military command, Central Command or CENTCOM, in the early 1980s. As CENTCOM developed, major basing facilities were developed in Saudi Arabia and a large air and naval base was constructed on the Indian Ocean island of

Diego Garcia, a British possession leased to the United States, after the Ilois inhabitants had been removed to Mauritius and largely abandoned. Although CENTCOM was developed as a regional aspect of the Cold War, its facilities were readily available for use against Iraq, forming the basis for the coalition assembled to evict Iraq from Kuwait in 1991.[15]

During the rest of the 1990s, the US Navy and Marine Corps underwent some interesting changes as they embarked on the process of contributing to taming the jungle. Essentially, the process was one of divesting excess Cold War baggage while preserving and enhancing those forces likely to be of greatest value in controlling the new world disorder. Between 1989 and 1999, the US Navy decreased in size from 584,000 to 370,000. With the decrease went many warships but the emphasis was primarily on cutting back anti-submarine forces. In 1989 there were 14 aircraft carriers, five of them nuclear-powered, yet by 1999, there were still twelve, nine of which were nuclear-powered. Similarly, there were very few cuts in large amphibious ships. In other words, the US Navy's capacity to project power was only slightly diminished, even though the principal focus of that power during the Cold War era had been reduced to a pale shadow of its former power. The developments in the US Marine Corps were even more marked. Both the US Air Force and the Navy lost well over a third of their total personnel, whereas the decrease in the Marine Corps, from 195,000 to 171,000, was barely a tenth.[16]

Both the navy and the marines see their roles in the future in terms of the need to protect US interests in regional conflicts wherever they occur. In doing so, they are able to deploy forces that are very much greater than any other state. A single US aircraft carrier battle group is more powerful in its military capability than the aircraft carriers of Britain and France combined. The US Marine Corps is larger than the entire British Army and Royal Navy combined.

Of the greatest significance in the context of US ascendancy over the next two decades or more is the manner in which the global reach of the US Navy and Marines has been maintained, if not enhanced, at a time of cut-backs throughout the US armed forces. The various components – carrier battle groups, sea-launched cruise missiles, amphibious forces, overseas basing and pre-positioning – all contribute to a potential for 'keeping the violent peace' that is unmatched.

In many respects this is nothing new, as it was a persistent feature of the Cold War posture. For the marines it goes much further, and has strong echoes of the manner in which the marines were used to maintain US interests in Central America in the early years of the twentieth century, described memorably by General Smedley E. Butler writing in 1935:

I spent thirty-three years and four months in active service as a member of our country's most agile military force – the Marine Corps. I served in all commissioned ranks from a second Lieutenant to Major-General. And during that time I spent most of my time being a high-class muscle man for Big Business, for Wall Street and for the bankers. In short, I was a racketeer for capitalism. Thus I helped make Mexico and especially Tampico safe for American oil interests in 1914. I helped make Haiti and Cuba a decent place for the National City Bank to collect revenues in... I helped pacify Nicaragua for the international banking house of Brown Brothers in 1909–1912. I brought light to the Dominican Republic for American sugar interests in 1916. I helped make Honduras 'right' for American fruit companies in 1903.[17]

Butler's candour recalls an era when US business interests were expanding in Central America and required, in extreme circumstances, the use of military force to ensure their security, either against local regimes or against rebellions. The global picture in the early twenty-first century is far more complex and has more business actors. In the early twentieth century, European powers had massive influence in most of Asia, Africa and much of South America. In relative terms, the United States is far more powerful and, moreover, has business activities that frequently interlock with interests in Europe and East Asia. What is dominant, though, is the US capacity to project force, a capacity on a global scale that bears comparison with the use of the Marine Corps, in Latin America, over 80 years ago.

Special operations, counter-insurgency and counter-terrorism

Of the four branches of the US armed forces, the army has faced the greatest problems since the end of the Cold War, experiencing the most substantial cuts and losing 300,000 people or 40 per cent of its strength. Even so, the make-up of the army has been changed to preserve rapid reaction and long-range strike. Thus in the ten years after 1989, the army disbanded two of its four armoured divisions but retained its two air assault and airborne divisions. In many ways, this parallels the changes in the navy, with both forces cutting back vigorously on 'Cold War' capabilities, while preserving others. The navy's anti-submarine forces have been cut but force projection is maintained. Similarly, gone are the days of massive tank armies facing the Warsaw Pact in Central Europe, but efforts are made to maintain rapid reaction and deep strike capabilities.

The army is particularly affected by the 'body bag' syndrome, and a feature of army operations overseas is to put a premium on protecting its troops, to the extent of their living in fortified compounds even when engaged in peacekeeping operations. For the past ten years, the US Army has been fighting something of a rearguard action to preserve as much of its combat capability as possible, and two of the main features have been acquiring weapons for long-range strike and putting an increased emphasis on special operations forces, particularly geared to counter-insurgency, both seen as crucial elements in the army's posture in the coming decades.

Apart from helicopter gunships, the core weapon for deep strike against targets in regional conflicts is the Army Tactical Missile System (ATACMS), a surface-to-surface ballistic missile that can carry up to 1,000 anti-personnel grenades over a distance of 150 miles. In an intensive re-equipment programme during the 1990s, the army has acquired over 800 launchers capable of firing this missile. One report, soon after it was first deployed, couched it in terms of competition with the air force in that it:

> ...gives the service 'a significant leg-up' over the Air Force, which relies on piloted aircraft that react more slowly. The ATACMS can be used to destroy a target at long range while Air Force pilots are still en route...[18]

Use of ATACMS in regional conflicts is one of the few force projection systems available to the US Army, but it is working hard to maintain its status in one other area – special operations forces. As with the marines, the army special operations forces act principally in low intensity conflicts, working with the navy and air force in US Special Operations Command (USSOCOM), based at Fort Bragg in North Carolina. Although this is relatively small, with less than 50,000 people, it is still nearly half the size of the British Army and operates a wide range of aircraft, helicopters and ships. It expects to increase its spheres of operations in an era of diverse conflicts and security interests in the South, and has a major re-equipment programme under way. This includes a series of upgradings to support aircraft and helicopters, new long-range support craft with an open-ocean range of over 1,000 miles and the provision of newly modified submarines for secret delivery of forces into hostile areas. There has even been an acknowledged expansion in some of the forces, with the US Navy's SEALs (sea/air/land) nearly doubling in size in the early 1990s.[19]

Another indication of changing priorities is the increase in training available to friendly regimes, especially in Latin America. From the 1950s to the 1980s, US forces were involved in many internal conflicts, most commonly aiding conservative governments fighting left-wing rebels. Many of the conflicts were part of the Cold War confrontation, with rebels aided on occasions from Cuba and Eastern Europe, and many of the activities, including those of the School of the Americas, were seen as controversial, not least because of human rights abuses.

With the Cold War ten years distant, the training of foreign armies, especially those involving US special operations forces, has expanded. Much of it appears at first sight to be directed at anti-narcotics action, but it all too commonly involves counter-insurgency training in support of local elites. In 1998, some 2,700 special operations troops were involved with training the armed forces of every one of the 19 Latin American states and nine Caribbean states, including armies in Guatemala, Colombia and Suriname that have been widely criticised for human rights abuses.[20]

NATO and European allies

Although European members of NATO are collectively larger than the United States, the capacity of these countries to project military power is limited, certainly in comparison with the United States. Few European NATO members specialise to any great extent, so all attempt to provide a wide range of forces, with individual capabilities being a fraction of those of the United States. Over-riding all of this is the vexed question of the future of NATO. As an alliance it is popular in Eastern Europe, not least as former Warsaw Pact states see it as providing security against a resurgent or unstable Russia. For Russia, though, any increase in NATO capabilities or any spreading of its influence is seen as a dangerous and entirely unwarranted extension into Russia's sphere of influence. This adds to the near-paranoia over western commercial involvement in the former Soviet republics of the Caucasus and Central Asia.

NATO has other stresses built into its evolution. One is that European NATO, with its numerous small armies, is wholly unable to engage in large-scale military action without the United States, a reality demonstrated by the Kosovo War in 1999. This leads to stresses at two levels. One is that the US itself wants its European allies to share more of the burden, a view complicated by the fact that one or two European countries, not least Britain, feel that they are carrying too much of a commitment themselves.

The second aspect is that some circles of influence in Europe want an increased European role in security issues, not so much in support of the United States, but more as providing another centre of power and influence. This view, particularly strong in France, seeks a strong European defence identity, allied to the development of the European Union's foreign and security policy. At first sight, there would seem to be an area of overlap, with the 'pro-Europe' orientation also serving to reduce the European security burden currently taken on by the United States. In practice, it is not so simple.

Essentially, the ideal position for the United States in the coming decades would be for Europe to develop integrated military forces that can operate primarily within Europe, but preferably with some US involvement. Outside of Europe, though, the key player would be the United States, with its formidable global power projection capabilities. There might be occasions when it would operate with NATO, or with individual NATO states, but these would be essentially subservient. The end result would be that the US would not have to worry excessively about security in Europe, and would be able to devote its military capabilities to the wider global security threats.

The 'pro-Europe' view, though, is that Europe should not only develop a defence identity that counterbalances US power and influence within Europe, but that it should also have some capability to operate 'out of area', with a degree of military power that enables it to curtail or at least limit US control of major military operations.

This underlying tension is likely to persist well into the twenty-first century, but, meanwhile, the larger European states have progressively adapted their armed forces in much the same way as the United States, but at much lower levels. Britain, for example, still persists in over-reaching itself with its residual great power pretensions, but its armed forces have moved towards rapid deployment, maintaining an amphibious capability and carrier-based air power, even as armoured forces and anti-submarine forces have been cut back.[21] France, too, persists with pretensions of global reach, though most are directed towards Africa.[22] Together with Spain and Italy, much of the re-orientation of military postures in the 1990s was away from the East and towards the South. In other words, as the Soviet 'threat' receded, so a perception of threat from a violent and disorderly North Africa has resulted in the maintenance if not strengthening of naval forces and projection capabilities in the Mediterranean.

Among the more powerful military states of NATO Europe, a perception of a volatile unstable world with diverse threats to international security is shared with that of the United States. There is little pretence that individual countries can begin to match the security control that can be exercised by the US, and an unanswered question concerns NATO's role. The talk is of 'outreach', an unspoken desire to 'balance' US military power, but how NATO is going to be able to have a piece of the action without being beholden to the US remains entirely uncertain.[23]

Missile defences and the control of space

In preparing to ensure international security, the United States seeks a range of new technologies and force postures. Many of these relate to force projection and long-range strike, but one of the principal areas of concern, and one that is proving difficult to counter by existing military technologies, is defence against attacks with ballistic missiles. This concern has resulted in a considerable impetus towards developing missile defences, many of them using technologies and systems originally envisaged as part of the Strategic Defence Initiative (SDI) or 'Star Wars' programme during the closing stages of the Cold War in the mid-1980s. In one particular area, that of directed energy weapons, intensive research and development is beginning to lead to forms of technology that may amount to a revolution in warfare. At the centre of this are two weapons programmes, one medium-term and one long-term and both experimental – the airborne laser and the space-based laser respectively.

During the mid-1980s, the primary focus of SDI was the substantial force of multi-warhead ICBMs and SLBMs being developed and deployed by the Soviet Union. To the Soviets, though, the SDI programme itself was a threat. Although they were undertaking similar research, there was a recognition that the United States had a technological 'edge', and there was therefore the uncomfortable prospect of the US developing missile defences which, with its own offensive missiles, might give it an advantage in the event of a central nuclear exchange.[24]

In the event, the collapse of the Warsaw Pact, democratisation in Eastern Europe and the dismemberment of the Soviet Union all contributed to the ending of the East-West confrontation, and this was accompanied by some progress in strategic nuclear arms control with the START I and START II negotiations. As a result, funding for Russian missile defences collapsed and the SDI programme in the United States was substantially curtailed, many of the remaining programmes within the initiative being handed over to the smaller Ballistic Missile Defense Organisation in 1993.

Even as this was happening, though, the overall concept of ballistic missile defence was getting a new lease of life, partly because of the pro-liferation of ballistic missiles in Asia and the Middle East, and partly because of the attacks by Iraqi Scud and Al Hussein missiles during the 1991 Gulf War.[25]

The Gulf War missile attacks were significant for the United States in three ways. The first was that the attacks on Saudi Arabia and especially Israel had profound political effects. One of the greatest concerns for the US was that Iraq might succeed in dragging Israel into the war, making it far easier for Iraq to gain support in the region. The US had to expend con-siderable energy in persuading Israel not to retaliate for the missile attacks, and this included emergency provision of Patriot air defence missiles and the diversion of considerable resources to try to locate and destroy the mobile missile launchers. Few of the launchers were found, and the Patriot missiles proved singularly ineffective in intercepting the Scuds.

The second factor was that, although the missiles were inaccurate and unreliable, some did hit their targets. Towards the end of the war, on 25 February 1991, a missile hit a storage and billeting depot in Dhahran, Saudi Arabia, killing 28 people, the greatest loss of life experienced by coalition forces throughout the war. The third factor, not made public at the time, was that one other Scud incident came close to being a much greater disaster for the US forces. On 16 February, a missile narrowly missed a large pier complex in the Saudi port of Al Jubayl. The missile landed in the sea some 300 yards from the US Navy's aviation support ship *Wright* and close to the large amphibious warfare ship *Tarawa*, both of which were moored alongside a pier complex which included a large ammunition storage dump and a petrol tanker parking area.[26]

This Gulf War experience of missile attack was profound, given that the Iraqi Scud and Al Hussein missiles were crude by any standards, using missile technology that was up to 40 years old. Coupled with fears of missile development and proliferation by North Korea, Iran and other states, the US moved to revitalise its missile defence research. The emphasis initially was on threats to US forces operating in regions of conflict away from the United States, but advocates of missile defence also promoted the idea of developing a national missile defence for the continental United States, not necessarily aiming to provide protection against a mass missile attack as in the Cold War era, but sufficient to provide possible defences against 'rogue' states, accidental missile launches or some kind of future conflict with Russia or China.

Over the past ten years, ballistic missile defence has gone through a series of phases. Initially, there was a sustained programme to improve the Patriot missile, the so-called PAC-3 system, and to help Israel fund a similar missile, the Arrow. Both are now being deployed, although there are considerable doubts as to their effectiveness. Beyond these two systems, the US Navy is developing an anti-missile system that would use modified standard missiles carried on warships and able to be moved to regions of potential conflict, and there is also a heavily-funded 'super-Patriot' missile the Theatre High Altitude Area Defense (THAAD) system.[27]

THAAD has experienced considerable problems, although its development is continuing, at considerable cost. It is, in any case, subject to one fundamental problem in that it is only capable of intercepting a missile towards the end of its trajectory, as it approaches the target. If a missile has already dispersed multiple warheads or canisters, such terminal interception has little or no effect.

The sub-munitions canisters could contain chemical or biological warheads, although problems with the high temperatures reached on re-entry into the earth's atmosphere would make the survival of such payloads difficult to ensure. Of greater concern would be the use of radiological warheads, with the sub-munitions containing cobalt-60 or strontium-90, the intention being to contaminate the target area, whether it be a military base, the financial centre of a city or an industrial centre, rendering any of them unusable.[28]

To counter this problem, the US Air Force has embarked on a major research and development programme to provide 'boost-phase interception' destroying a missile in the first minute or two after launch, when it is still in powered flight. At this time, before any sub-munitions have been dispersed, the missile is very visible because of the heat of the rocket exhaust, and is under considerable mechanical stress because of the acceleration. Some plans seek to develop UCAVs, pilot-less aircraft carrying missiles that could patrol a possible launch area and would then home in on newly-launched missiles. There are many problems with such a system, and the chosen weapons now being developed are the Airborne Laser (ABL) and its successor, the Space-Based Laser (SBL). These laser weapons are in an early stage of development, and face many technical and financial hurdles, yet they represent the first stage of what is likely to be a revolution in power projection – the use of directed energy weapons in warfare.

Following the intensive military development of lasers in the late 1970s and 1980s, several experiments were conducted in the early 1990s that suggested that a powerful laser, mounted on a modified Boeing 747, might be developed to destroy boost-phase missiles. Substantial funding was provided from 1996, and three large defence contractors, Lockheed-Martin, Boeing and TRW have since worked with the US Air Force Research Laboratory at Kirtland Air Force Base in New Mexico. Depending on funding and technical progress, a prototype airborne laser is planned to be completed by 2005, with deployment within a further five years.[29]

The basis of the ABL is a powerful 2–3 megawatt Chemical Oxygen-Iodine Laser carried on a 747 and directed through a complex set of optics at targets up to 400 miles away. Under operational conditions, and in the event of a regional crisis in which US interests are threatened by ballistic missile attack, it will be possible for an ABL with augmented crew to fly from the continental United States to the crisis area within 48 hours, carrying a full magazine of laser fuel and supported by aerial refuelling, making it independent of forward basing.[30]

In practice, though, the normal deployment pattern will be for five aircraft and supporting tankers and transport aircraft to deploy to bases in friendly territory, from where continuous 24 hour patrols can be maintained by two aircraft at a time. The aircraft will remain in 'friendly' air space, able to track missiles as they emerge from cloud cover, lock on to them and lase them for up to a minute. Each ABL will carry enough fuel to 'fire' up to 40 shots, each capable of destroying a missile under optimal conditions. In short, the ABL is a directed energy weapon that is intended to be capable of destroying ballistic missiles accelerating after launch, by focusing a powerful laser beam on them at the speed of light, from a range of up to 400 miles in secure air space until they are irreversibly damaged.

The airborne laser is intended to counter ballistic missiles where the US Air Force can operate within range of launch sites. It is clearly intended for use principally in the Middle East and East Asia, but its follow-on, the space-based laser, would be a global weapon. This is a much longer-term endeavour and would be developed through to 2015 and beyond. It builds on many of the SDI technologies of the 1980s, as well as the massive experience in satellite technology and space launchers that the US has acquired over half a century. Each SBL would be 65 feet long and weigh over 17 tons, using a powerful laser to destroy missiles within ten seconds, with re-targeting possible in as little as half a second. At least twelve and possibly 24, satellites would eventually be deployed in low Earth orbits of about 650 miles.[31]

Both the airborne laser and its space-based successor are new types of weapon that remain highly experimental. They are controversial within the Pentagon, not least because they are very costly and compete with other programmes. Both may also face severe technical problems and it is possible that the ABL could be postponed or even cancelled. Against this, a powerful lobby has developed in support of the programmes, many variants are already being proposed and the overall concept of directed energy weapons is proving very attractive.

In the short term, this is because of the perceived threat from missile proliferation, and problems with other forms of missile defence may even result in a speeding up of directed energy research. Beyond this, though, is the idea that directed weapons represent the beginning of a new form of warfare. If a directed energy weapon can be produced that can destroy a fast-moving missile from 400 miles away, why cannot similar technologies be adapted for destroying all kinds of targets? In this respect, directed energy weapons come close to being 'ideal weapons', and whoever is able to develop and produce them could acquire a particular form of military superiority.

In theory, a weapon is simply a device for transmitting energy from a source to a target in order to damage or destroy the target. This is true for a club, spear, arrow, bullet, shell, bomb, missile or even nuclear weapon. There are a few exceptions, such as biological weapons, although even a biological weapon 'disrupts' a target. 'Ideal' weapon characteristics include extreme precision, very long range, great speed, repeated attack and invulnerability and resistance to counter-measures. A space-based laser could operate at the speed of light, over ranges of hundreds of miles, with great accuracy, repeatedly and, unless an opponent had the means of destroying a satellite, it would be invulnerable. Some countermeasures might be possible but, in other respects, such a weapon would represent a near-revolution in warfare.

Such an analysis might seem far-fetched, but the implications of new generations of directed energy weapons are already being recognised. A major problem with lasers is that they can be weakened in passing through the atmosphere, so one research effort is directed towards combining them with other forms of directed energy such as particle beams. More generally, US defence planners are already investigating ways of using the airborne laser for offensive purposes against a range of targets. The US Air Force set up a study, Directed Energy Applications for Tactical Air Combat (DEATAC) in 1998, one aim of which was to study ways in which the ABL could be used for a range of roles in addition to missile defence. According to the chair of the study, former USAF Chief of Staff General Ronald R. Fogelman:

> I believe that directed-energy weapons will be fundamental to the way the Air Force fights future wars. This study, which I am pleased to be part of, will help prepare us for the changing face of warfare. It is an important step in pursuing the potential of directed-energy technologies. [32]

This thinking extends to the space-based laser, thought by some to be revolutionary in its implications, not unlike the 'death ray' beloved of science fiction writers. Although initially seen as a means of attacking boost-phase missiles, it already has potential for attacking ground-based targets. The successor to the B-2 stealth bomber might not even be a bomber at all, but a space-based directed energy weapon. [33]

US Space Command has developed a Long Range Plan for the period through to the year 2020 that is based on the view that it is essential for the United States to have clear and unequivocal control of space. This must include what is termed 'world-wide situational awareness', an ability to defend against ballistic and cruise missiles from space as well as an ability to hit ground targets. It also means being able to defend satellites and other space-based vehicles from attack as well as an ability to destroy any other state's space-based systems. [34]

The wider view that it is essential for the United States to be the world's dominant space power has strong support throughout the US defence community, and the role of directed energy weapons in this process will probably be central to this task. Their other function – extending the ability to destroy missiles to the ability to attack a wide range of targets on the ground – is of particular interest to many military planners. It is possible, at present, for the US to target virtually anywhere on earth with a conventionally-armed cruise missile. This is regarded as a major step forward in force projection, not least because it does not put American lives at risk. Even so, cruise missiles take time to reach their targets, they must be launched from ships or aircraft that are within range and they are of little use against mobile targets.

By contrast, a space-based directed energy weapon could be used with impunity and almost instantaneously, operating anywhere in the world, even hitting moving targets. In short, it is a very seductive idea, one that appeals to political and military opinion formers and could potentially yield a funding bonanza to the military-industrial-academic complex.

Keeping the violent peace

This chapter has concentrated mainly on the United States, seeking to assess the changes in its defence posture since the ending of the Cold War, and likely developments in the next couple of decades or so. Some attention has been paid to other states, but it is the US that is dominant, both in terms of military power and economic leadership. The view from the security community is that the Cold War was won, that there is no one state that can challenge US dominance, but that there will be many smaller security problems to face.

In this paradigm, Russia is in disarray and could be a source of instability or, just possibly, a resurgence, and China is growing in power and could eventually pose a threat to US leadership. There are distinct threats to regional interests, primarily in Eastern Asia and the Middle East, and there is a deep concern with 'rogue states', a small and disparate collection of states that seek, in different ways, to challenge the US and the West. Overlying all of this are concerns about the proliferation of nuclear, chemical and especially biological weapons and ballistic missiles, and a belief that there will be a particular vulnerability to paramilitary action and terrorism.

This 'jungle full of snakes' will present many problems of control, most of them regional and distant from the United States itself, but US military forces have already undergone a transition from their Cold War posture and are involved in various processes of potential military control, with a further major development no more than a decade away.

In the near future, US forces will maintain and enhance the ability to project force anywhere in the world by a variety of means. The air force will have global reach using its strategic bombers, and will be capable of rapid regional build-ups using its air expeditionary wings. Use of cruise missiles and other stand-off weapons, stealth bombers, unmanned aerial vehicles and air- and space-based surveillance and reconnaissance will all make it possible to fight wars 'at a distance' and with little risk to American lives.

The navy will continue to maintain carrier-based power and further generations of cruise missiles, and the marine corps will suffer little in the way of cuts as it preserves and enhances its abilities in amphibious warfare. The army loses out most, but hangs on to power projection, and puts particular emphasis on special operations and counter-insurgency training. By all these means, the US maintains the power to intervene at times and places that are considered necessary to protect its interests. It may operate in coalition with allies, especially in Europe, but it will remain the lead player in global terms while being content to let the Europeans take a rather more significant, and expensive, defence role in their own limited region.

Countering weapons of mass destruction will be a priority, with a continuing reliance on modernised nuclear forces if that should prove necessary, and defence against missiles, whether in distant regions or for protecting the United States, will be a major issue. Control of space will be a pre-requisite for continued global military power. In the longer term, but within two decades, there is a promise of entirely new forms of military power, especially directed energy weapons, that could well greatly enhance US military capabilities and prove almost impossible to counter by conventional military means.

In short, the next 30 years will present challenges to US global power, but these will not be excessive and can be readily met. There are many uncertainties and the world is likely to prove volatile, with diverse threats to the US in particular and western-orientated political power in general. Even so, there is essentially a westernised world system now taking hold in a unipolar world in which one state, the US, is dominant. It will be possible 'to keep the violent peace'. It is a comforting view but it is wrong.

The New Security Paradigm

A local rebellion in a global context

On 1 January 1994, a rebellion broke out in the southern Mexican province of Chiapas. It was timed to coincide with the coming into force of the North American Free Trade Area (NAFTA), an agreement between the United States, Canada and Mexico that was seen by the rebels as another example of the free market trends that would further marginalise the majority of the people of Chiapas into greater poverty.

A rebel source gave the reasons for the revolt:

> We have nothing, absolutely nothing – not decent shelter, nor land, nor work, nor health, nor food, nor education. We do not have the right to choose freely and democratically our officials. We have neither peace nor justice for ourselves and our children. But today we say enough![1]

The rebels called themselves the Zapatista National Liberation Army (ZNLA), after Emiliano Zapata, a leader of the 1910–17 rebellion in Mexico that resulted in the break up of many of the major land-holdings and some measure of land redistribution to poorer people. In several days of violence, over 150 people were killed as the Mexican Army moved in to put down the rebellion. Although mainly confined to Chiapas Province, there were car bombs in Mexico City and Acapulco and an attack on electricity supplies. In Chiapas itself, the rebels took control of a number of towns and villages.[2]

Harsh measures were used in initial efforts to suppress the rebellion, but these were followed by attempts at negotiation. Although the rebellion subsided from its original intensity, the issues that lay behind it remained largely unresolved and the activities of the ZNLA continued for the rest of the decade, aimed at those elites and their sources of power that control the economy of the country as a whole and of Chiapas in particular. Two features of the rebellion have been the persistent attempts of rebel leaders to communicate their motives to a wider audience, not least through the Internet, and their insistence that the Zapatista rebellion must be seen in the context of a much broader division of global wealth and poverty.

This linking of the rebellion with the workings of the global economy has caused consternation in government circles in Mexico and the United States, running directly counter to received wisdom. The almost universal view in such circles is that NAFTA is an important regional contribution to an era of free trade that is, in turn, a necessary precondition to the effective working of a global liberal market economy. Any contrary view is considered to be retrograde if not Luddite, and the idea that a peasant rebellion could be couched in terms of a revolt against free trade can only be comprehended if the rebels can be considered illiterate (not an easy matter when their leaders use the Internet with such skill and sophistication) or at least misguided in the extreme.

The Zapatista rebellion is an indicator of a much broader global trend that constitutes the security paradigm that is now evolving, a paradigm that is quite different from the Cold War era. At the heart of this paradigm are three factors or 'drivers', the widening wealth-poverty divide, environmental constraints on development and the vulnerability of elite societies to paramilitary action. The paradigm is not new – it has been evolving largely unnoticed for at least a couple of decades, and there have already been numerous indicators.

One way of recognising this is to visualise conflicts of the past half century either as 'epilogue' or 'prologue' wars. The epilogue wars are those that are mainly indicative of past trends. There are many examples, notably the numerous wars of de-colonisation or liberation that were prevalent in the 1950s and 1960s and persisted in some parts of Africa through the 1970s. Examples are Indo-China, Indonesia, Malaya, Kenya, Cyprus, Aden and Algeria in the 1950s. Other epilogue wars are the numerous 'proxy' wars of the Cold War era, some of them immensely costly in human terms. The Korean War, with 3 million people killed, stands out, as does Vietnam and, more recently, Afghanistan, but many of the conflicts in sub-Saharan Africa and Latin America had strong Cold War elements.

The Zapatista revolt and the Gulf War of 1991 are both prologue wars, indicative of future conflict, but there are many others, not least Peru in the 1980s and Algeria and South Lebanon in the 1990s. Both the Zapatista rebellion and the Gulf War illustrate components of the trend in international insecurity that together amount to a paradigm shift. The Zapatista revolt is an example of an anti-elite rebellion exacerbated by the growing wealth-poverty divide, and the Gulf War was essentially a resource war, fought over the control of Persian Gulf oil between an autocratic leader with regional ambitions and a powerful coalition of oil-importing states.

The impact of environmental constraints on an economically divided world has been recognised for several decades, although its security implications have only recently become apparent. It was, for example, put succinctly by Palmer Newbould at the time of the UN Conference on the Human Environment in Stockholm, back in 1972:

> My own view is that however successful population policies are, the world population is likely to treble before it reaches stability. If the expectation of this increased population were, for example, to emulate the present lifestyle and resource use of the USA, the demand on world resources would be increased approximately 15-fold; pollution and other forms of environmental degradation might increase similarly and global ecological carrying capacity would then be seriously exceeded. There are therefore global constraints on development set by resources and environment and these cannot be avoided. They will require a reduction in the per caput resource use and environmental abuse of developed nations to accompany the increased resource use of the developing nations, a levelling down as well as up. This conflict cannot be avoided.[3]

Unless there was a change in political and economic behaviour, the end result of the growing pressures of human demand would, according to Edwin Brooks writing at the same time, result in a 'crowded, glowering planet of massive inequalities of wealth buttressed by stark force yet endlessly threatened by desperate people in the global ghettos of the underprivileged'.[4]

At the root of this prognosis lie the two themes of socioeconomic polarisation and environmental constraints.

The wealth-poverty divide

Although the centrally-planned economies of the former Soviet Union and Eastern Europe represented a significant part of the population of the industrialised world for more then 50 years, their role in the world economy was relatively small. For the past century, most of the world's people have experienced a mixed economy with an emphasis on the capitalist model.

Until the early post-war years, most of the global economy was under the direct or indirect control of a small number of often competing states. Africa and most of Asia were under colonial control, and the key sectors of the economies of most of Latin America were closely linked to western business interests, especially in the United States and Britain. The de-colonisation process of the post-war years resulted in the transfer of varying degrees of political power, although it often involved a transfer from colonial elites to local elites. In the last 20 years of the century there was an acceleration in market and trade liberalisation and a decrease in state activity, a process that was accelerated by the collapse of most elements of the centrally planned alternative in the former Soviet Union and Eastern Europe.

The world economy is now a largely unimodal liberal market system, as distinct from the more bimodal system of the Cold War years. Both during and since the Cold War, this liberal market system has delivered economic growth, although with variable success, but has been persistently unsuccessful at delivering social justice. Put simply, the end result has been the success of the few at the expense of the many. The 'few' may number over a billion, but the 'many' are over four times that number. Socioeconomic disparities are growing and extreme poverty is experienced by a substantial proportion of the world's population. The actual numbers are massive – between one and two billion – and show little sign of any decrease; they may even be increasing as the world's population continues to grow by over 80 million each year. Along with them are three billion more people who are substantially marginalised as the world's elite surge ahead.

The liberal market system is not delivering economic justice and there is a decline in welfare across much of the system, a process exacerbated by the erosion of publicly-funded welfare provision. During the Cold War, there were powerful motives in the liberal market economies to ensure the maintenance of social stability, not least through welfare provision. This was particularly obvious in Western Europe in the immediate post-war era, but was a feature of western policies in many countries across the world. With the ending of the Cold War, and the perhaps temporary ascendancy of a single economic system, these motives have declined and so has public welfare provision, not least as a result of structural adjustment and similar programmes encouraged by multilateral bodies such as the International Monetary Fund.

Roots of the divide

International wealth in the past five decades has persistently transferred from the poor to the rich. The main engine of this inequality has been the post-colonial trading system and its endemic imbalances, expressed especially in the deteriorating terms of trade borne by most ex-colonial states in the 1950s and 1960s, but continuing through to the 1990s with the brief exception of a two-year commodity price boom in the early 1970s. More recently this situation has been exacerbated by two factors. One is the debt crisis which, though it peaked in the 1980s and is now subject to some modest relief, is still a huge hindrance to the development potential of most Southern states. The other is the process of corporate globalisation, especially in the exploitation of labour markets, where corporations can search persistently for the cheapest sources of labour.

The three successive 'drivers' of international wealth divisions are all inextricably linked to the liberal market: trade problems, the debt crisis and labour rights. The first relates to trading patterns that date from the early post-colonial era but which evolved from the colonial experience itself. The majority of world trade, then as now, was between the wealthy industrialised states, but an important sub-set was the pattern of North-South trade where former colonies traded a wide variety of primary commodities, from copper, tin and bauxite to coffee, cocoa and tea, with industrial consumers, in return for manufactured products. Inefficient import substitution had some impact, but the fundamental problem was the decline in terms of trade as primary commodity prices declined relative to manufactured imports. The problem was put bluntly by Tanzania's Julius Nyerere in 1971:

> When we were preparing our first Five Year Plan, the price of our sisal was 148 British old pounds before devaluation – 148 pounds per ton. We felt this price was not likely to continue so we planned on the basis that we might average 95 pounds per ton. It dropped down to less than 70. We can't win. In 1963, we needed to produce 5 tons of sisal to buy a tractor. In 1970, we had to produce 10 tons of sisal to buy that same tractor.[5]

A small number of oil-producing states were partly insulated from this trend, and some East Asian countries such as South Korea and Taiwan got huge economic aid from the West because they were considered to be front-line states in the Cold War. These were exceptions – overall, non-oil-producing Third World states experienced a 32 per cent increase in import prices from the mid-1950s to 1972, compared with just an 11 per cent increase in export prices. According to the UN Conference on Trade and Development (UNCTAD), in 1972 the deterioration in terms of trade for third world countries over this period was:

> equivalent to a loss, in 1972, of about $10,000 million, or rather more than 20% of these countries' aggregate exports, and considerably exceeding the total of official development assistance from developed market economy countries to developing countries in Africa, Asia and Latin America (some $8,450 million in 1972). In other words, there was, in effect, a net transfer of real resources, over this period, from developing to developed countries, the flow of aid being more than offset by the adverse terms of trade of the developing countries.[6]

The figures given are at 1972 prices, before the inflation of the mid-1970s set in – if put in current prices, the loss of terms of trade would be closer to $80,000 million each year. Furthermore, UNCTAD contrasts the loss of terms of trade with official development assistance. But such assistance was, and is, commonly in the form of loans requiring repayment, or 'tied' to the buying of goods and services from the 'donor' country. Even ignoring these, there was a net wealth flow from the poor South to the rich North. If they are included, the extraction of wealth from poor to rich was little short of remarkable.

During the 1960s efforts were made to reform world trade to favour third world states, most notably in the first UNCTAD blueprint, *Towards a Trade Policy for Development* in 1964, known more popularly as the Prebisch Plan after UNCTAD's first Secretary-General, the Argentinian economist Raul Prebisch. The Prebisch Plan embraced commodity agreements, compensatory finance, tariff preferences, control of invisibles, regional industrialisation and substantial improvements in the quantity and quality of aid to produce an integrated programme to foster rapid development. It formed the basis for UNCTAD bargaining for almost a decade but made little progress against the substantial economic interests of the North, especially those of the major primary commodity importers, the UK, France, West Germany, Japan and the United States.[7]

With few exceptions, Third World commodity producers failed to achieve the unity required to enforce price increases for their exports. There was an extraordinary irony in the fact that the one group that succeeded, the Organisation of Petroleum Exporting Countries (OPEC), achieved substantial if temporary benefits for its own members but set up the conditions for a debt crisis stretching over two decades.[8]

Between October 1973 and May 1974, OPEC acted effectively as a cartel and presided over an increase in crude oil prices of over 400 per cent. The prices held for more than two years, declined somewhat and then increased massively in 1979/80 because of regional oil supply disruptions consequent on the Iranian Revolution and the outbreak of the Iran-Iraq War. While the economies of many industrialised oil-importing states were hindered, those of Third World states came close to being crippled, resulting in heavy borrowings on international money markets leading to massive problems of debt within a decade.

For a very brief period, from 1973 to 1975, the oil price increases coincided with a generalised commodities boom.[9] This put some pressure on industrialised countries to negotiate a reformed international commodity trading system, and a special session of the UN General Assembly early in 1974 advocated a New International Economic Order embracing many of the features of the Prebisch Plan of a decade earlier. By early 1975, though, the 'stagflation' affecting many industrialised states resulted in a collapse of commodity prices and an immediate loss of interest in trade reform. The New International Economic Order, involving fair trade for the South, was lost.

Furthermore, by the mid-1990s the effects of the debt crisis were to be an extraordinary handicap on development prospects. For many third world states, servicing the external debt, let alone repaying the debt capital, was absorbing a significant proportion of total export earnings. Even by the late 1990s, debt servicing still accounted for a quarter or more of export earnings for countries right across the South, including Algeria, Bolivia, Chile, Colombia, Ethiopia, Ghana, Indonesia, the Ivory Coast, Kenya, Mexico, Morocco, Mozambique, Pakistan, Peru and Zambia. Sub-Saharan Africa was particularly badly affected by debt. In 1997 it owed creditors $234 billion and had already paid $170 billion in debt servicing, with this costing around four times the health and education budgets each year.[10]

During the course of the decade, some attention was paid by the Group of Seven (G7) leading industrial states to this core handicap on development, but most of the responses amounted to a re-scheduling or, at best, some limited direct relief. Even some more systematic responses in 1999 accounted for only a minority of the overall debt problem of southern states. Taking the continuing problem of terms of trade together with indebtedness, the poor South continued to see wealth transferred to the rich North right through into the new millennium.

However, a further factor was becoming more significant. From the early 1980s, the rapid spread of the free market paradigm led to the partial retreat of the state from welfare and social support in many parts of the world. While it took root with greatest fervour in the United States and the UK, it had a profound influence on multilateral finance organisations such as the IMF and the World Bank, with structural adjustment of Third World economies towards an unfettered market often being a condition for aid.

A frequent casualty has been labour rights, reversing a trend stretching back three-quarters of a century. The founding of the International Labour Organisation (ILO) in 1919, in the aftermath of the First World War and the Russian Revolution, led on to the ILO Convention stipulating minimum working conditions such as the 48-hour week and 8-hour day. While many of the wealthier countries moved progressively towards such norms over the following half century, often 'encouraged' by strong trades unions, these labour rights were rarely observed in the majority world of the South, where the informal sector of the economy flourished without regulation.

In the past quarter century, enhanced by the increased availability of a trained but underemployed workforce and by ease of movement of capital and production, it has been possible for production of a wide range of consumer goods to be transferred to Southern states. These have typically been controlled, either directly or indirectly, by transnational business interests that have sufficient flexibility and purchasing power to be able to seek out the cheapest labour markets, whatever the conditions of the workers. This is made easier by chronic underemployment in many regions. In sub-Saharan Africa, for example, some 75 per cent of the workforce works on the margins of the formal economy and there are 16 million child labourers aged between 10 and 14.[11]

In the churchyard of the town of Kirkheaton near Huddersfield in West Yorkshire there is a monument to 18 girls, the youngest aged nine, burnt to death in a mill fire in 1818. Ten miles away another monument outside Silkstone Parish Church near Barnsley records a flood in a local coal mine in 1838 in which sixteen boys and ten girls died, most aged under twelve years and the youngest only seven. If such disasters were to occur in present-day Britain, or indeed in any other western country, there would be outrage. But they do happen, frequently, the only difference being that they have been 'exported' to countries of the South.

The widening of the rich-poor divide

At the start of the twenty-first century there is endemic deep poverty affecting over a billion people. There is also a steadily widening gap between a rich minority of the world's population (located primarily, but not solely, in North America, Western Europe and Japan) and most of the rest. One of the crudest measures is that the 300 or so dollar billionaires in the world are collectively as wealthy as the poorest 2.4 billion people. In 1960, the richest 20 per cent of the world's people had 70 per cent of the income; by 1991 their share had risen to 85 per cent while the share of the poorest 20 per cent had declined from 2.3 per cent to 1.7 per cent. Put another way, the ratio of global inequality had nearly doubled.[12]

It is also notable that the rich-poor gap widened at a faster rate in the 1980s, as free market liberalisation increased. There are early indications that there has been a further widening in the late 1990s, a consequence of the severe economic problems affecting first South East Asia and then South Asia, Africa and Latin America.

This widening rich-poor divide contrasts markedly with an implicit assumption of most current economic thinking that economic growth is part of the world-wide phenomenon of globalisation that is delivering economic growth for all. This is not so. As John Cavanagh remarked:

> More than three-quarters of the new investment into the developing world goes into China and nine other rapidly growing countries. A new global apartheid of 24 richer countries, a dozen rapidly developing countries and 140 that are growing slowly or not at all becomes one of the major new threats to global security.[13]

The global divisions are even repeated in some apparently successful Southern states. After Mexico became a member of NAFTA in 1994 and experienced the peso crisis of that year, there was an expectation of rapid economic growth. Overall there have been many developments, but:

> ... the gap between rich and poor in Mexico is enormous, and it has widened since the peso devaluation. But just as large is the gap in the country's economic recovery, which seems to have taken hold at only the highest income levels and skipped the all-but-forgotten places.[14]

What is happening in individual countries of the South, and much more harshly across the world, is an increasing rich-poor divide. All the indications are that this will continue over the next 30 years, and may even accelerate, with the development of a trans-state global elite surging ahead of the rest. This elite, of rather more than one billion people, a sixth of the world's population, lives mainly in the countries of the North Atlantic community, Australasia and parts of East Asia.[15]

The distribution in these regions is not uniform, and there are substantial problems of poverty in a number of advanced industrialised states such as the United States.[16] Nor are the poorer states of the South uniformly poor. In some countries, the rich elites represent a tiny minority of the population, but others such as Brazil have quite substantial middle and upper classes, living apart from the majority poor and ever-conscious of their own security vulnerabilities.

Southern elites frequently work very closely with the business interests of major trans-national corporations based primarily in the North and these, too, put a premium on the security of their expatriate personnel and local associates. In the case of energy and mining companies, this will commonly extend to maintaining their own security forces, private armies that ensure the safety of their operations while providing lucrative and welcome employment for recently retired members of special operations forces and others from the armies of the North.

There is a further key factor in the global socioeconomic polarisation. In the past four decades, there has been substantial progress in some aspects of development in the South, often achieved against the odds and in a global economic environment that works more in the interests of the states of the North. Progress has been particularly marked in the field of education and literacy and there is current progress in communications. An effect of this is that an increasing number of marginalised people in the South are aware of the fact of their marginalisation and of the rich-poor gap.

Revolts from the margins

Such a circumstance, the combination of a widening rich-poor gap with an increasingly knowledgeable poor, is leading to a 'revolution of unfulfilled expectations', a prominent feature of many insurgencies and instability in Latin America, North Africa and the Middle East. The Zapatista rebellion is a clear recent example. Another is the far more radical Sendero Luminoso (Shining Path) movement in Peru, developing from the teachings of Abimael Guzman in the 1970s. Sendero may be in retreat, but its tough and often brutal quasi-Maoist ideology took root among the poor both of the high Andes and in the urban shanty towns of Lima and other cities, resulting in a long and bitter conflict with the Peruvian Army that saw some 25,000 people die.[17]

A similar revolt from the margins is evident in other countries, with much of the attraction of organisations such as Hamas coming from their ability to offer a way out of exclusion. Hamas has been prominent in its social agenda, a programme of social welfare and education running parallel with radical insurgency action against the Israelis. Hamas is marginalised as a straightforward terrorist organisation bent on the destruction of the Israeli state, with little attempt made to study the reasons for its development. But Hamas cannot be understood without recognising the position of tens of thousands of young Palestinians growing up in the fifty-year-old refugee camps of the Gaza strip.

Of concern in France, if less widely recognised in the rest of Europe, is the bitter civil war in Algeria that has claimed 100,000 lives in less than a decade. It has been a war fought between a repressive government and radical (and often extreme) fundamentalist groups who gather support from among the millions of marginalised people, especially unemployed young men, who are largely excluded from the Algerian economy.

A combination of incompetent and corrupt government and a severe economic downturn in the late 1980s led in 1988 to riots, disturbances, repression by the armed forces and a state of emergency. A cautious move towards elections enabled the Islamic Salvation Front (FIS) to gain much public support in the early 1990s, winning an overwhelming majority of seats in the first round of elections in December 1991. Before the second round, the military intervened to prevent the FIS taking power, setting in motion a bitter and protracted conflict lasting the rest of the decade.[18] The conflict in Algeria, with its violent effects felt in France, may well be a prototype conflict for the next several decades.

One of the most spectacular examples of a revolt from the margins was the uprising in many parts of Indonesia in 1998, with incidents in Djakarta described vividly by one journalist as the dispossessed rising out of the shanty towns to loot the shopping malls of the rich.

Environmental limits to growth

The violent effects of increasing socioeconomic polarisation are already apparent, with a likely trend towards further instability and conflict. On its own this is, at the very least, a matter of real concern. It might therefore be argued that such a trend will be recognised, and that sufficient economic reforms might be put in place to curb an excess of insecurity. There are few signs of this happening and it would, in any case, have little effect unless it was part of a recognition of the second global trend, the growing impact of environmental constraints on human activity.

In essence, the limitations of the global ecosystem now look likely to make it very difficult if not impossible for human well-being to be continually improved by current forms of economic growth. This is certainly not a new prognosis and it formed a central part of the frequently derided 'limits to growth' ideas of the early 1970s. Those ideas stemmed from some of the early experiences of human/environment interaction, notably the problems of pesticide toxicity, land dereliction and air pollution, all initially significant problems in industrialised countries.

The earliest indications came in the 1950s with severe problems of air pollution affecting many industrial cities, most notably a disastrous smog episode in London in 1952, responsible for the death of some 4,000, mostly bronchitic and elderly, people. A decade later came the recognition of the effects of organophosphorus pesticides on wildlife, a process greatly stimulated by a single book, Rachel Carson's *Silent Spring*. Later in the 1960s there were environmental disasters in Europe including a massive fish kill in the Rhine, the wrecking of the *Torrey Canyon* oil tanker near the Scilly Isles and the killing of over 140 people, mostly children, when a coal mining waste tip engulfed a school in the village of Aberfan in Wales.

By the early 1970s environmental concern was sufficient to stimulate the first UN Conference on the Human Environment in Stockholm. Although initially likely to be concerned with the environmental problems of industrialised states, the Stockholm meeting was substantially influenced by an early systems study of global environmental trends, *Limits to Growth*, published a few months earlier.[19] While widely criticised as a somewhat crude simulation study of the global system, *Limits to Growth* was seminal in introducing the idea that the global ecosystem might not be able to absorb the overall effects of human activity, especially those stemming from the highly resource-consumptive and polluting lifestyles of the richer states of the industrialised North.

The early signs of environmental problems have been joined by much more significant changes in the past two decades. Air pollution has been recognised as a regional phenomenon through the experience of acid rain, and a global problem, the depletion of the ozone layer, began to be recognised as serious in the 1980s. Ozone depletion has a significance as being the first major global effect of human activity. It resulted from the effects of a range of specific pollutants, chlorfluorocarbons (CFCs) and related chemicals, on the thin layer of ozone in the upper atmosphere that normally shields the earth's surface against excessive amounts of ultra-violet radiation.

While the potential for an ozone depletion problem was recognised in the 1970s, concern was hugely boosted by the discovery in the early 1980s of an annual 'ozone hole' over the Antarctic each spring. The problem was brought under some degree of control by international agreements, specifically the Vienna Convention in 1985 and the Montreal Protocol two years later, but still had a large effect on environmental thinking – this was a human activity that was having a discernible and potentially devastating impact on the entire global ecosystem.

Other problems developing on a global scale also rose to prominence. They included desertification and deforestation, the latter having an immediate effect in terms of soil erosion and flooding, and the salinisation of soils, especially in semi-arid areas. Other forms of resource depletion became evident, most notably the decline in the resources of some of the world's richest fishing grounds, not least in the continental shelf fishing grounds of North America and Western Europe.

Problems of water shortages and water quality are already severe in many parts of the world. Around half of the population of Southern Asia and Africa does not have access to safe drinking water, and 80 per cent of diseases in these areas stem from unsafe water. At a more general level, there have been tensions between states over the status and use of major river systems. The 1959 agreement between Egypt and Sudan resulted in joint control over the mid-Nile waters, but Ethiopia controls 85 per cent of the sources of the Nile, with Sudan and Egypt having the prime dependencies. Similarly, the Ganges and Brahmaputra rivers are essential to Bangladesh, with its rapidly growing population. Schemes for joint utilisation exist with India and Nepal, but Bangladeshi requirements and Himalayan deforestation remain twin pressures.

A more specific source of potential conflict is the substantial Turkish programme of dams, hydro-electric and irrigation programmes on the upper waters of the Tigris and Euphrates rivers in South East Anatolia, rivers which are subsequently essential to the economic well-being of Syria and Iraq. Also in the Middle East, a much smaller-scale problem (that forms a largely hidden part of Israeli-Palestinian negotiations) is found in the West Bank. Winter rainfall on the West Bank hills provides water not just for the West Bank, but also for much of Israel in the form of underground aquifers flowing westwards towards the Mediterranean. Any long-term settlement will require a fair sharing of the water resources that will be very difficult to achieve given the already heavy use of water by Israel and the increasing water demands in both Israel and the West Bank.

In some parts of the world a persistent failure to come to terms with human environmental impacts has produced near-catastrophic results. Nowhere was this more evident than in many parts of the former-Soviet Union, where a drying-out of the Aral Sea, massive problems of pesticide pollution and the radioactive contamination of Arctic environments are the most obvious examples.

Individual problems of pressures on land, water, fisheries and other resources are likely to increase, notwithstanding some successful cross-border agreements, as population growth and increases in per capita resource consumption combine in their effects. Even so, two much broader global phenomena will have a more profound impact on global security: the 'resource shift' and climate change.

The resource shift and resource conflict

The resource shift is a centuries-old phenomenon that stems from the original industrial revolutions of Europe and North America feeding initially on domestically-available raw materials, whether coal, iron ore, copper, tin, lead or other non-renewable resources. In the nineteenth century, European industrial growth was based largely on such resources mined within Europe, and the much more resource-rich United States could continue to be largely self-sufficient until the latter half of the twentieth century.

In the past century, the industrialised North has become progressively more dependent on physical resources from the South, as its own deposits of key minerals, ores, coal, oil and gas have become progressively more costly to extract. This resource shift has meant that certain physical resources have acquired a strategic significance that, in a number of cases, already results in actual or potential conflict.

Zaire, for example, has had much of its politics in the 40 years since independence dominated by competition for the control of Shaba Province, formerly Katanga. This has included outright violence during the civil war after independence in 1960, and rebellions in Shaba in 1977 and 1978 that were helped by Eastern Bloc aid from neighbouring Angola and were controlled by Franco-Belgian military interventions with logistic support from NATO. At the root of these conflicts have been the formidable mineral deposits of Shaba. Of these, the best known may be copper and industrial diamonds, but of at least as great significance are the cobalt mines around Kolwezi and Mutshatsha, these deposits representing about half of known world reserves in the late 1970s. With cobalt a key component of ferro-cobalt alloys used in ballistic missile motors, jet engines and other defence-related products, preventing the control of the Shaba deposits falling into the hands of leftist rebels was a priority.[20]

The protracted and bitter 25-year conflict for the control of Western Sahara between Morocco and the independence-seeking Polisario Front has complex causes, but a central factor is the massive reserves of rock phosphates at Boucraa in the north of the country. Rock phosphates form the basis of phosphate fertilisers, one of the essential components of compound fertilisers used throughout world agriculture. On its own, Morocco is the world's main exporter of rock phosphate, but with the Western Sahara reserves it achieves near dominance.[21]

Elsewhere in Africa illicit trading in diamonds has fuelled conflicts in Sierra Leone[22] and Angola, much of the western support for South Africa during the apartheid years was a consequence of South Africa's dominance of the gold and platinum markets. Russian determination to maintain control of parts of the Caucasus is due, in part, to access to Caspian Basin oil.

Even so, transcending all of these is the geo-strategic significance of the oil reserves of the Persian Gulf region, reserves that are both remarkably plentiful and cheap to extract. At the end of the twentieth century, some two-thirds of all the world's proved reserves of oil were located in Persian Gulf states with production costs typically around $3 a barrel compared with up to $12 a barrel for oil from more difficult fields such as the North Sea or Alaska.

When the Iraqi army occupied Kuwait in August 1990, Saddam Hussein's regime added Kuwait's oil fields to its own even larger deposits, gaining control of 19.5 per cent of all of the world's known oil reserves. Saudi support for the subsequent coalition military build-up stemmed, to a large degree, from a fear that the Iraqis would go on to seek control of the massive Saudi oilfields close to Kuwait. With Saudi oil then representing over a quarter of all known world oil reserves, the western coalition perceived the Iraqi regime as threatening to control 45 per cent of the world's oil, an entirely unacceptable prognosis demanding reversal.

The exploitation of world oil reserves is a remarkable example of the resource shift in that the world's largest consumer of oil, the United States, was until the early 1970s self-sufficient, but is now a massive oil importer. During the 1990s, in particular, the United States progressively ran down its own reserves of easily extracted oil, while new reserves discovered elsewhere in the world typically increased the holdings of many countries. To be specific, the US had reserves totalling 34 billion barrels in 1990; these decreased by more than a third during the 1990s, whereas the proven reserves of Saudi Arabia, Iraq, Kuwait and the United Arab Emirates, all much larger than those of the US, actually increased. Thus, in all of these states, the discovery of new reserves exceeded production. By the year 2000, all the major industrialised states of the world, except Russia but including China, were becoming progressively more dependent on Persian Gulf oil, even allowing for the deposits of the Caspian Basin.

Overall, and throughout the twentieth century, the industrialised states of the North have become progressively more dependent on the physical resources of the South, a trend set to continue well into the twenty-first century. As a potential source of conflict it is a core feature of the global economy.

Climate change

Of the many environmental impacts now being witnessed, one stands out above all the others – the development of the phenomenon of climate change as a result of the release of so-called greenhouse gases, especially carbon dioxide and methane. One of the most fundamental of modern human activities, the combustion of fossil fuels, is demonstrably affecting the global climate. Among the many effects already apparent and likely to accelerate are changes in temperature and rainfall patterns and in the intensity of storms.

The greenhouse effect caused by increases in gases such as carbon dioxide in the atmosphere has been recognised for some decades, and it was initially expected to have its most notable impact in terms of increases in atmospheric temperature – hence the use of the term global warming. In the past two decades this has become recognised as a pronounced oversimplification of much more complex changes in the world's climate, including considerable regional variations. It has also been more widely recognised that there are substantial natural climatic cycles, some of which, such as the El Nino effect in the Pacific, may also be affected by human activity. Furthermore, other forms of atmospheric pollution resulting from human activity might even counter the effect of the greenhouse gases.

A further complexity is that it has been generally believed that the more pronounced effects of climate change would happen in temperate regions, with tropical latitudes largely buffered against substantial change, a belief based on some historical evidence that the tropics had been least affected by earlier natural climatic cycles. The expectation has been that there would be substantial effects on north and south temperate latitudes and on polar regions. The former might variably involve changes in rainfall distribution, increases in temperature and increased severity of storms. There would be gainers and losers but the major effects of global climate change would be felt, by and large, by richer countries that would best be able to cope. Some commentators saw it as ironic that those countries that had contributed most to greenhouse gas production would be the countries most affected by climate change.

But it was known that not all the effects of climate change would impact on temperate latitudes, and two effects have long been expected to cause substantial problems for poorer countries. One is the likelihood of more severe storms, especially cyclones. While rich industrialised countries may be able to cope, albeit at a cost, it will be well beyond the poor countries' capabilities to handle the changes affecting them. There are examples of this across the world, and it is sometimes possible to contrast the impact of such disasters on rich and poor countries. In 1992, Hurricane Andrew hit parts of the United States, killing 52 people and causing damage estimated at $22 billion, over 70 per cent of it covered by insurance. Six years later, Hurricane Mitch hit Honduras and Nicaragua. The death toll was 11,000, and less than 3 per cent of the $7 billion damages was insured.[23]

The other effect is the risk of sea level rises, stemming partly from an expansion of the oceans consequent on increases in temperature and partly from a progressive, if slow, melting of polar icecaps. Effects of both of these trends would be severe on a number of poorer countries, partly because some of the heaviest concentrations of population are in low-lying river deltas, but more particularly because of the lack of resources to construct adequate sea defences.

Such problems have been recognised for some time, but more recent analysis of climate change, over the past five to ten years, suggests another pattern of effects that is likely to have much more fundamental global consequences. Although predictions are tentative, evidence has accumulated that the anticipated buffering of climate change in tropical regions may not happen, or at least may be far less pronounced. In particular, there are likely to be substantial changes in rainfall distribution patterns across the tropics, with the overall effect being far less rain falling over land and more falling over the oceans and the polar regions. With the exception of parts of equatorial Africa, almost all the other tropical and sub-tropical regions of the world are likely to experience a 'drying out'.[24]

The impact of this is likely to be fundamental in terms of human well-being and security. Across the world as a whole, the great majority of people live in these regions, most of the countries are poor and most produce their own food, primarily from staple crops dependent on adequate rainfall or irrigation. Much of the food is still produced by subsistence agriculture. Most of the heavily populated areas are the major river valleys and fertile deltas, including the Nile, Indus, Ganges, Brahmaputra, Mekong and Chanjiang (Yangtze) and areas of high natural rainfall across Latin America, sub-Saharan Africa and South East Asia.

A substantial drying-out across the tropics will have a far greater effect than any likely impact on temperate latitudes for two reasons. One is that the basic ecological carrying-capacity of the land – its ability to support given human populations – will decline, and the second is that poor countries will have massive difficulties in trying to adapt their agricultural systems to limit the loss in food production.

Uncertainties and insecurity

Some of the most substantial changes of the last half century have happened with little warning. Perhaps the most serious crisis of the Cold War, over the Cuban missiles in 1962, came virtually out of the blue. The oil price rises of the early 1970s were almost entirely unexpected, the anticipation throughout the West being of an era of cheap and plentiful oil. The Iraqi invasion of Kuwait in 1990 erupted out of nowhere in a matter of weeks. These are examples of political crises, albeit two of them with resource overtones, but it is also the case that assessing environmental trends, especially at the global level, is frequently difficult – pesticide toxicity in the 1960s, acid rain in the 1970s and the sudden intensity of ozone depletion in the 1980s being among a number of examples.

There has been considerable progress in the study of the global ecosystem in the past half century, especially in terms of the knowledge of the mechanisms of biogeochemical cycles, oceanic systems and the global climate, but all of these are, at the very best, imperfectly understood. As a consequence, there is every possibility that many current expectations concerning human environmental impacts may be incorrect. It is possible that some of the warnings now being made, including those discussed above, may turn out to be excessive as natural control mechanisms come into play and moderate the effects of the impacts.

This might be considered reassuring, but there are several reasons for thinking that such optimism is unwarranted. The first is that many of the expected effects are likely to prove costly and politically unwelcome. As a result, where significant environmental research is undertaken in publicly-funded centres, whether government laboratories or universities, there is a tendency for researchers to be cautious in their conclusions. If the implications of your research results are unpalatable, you tend to be very careful in ensuring that you are as certain as you can be with the evidence. The second is that there is growing evidence from various long-term fossil and other evidence, that the global ecosystem, especially its climate, has been much more volatile than was previously thought. In other words, natural 'buffering' systems may not have coped with change in the past. Finally, the time-scales of human interaction are much more immediate in terms of 'ecosystem time' than anything short of rare natural cataclysms such as a massive meteor or comet striking the earth (one explanation for the extinction of the dinosaurs).

Humans evolved over several million years, but only spread right across the world by 20,000 years ago, numbering perhaps five million before they learnt to farm 10,000 years ago. Cities and empires have developed in the past 5,000 years but environmental impacts were limited in extent and confined to a few locations until the start of the industrial revolution just over 200 years ago. Only since then have there been major regional impacts and only in the past 100 years can these be said to have 'gone global', with most of that effect coming in the closing decades of the twentieth century. In other words, a global ecosystem evolving over several billion years was hardly affected by its most intelligent species until the most recent century, but that one species is engaging in activities that do just that. In such circumstances, it is probably wise to err on the side of caution and expect the unexpected to be a cause of further problems rather than a solution to them.

Forms of conflict

To summarise the argument so far, the current economic system is not delivering economic justice, and there are now firm indications that it is not environmentally sustainable. This combination of wealth disparities and limits to current forms of economic growth is likely to lead to a crisis of unsatisfied expectations within an increasingly informed global majority of the disempowered.

Such a crisis is increasingly seen from the North as a threat. As Wolfgang Sachs puts it:

The North now glowers at the South from behind fortress walls. It no longer talks of the South as a cluster of young nations with a bright future, but views it with suspicion as a breeding ground for crises.

At first, developed nations saw the South as a colonial area, then as developing nations. Now they are viewed as risk-prone zones suffering from epidemics, violence, desertification, over-population and corruption.

The North has unified its vision of these diverse nations by cramming them into a category called 'risk'. It has moved from the idea of hegemony for progress to hegemony for stability.[25]

In Sachs' view, the North has utilised the resources of the South for generations but has now come up against environmental limits to growth:

Having enjoyed the fruits of development, that same small portion of the world is now trying to contain the explosion of demands on the global environment. To manage the planet has become a matter of security to the North.[26]

Managing the planet means, in the final analysis, controlling conflict and, within the framework of the development/environment interaction, several issues are likely to come to the fore, stemming from migratory pressures, environmental conflict and anti-elite violence. None of these is new and there are recent examples of all.

Potential sources of conflict stem from a greater likelihood of increased human migration arising from economic, social and especially environmental desperation. This movement will focus on regions of relative wealth and is already leading to shifts in the political spectrum in recipient regions, including the increased prevalence of nationalist attitudes and cultural conflict. Such tendencies are often most pronounced in the most vulnerable and disempowered populations within the recipient regions, with extremist political leaders and sections of the popular media ready to play on fears of unemployment. This trend is seen clearly in western Europe, especially in countries such as France and Austria, where antagonism towards migrants from neighbouring regions such as North Africa and Eastern Europe has increased markedly. It also figures in the defence postures of a number of countries, with several Southern European states reconfiguring their armed forces towards a 'threat from the South' across the Mediterranean.

There are already some 30 to 40 million people displaced either across state boundaries or within states, and this figure is expected to rise dramatically as the consequences of global climate change begin to have an effect. The pressures are likely to be particularly intense from Central into North America, Africa and Western Asia into Europe and South-East Asia towards Australia. The most probable response will be a 'close the castle gates' approach to security, leading in turn to much suffering and not a little 'militant migration' as marginalised migrants are radicalised.

The second area of conflict concerns environmental factors, especially the control of physical resources. Locally, over issues such as land and water, it may be restricted primarily to Southern states, though even this could have an impact on Western interests by exacerbating socioeconomic marginalisation with concomitant pressure on migration and insurgency. In other respects, however, it is likely to have a more global impact.

These stem from the effect of the resource shift, especially the remarkable concentration of oil and also gas reserves in the Persian Gulf region. The stability and control of this region is recognised across Western military circles as essential for Western security, and local 'threats' will be countered by whatever means are necessary.

While oil is by far the top-ranking strategic resource, there are others of significance. These include minerals yielding ferro-alloy metals such as cobalt and tungsten, catalytic metals such as platinum and anticorrosion metals, together with certain non-metallic minerals such as rock phosphate and industrial diamonds. Here again, resources are increasingly located outside the industrialised countries, even including the United States, Canada and Russia.

Perhaps least easy to assess is the manner in which an economically polarised and increasingly constrained global system will result in competitive and violent responses by the disempowered, both within and between states. There are already many examples of such actions, whether the Zapatista revolt in Mexico, or movements stemming from the disempowered in North Africa, the Middle East and Southern and South East Asia.

At an individual and local level, much of the response from the margins takes the form of criminality, usually by young adult males and directed not just against wealthier sectors of society but often against the poor and unprotected. For middle-class elites in many Southern states, though, security is an every-day fact of life, with people moving from secure work places through travel in private cars to gated communities and leisure facilities with 24-hour protection. For the richest sectors of society, security extends to armed bodyguards and stringent anti-kidnapping precautions, with a host of specialist companies offering their services.

This is the environment that is already the norm throughout most countries of the South and the widening rich/poor gap suggests it will get worse. But the more difficult and potentially more important problem stems from substantial new social movements directed, often with violence, against the elites. Predictions are difficult but four features are relevant.

The first is that anti-elite movements may have recourse to political, religious, nationalist or ethnic justifications, with these frequently being fundamentalist, simplistic and radical. Many recent analyses focus on the belief systems themselves, with much emphasis placed by Western writers on religious fundamentalisms, especially within the Islamic world. While such religious movements are significant, they are far from being alone in serving as a motivation against marginalisation and for empowerment, with ethnic, nationalist and political ideologies, cultures or beliefs also being of great significance. At times, it is as if the Islamic threat is being erected to replace the Soviet threat of the Cold War years, an attractive yet thoroughly dangerous simplification of a much more complex set of processes.

The second feature is that anti-elite movements may be more prevalent in the poorer states and regions of the world, and they may therefore be considered of little concern to the relatively small number of wealthy states that dominate the world economy. But in an era of globalisation, instability in some part of the majority world can have a considerable effect on financial markets throughout the world, making the security of local elites of real concern to the West. Wealthy states are dependent on resources from the South, on cheap labour supplies and on the development of new markets for their advanced industrial products. A civil disturbance in a country of the South 50 years ago might have had its effect in the North within weeks. Now, it can be within minutes.

Thirdly, there is a perception across much of the majority world that a powerful and firmly rooted Western hegemony is now in place and a very widespread response is one of real antagonism to this control of the world economy. It is easy to assume, from a Western ethnocentric position, that antagonisms are most likely to be directed from the margins at local elites. This is not necessarily the case. There is, instead, every chance that it is the Western economic dominance that will be blamed for marginalisation, not the activities of local elites.

Finally, there is sufficient evidence from economic and environmental trends to indicate that marginalisation of the majority of the world's people is continuing and increasing, and that it is extremely difficult to predict how and when different forms of anti-elite action may develop. It was not predictable that Guzman's teachings in Peru would lead to a movement of the intensity and human impact of Sendero Luminosa, nor was the Zapatista rebellion in Mexico anticipated. When the Algerian armed forces curtailed elections in 1991 for fear that they would bring a rigorous Islamic party to power, few predicted a bloody conflict that would claim many tens of thousands of lives.

What should be expected is that new social movements will develop that are essentially anti-elite in nature and will draw their support from people, especially men, on the margins. In different contexts and circumstances they may have their roots in political ideologies, religious beliefs, ethnic, nationalist or cultural identities, or a complex combination of several of these. They may be focused on individuals or groups but the most common feature is an opposition to existing centres of power. They may be sub-state groups directed at the elites in their own state or foreign interests, or they may hold power in states in the South, and will no doubt be labelled as rogue states as they direct their responses towards the North. What can be said is that, on present trends, anti-elite action will be a core feature of the next 30 years – not so much a clash of civilisations, more an age of insurgencies.[27]

Revolt of the middle kingdoms

States that may be led by radical anti-Western regimes or dictatorships can readily be regarded as rogue states, a catch-all term increasingly applied to smaller states considered to threaten regional Western interests. But beyond them are much more powerful states that may have their own entrenched elites yet are unwilling to accept a global polity dominated by a Western military, political and economic alliance. China, India and Iran are all examples of states who, in many ways, seek to challenge a Western hegemony, and many of their attitudes and outlooks are shared by numerous other states of the South.

There are many examples of these divergent views and outlooks. Opposition to the further development of trade reforms through the World Trade Organisation is widespread in the South, with such reforms seen primarily to benefit powerful Western market economies and transnational corporations (TNCs). There remains resentment at the attempts to force through a Multilateral Agreement on Investments (MAI) with its 'small print' likely to disadvantage weaker Southern states in their dealings with TNCs.

There is a deep and persistent bitterness at the entrenched attitudes of Northern states towards problems of the global environment. Across much of the South, it is believed, with not a little passion, that Northern states have been primarily responsible for the development of global environmental problems yet are deeply reluctant to accept responsibility or to take remedial action. In particular, as the changes in the climate take effect due primarily to pollution from the industrialised world, poorer countries will be far less able to cope with the changes, yet they will be expected to curb or limit their industrial development while the North pays little more than lip-service to the critical need to curb its polluting profligacy.

The perception of hypocrisy extends to many other areas. In the arena of weapons proliferation and arms control, numerous Third World states see Western attitudes to controlling nuclear proliferation as a classic case of 'do as we say, not as we do', a view taking on an added dimension with the United States failing to ratify the Comprehensive Test Ban Treaty. The 1990 Iraqi invasion of Kuwait was roundly condemned across the world, yet the subsequent Gulf War was widely seen as a Western military action, mounted as soon as the necessary forces had been assembled, that had far more to do with maintaining control of Gulf oil than correcting a wrong, and which sidelined the UN into the bargain.

Even the NATO bombing of Serbia in 1999 was seen as a 'remote control' example of economic targeting – causing $60 billion of damage to the Serbian economy by an alliance deeply unwilling to take risks with its own military, and once again readily by-passing the UN. For public opinion in much of the West, the Serbia/Kosovo War was a just war against an aggressive regime. In much of the rest of the world, it was a selective war using selective force against an objectionable regime, yet one that was no worse than many that continue to maintain friendly relations with the West.

Many of the new parameters of insecurity may operate at sub-state level, and will be directed at local elites and their collaborative Western interests, but they will operate within the context of a broader 'axis of disagreement' between Western governments and many states of the South. While this may not deteriorate into conflict, it could further encourage a perception of 'the civilised West versus the rest'. Moreover, 'the rest' may include powerful countries capable of aiding sub-state groups and vulnerable states in many ways, not least through the export of military technologies and associated expertise. During the Cold War, the West saw the Soviet bloc as the ever-dangerous ideological giant, encroaching on and threatening the free world. It will be all too easy for Western attitudes to a new world disorder to coalesce into a perception of 'them and us', a combination of insurgencies and competitive Southern states threatening the peace, security and economic well-being of the West, the new barbarians versus the self-styled custodians of civilised values.

6

Losing Control

The security outlook from the West is that the early years of the new century will be an era of multiple but unpredictable threats to US and other Western interests, stemming mainly from 'rogue' states, terrorists and possibly China or Russia. The importance of strategic resources such as oil is recognised, there is a perception that there may be an increasing tendency towards anti-elite rebellions, but it is much more common to view any anti-Western action as motivated by religious fundamentalism or nationalism.

There is an underlying assumption, bordering almost on an article of faith, that the normal and, indeed, only rational form of political and economic behaviour is the free-market economy overseen by Western democracies. Anything else is frankly irrational and potentially threatening to peace, stability and civilised values. In this paradigm very little consideration is given to the security impact of environmental limitations and there is almost no concern about the widening socioeconomic divisions. These are certainly not seen as parameters of insecurity or 'drivers' of future conflict.

The previous chapter puts a very different case, arguing that socioeconomic divisions and environmental constraints will be core factors in determining levels of international insecurity in the next three decades. Predicting the precise nature and occurrence of rebellions, insurgencies, anti-elite action and the effects of pressures of migration may not be possible, but it is an eminently reasonable prognosis that underlying trends will lead to many such crises, given the recent experience of a number of countries of the South, especially when coupled with global economic and enviromental trends. Moreover, these will frequently be seen as threats to Western security. Environmental conflicts may indirectly affect Western economic interests and political allies, especially the elites of those states experiencing the conflicts, and there is a likelihood of direct threats to Western interests if strategic resources such as oil are subject to disruption.

On present trends, the common response to this range of conflicts will be one of regaining and maintaining control, rather than addressing root causes. This will depend on the maintenance of appropriate security and intelligence capabilities, with aid for local and regional elites from Western states, especially the US, where necessary. As we have seen, a prominent feature of the recent post-Cold War years has already been the reconfiguring of the military forces of Western powers towards long-range intervention with rapid deployment capabilities.

In addition, there is an increasing use of private security organisations which go well beyond the level of personal bodyguards, for the local protection of mines, oil-fields, factories and other expatriate business interests, as well as local elites. Privatised security now extends to the provision of what are essentially well-equipped mercenary armies and paramilitaries, employed by elites, transnational corporations or even governments. Such mercenary forces are not new, and were a fairly common feature of the final stages of decolonisation, but they have increased in power and capability in a number of countries of the South, notably in Latin America.

Overall, the process is one of keeping the lid on dissent and instability – 'liddism' – by means of public order control that will, when necessary, extend to the use of military force. For the most part, little attention is paid to the fundamental causes of instability, the economic processes that continue to ensure the marginalisation of the majority world and the failure to address core problems of the global environment. The old security paradigm survives – maintain control, maintain the status quo, do not address the underlying problems.

Quite apart from the raw injustics of the present world order, such a paradigm is threatened with obsolescence on its own terms in that it fails to recognise the innate vulnerabilities of Western elite society and its associates. Barnett talks about the increasing ability of the weak to take up arms against the strong and Brooks presents a picture of a crowded, glowering planet (see previous chapter). Both touch on significant changes that have taken place as industrial societies have become more susceptible to disruption, and proliferation of military technologies is providing 'force equalisers', weapons that are within the reach of intermediate states and paramilitary groups that can be used in what is frequently being called 'asymmetric warfare' to counter much more advanced military power.

The ability of 'the weak to take up arms against the strong' is a feature of the post-Cold War era that is recognised by some military analysts but is not widely discussed (except in the US where there is a persistent concern with terrorist threats to its interests). There are many recent illustrations, with some of the more publicly acknowledged examples relating to the proliferation of ballistic missiles. Missile proliferation is being met with a very vigorous political and military response, not least because of a belief that such missiles may be armed with relatively cheap weapons of mass destruction such as anthrax.

The availability of such weapons also causes concern in relation to paramilitary action, and much of the basis for this concern relates to perhaps the most remarkable recent example of the development of biological weapons, one that pre-dates the ending of the Cold War yet has implications that may last for decades. It concerns the activities of the Iraqi regime of Saddam Hussein in the 1980s and certain aspects of the 1991 Gulf War, both features of the Iraqi war effort that are rarely addressed when analysing the significance of that conflict.[1]

The Iraqi biological weapons programme and its implications

During the course of the 1970s, Saddam Hussein gradually took control of the Ba'ath Party and of Iraq, formally taking power in 1979. Although Iraq only had a population of around 20 million, it had benefited greatly from the massive surge in oil prices in 1973–74 and the regime had ambitions to promote the country as the major regional power. In doing so it was helped by several factors, not least the status of its neighbours. Syria and Egypt were preoccupied with their ongoing conflict with Israel, and neither had the backing of the huge oil reserves of Iraq and the other Gulf states. Saudi Arabia certainly had oil, but was politically backward with an almost indecipherable feudal system of power-seeking among hundreds of princely familes. Iran, under the Shah, not only had oil, but also a large population and an autocratic ruler with great ambitions. It was the greatest threat to Iraq's regional power ambitions, but by the late 1970s Iran was facing internal dissent. Iran was also reported to be in the early stages of developing nuclear weapons and Israel already had an operational nuclear arsenal and probably had chemical and biological weapons as well, together with a modern air force and ballistic missiles.

Faced with the power bases of Israel and Iran, one feature of the Iraqi military expansion was a commitment to developing weapons of mass destruction together with appropriate delivery systems. By the end of the 1970s the regime had already begun to produce stocks of chemical weapons, both blister agents such as mustard gas and nerve agents such as sarin. Some consideration had been given to developing biological weapons but this had been abandoned, whereas a nuclear weapons programme was getting under way. This was based mainly on the plutonium route, for which an experimental facility, the Osiraq reactor, was being constructed near Baghdad. Israel recognised the significance of this development and destroyed the reactor in an air raid in 1981.

The Israeli Osiraq raid had a profound effect on Iraqi security thinking. While Israel was criticised for the raid by many states, little action was taken by its closest supporter, the United States, where the Reagan administration was content to see Israel take this pre-emptive action to control nuclear proliferation. From the Iraqi perspective it meant that any future plans to develop a deterrent would carry the permanent risk of Israeli intervention, especially if plans for weapons of mass destruction were centred on one or two high-value sites.[2]

Iraq responded by developing a multi-faceted programme of research and development with two related features. The first was that programmes were dispersed and had redundancy built into them. The nuclear programme concentrated henceforth on the uranium route, using several different methods of uranium enrichment including some obsolete methods such as calutrons. The development and production of chemical weapons was undertaken at several sites, and delivery systems included imported strike aircraft, Scud missiles with local modifications and experimental plans to develop a programme of very long-range rocket-assisted artillery pieces, leading up to the so-called 'super-gun'.

Second, Iraq recognised that its regional aspirations would be likely, at some stage, to involve a war with Israel, and that this would primarily be an air war. It therefore set about building a substantial number of dispersed air bases with hardened aircraft shelters, a command and control system with many underground bunkers and a force of Scud missiles and their longer-range Al Hussein variants. What made this all the more remarkable was that all of this was under way while Iraq was fighting a bitter and costly war against Iran, having gone to war when Iran was mistakenly believed to be vulnerable in the immediate aftermath of its revolution.

The 1980–88 Iraq/Iran War was significant to Iraq in one sense, in that it was seen as a bulwark for Western interests. To the United States in particular, with its memories of the recent hostage crisis, the Iran of the Ayatollahs was seen as a profound threat to the security of the Persian Gulf. With Iraq as a buffer state indirectly protecting Western interests, it was not difficult for it to acquire many forms of military technology from sources in the West. There may have been an embargo on arms sales to both Iran and Iraq, but the reality was that it was far more rigorously enforced on Iran. Even more significant was the persistent refusal of Western countries to take action against the Iraqi use of chemical weapons, even when this included the killing of thousands of civilians in an attack on the Kurdish town of Hallabjah in March 1988.

By the late 1980s the war with Iran had ended, helped not least by US military action against the Iranian Navy at the tail-end of the 'tanker war' in the Gulf, and Iraq was well on the way to developing and deploying weapons of mass destruction. Central to this effort was a remarkable programme of research and development of biological weapons that had commenced only a few years before.

Biological weapons research was initiated at Iraq's main chemical warfare centre at Muthana in 1985, with work starting on anthrax and botulinum toxin. Anthrax is a disease caused by a bacterium *Bacillus anthracis* that is usually fatal if the lungs are infected and there is no immediate antibiotic treatment. One feature of the anthrax organism is that it can form spores that are resistant to sunlight and desiccation, making it particularly suitable as a biological weapon. Botulinum is an extremely poisonous toxin produced by the bacterium *Clostridium botulinum*. Both organisms can be cultured in the laboratory, although they require specific growth media. Large-scale fermenters can be used to produce anthrax spores or botulinum toxin in bulk.

Progress in the new biological warfare (BW) programme was rapid, the work was transferred to another site at Al Salman and, within a year, laboratory and field trials had been conducted on animals including monkeys and sheep. A single-cell protein plant at Taji, normally used for producing animal feed, was taken over for large-scale production of botulinum toxin, while at Al Salman production of anthrax was rapidly scaled up.

By the end of 1987, just over two years after the start of the programme, the decision to go ahead with full-scale biological weapons production had been taken and in March 1988, an entirely new site was selected for BW production at Al Hakam which would also include a separate research facility. The centre was constructed at a remarkable rate and was largely completed within six months, while an intensive search was undertaken throughout Iraq for suitable equipment. Large fermentation units were brought in, botulinum production began in April 1989 and anthrax the following month. According to a UN Special Commission report, the Al Hakam facility produced 6,000 litres of concentrated botulinum toxin and 8,425 litres of anthrax in 1990 alone. During this whole process, the Iraqi BW programme sought equipment and growth media from abroad and also comandeered any relevant equipment from within Iraq.

Even this was only one part of the overall programme – as the Iraqi BW efforts gathered pace, a wide range of other potential biological warfare agents were examined. In 1988, work started on the bacterium that causes gas gangrene, *Clostridium perfringens*, the idea being that if cluster munitions are impregnated with this organism, the chances of wounds resulting in gas gangrene are greatly increased, severely stretching the medical facilities of the opposing forces. Also in 1988, studies commenced into aflatoxin, a relatively rare cancer-inducing mycotoxin (a poison produced by fungi of the genus *Aspergillus*). This formed part of a wider programme on mycotoxins, including some that can cause vomiting and diarrhoea and which, unlike most toxins, can be absorbed through the skin.

In a separate project, the Iraqis even investigated anti-crop warfare, developing a programme to produce large quantities of the plant disease organism that causes cover smut of wheat, a potentially devastating disease. Cover smut is a problem in many parts of the world, but it is probable that in the Iraqi case it was intended for use in economic warfare againt the wheat crops of Iran, the staple food of that country.[3]

The Iraqi BW programme also involved work on viruses. This included studies on a rotavirus causing diarrhoea which can lead to dehydration and death, and the virus causing haemorrhagic conjunctivitis. This is an acute disease of the eyes, causing extreme pain and temporary blindness, and likely to have an intensely debilitating effect on victims. It is also a disease that puts a severe strain on the medical facilities of any army that is the victim of an attack.

As the Iraqi work on anthrax and botulinum expanded into full-scale production, so a parallel programme was under way to produce weapons that could deliver the biological agents. Field trials of biological weapons commenced in 1988 and included work on 122mm rockets, bombs and spray tanks. They continued through to the middle of 1990, and were still under way when the Saddam Hussein regime took the decision to invade Kuwait in August 1990. This attack was followed by an immediate escalation of the crisis as coalition forces moved into the Gulf region. Within weeks, it was evident that the United States was not prepared to countenance the Iraqi take-over of Kuwait, and this became abundantly clear by October of 1990 when the initial substantial build-up of coalition forces in the Gulf was massively expanded.

The Iraqi regime faced the real probability of military action and embarked on a long programme of prevarication, coupled with the use of hostages to forestall a coalition military attack. Meanwhile, the biological warfare programme was greatly intensified and directed towards having useable weapons before coalition military operations could begin.

By January 1991, still less than six years after the whole BW programme was first initiated, Iraq had 166 bombs ready for use, 100 filled with botulinum, 50 with anthrax and 16 with aflatoxin. An emergency programme to produce warheads for the Al Hussein medium-range ballistic missile was initiated in August 1990. By January 1991, 13 missiles armed with botulinum warheads were ready, together with ten missiles with anthrax and two missiles with aflatoxin. The 25 missiles were deployed to four locations and remained there throughout the war.

These, and chemical warheads, were intended for use in the event of the destruction of Baghdad by nuclear weapons during the Gulf War. Moreover, authority to launch the missiles was pre-delegated from Baghdad to regional commanders, an extraordinarily risky move, giving rise to the possibility of unauthorised use of weapons of mass destruction during a fast-moving and, for the Iraqis, chaotic and increasingly disastrous military confrontation.

Perhaps the most significant feature of the entire process is that it is now known that the US intelligence community was aware of the major features of the Iraqi BW programme, including the assessment that the Iraqis were likely to use weapons of mass destruction if the survival of the regime was threatened. This was the subject of a National Intelligence Estimate prepared in November 1990, three months after the Iraqi invasion of Kuwait and two months before the start of Operation Desert Storm.[4]

One of the surprising features of the Gulf War was its abrupt end. After several weeks of intense bombing, a ground assault by coalition forces rapidly evicted Iraqi forces from Kuwait and moved in to control a substantial part of southern Iraq. During this four-day ground war, coalition troops engaged relatively weak sectors of the Iraqi army, with, at most, two of the eight Republican Guard divisions being damaged. It would appear that, for the Saddam Hussein regime, it was regime survival that was the dominant requirement, and this required the protection of the elite forces available to it.

Coalition forces were firmly entrenched within Iraq and would have been in a position to move towards Baghdad, backed by overwhelming air superiority, but the US leadership decided not to do so and sought an immediate cease-fire. While this involved relatively harsh terms for Iraq, it did not include the disarming of the armed forces out of the zone of conflict, and soon after the regime was able to put down rebellions in the Shi'ite south and Kurdish north with some ferocity.

The refusal of the US leadership to pursue the destruction of the regime has been explained by a reluctance to see Iraq dismembered and a concern over casualties in a further period of fighting. It is also likely that there was a recognised risk of the Iraqis escalating the war to use weapons of mass destruction if the very survival of the regime was threatened. It is not clear whether the Iraqi biological weapons would have been effective – the missiles that were fired in the war, with their conventional high-explosive warheads, were both inaccurate and prone to break-up during their flights. The point is that there was no way of knowing whether or not the BW-armed missiles and bombs would have worked, just that Iraq had invested heavily in developing them and had the weapons ready to use.

At the time of the Gulf War there were a number of statements from Western sources indicating that there would be a willingness to consider using nuclear weapons if the Iraqis escalated to the use of chemical or biological weapons in their war with coalition forces. There was an assumption that such an extreme action would only follow major coalition losses from such an Iraqi attack, but it was also assumed that the existence of this 'threat' may have deterred the Iraqis. However, it would seem that there was a double deterrent at work – US threats to retaliate with nuclear weapons, but an Iraqi capability to use chemical and biological warfare *in extremis*, if the US-led coalition went as far as threatening the survival of the regime.

Even since the Gulf War the issue of Iraqi biological weapons has been central to US policy. It was not until 1995 that the main features of the Iraqi BW programme became apparent to the UNSCOM inspectors, and in 1997 and 1998 Iraqi attempts to prevent further UNSCOM BW investigations led to a number of crises. These culminated in the 'Desert Fox' air strikes of December 1998, the abandonment of the UNSCOM process and the development of a new US policy of 'aggressive containment'. Throughout 1999, there were frequent air strikes by US and British planes. While all were claimed to be in retaliation to Iraqi provocation, the rules of engagement were remarkably wide and many different targets were hit. Even so, in the absence of any weapons inspection process, there were credible reports that Iraq was continuing with its biological warfare work, probably in underground research and development centres.[5]

The overall experience is significant in two respects. The first is that the Gulf War itself was an example of a weak power having the capability to deter a coalition of very powerful states ranged against it. Second, it shows how a state with an intermediate technical capability can develop weapons of mass destruction in a relatively short period of time – Iraq's entire biological weapons programme was the result of a process of research, development and production undertaken in just five years. Taken together, they illustrate the 'equaliser' effect of technology proliferation, an approach readily available to other states and also to sub-state groups, whether acting on their own or as clients of states.

Political violence and asymmetric warfare

The Iraqi development of biological weapons is an example of a force equaliser produced by a state, but the forms of conflict and insecurity resulting from socioeconomic polarisation and environmental constraints are also likely to involve sub-state actors, not least radical movements that engage in political violence against elites. Such movements may be allied to particular states, or they may be part of wider trans-national groups, and they may operate against local or overseas elites and centres of control.

Whether such forms of insecurity are sufficiently serious to affect Western states or alliances will depend, to a great extent, on whether the states prove to be vulnerable to paramilitary action and other aspects of asymmetric warfare. There are a number of indications that there are such vulnerabilities, stemming in part from the nature of modern urban-industrial states. Furthermore, it is also possible that such vulnerability is not easily countered by military force, either as currently deployed or as planned in the next one or two decades.[6]

During the past 30 years, many sub-state groups have targeted major centres of power and influence, whether in Beirut or Bologna, Buenos Aires or Tel Aviv. For the most part, paramilitary organisations have concentrated on police forces, the military and the political leadership of target states. It is also the case that most paramilitary organisations that are engaged in political violence have been relatively conservative in their tactics, concentrating either on bombings, kidnappings, assassinations or other traditional methods. For some, any economic impact has been secondary to political effects, but other groups have been more single-minded in seeking to do serious economic damage.[7]

There have been periods in recent history where particular forms of political violence have been prevalent. The extensive hijacking of commercial aircraft during the late 1960s and early 1970s was principally designed for publicity purposes, though the economic impact on the world airline industry was considerable. During the 1970s and 1980s a number of left-wing paramilitary groups in Europe targeted business leaders and company headquarters. In France, Action Directe's targets included a bomb attack on the European headquarters of the World Bank in Paris in 1982 and the assassination of the chairman of Renault, Georges Besse, in 1986.

The Brigate Rosse (Red Brigade), active in Italy in the 1970s and 1980s, conducted the majority of its operations against Italian business targets, including knee-cappings and assassinations. It also specialised in business kidnapping, extorting many millions of dollars in ransoms. The German Red Army Faction (known also as the Baader-Meinhof Gang) also targeted the business community, including the kidnapping of Hans-Martin Schleyer in 1977, the murder of Deutsche Bank Chairman, Alfred Herrhausen, in 1989 and Detlev Rohwedder in 1991.

Outside of Europe, one of the most protracted insurgencies, as we have seen, has been the Sendero Luminoso quasi-Maoist guerrilla army in Peru. SL has repeatedly targeted aspects of the Peruvian economy, with particular attempts at damaging wealthy sectors of society. To mark the first 100 days of emergency rule brought in by President Alberto Fujimori in 1992, SL exploded two car bombs in a wealthy quarter of Lima, killing 18 and wounding 140. Overall, 15 years of SL insurgency and police and military response in Peru from 1980 to 1995 has resulted in around 25,000 deaths and $22 billion of damage to the Peruvian economy.[8]

During the course of the 1990s there have been many examples of large-scale sub-state violence against centres of political and economic power, with a pattern emerging that suggests a persistent vulnerability of elite states and groups. Some of the most significant examples did not even have their intended effect, but are relevant nonetheless to any analysis of elite vulnerability. Three particular examples, in Colombo, Paris and Tokyo in the mid-1990s, are worthy of some examination, and two others, the attempt to destroy the New York World Trade Center in

1993 and the use of economic targeting by the Provisional IRA in Britain from 1992–97, yield more detailed lessons.

Colombo, Paris and Tokyo

The bitter conflict between the Tamil Tiger separatists (the LTTE) and the Sri Lankan government forces had been under way for twelve years in 1995 and, in October of that year, the Sri Lankan Army embarked on a costly campaign to oust the LTTE from what was perceived to be their core stronghold in the northern city of Jaffna. While the army succeeded, it was a hollow victory in three senses; most of the LTTE forces simply melted away to re-group in other areas, the action was hugely costly to the army, with over 600 killed, and the LTTE guerrillas responded by increasing their use of economic targeting against the Sri Lankan state, which had previously included bomb attacks on energy and communications targets in and around the capital city of Colombo.

The most substantial attack came on 31 January 1996, just seven weeks after the fall of Jaffna. In this incident, a suicide bomber drove a truck containing around half a ton of high explosive up to the entrance to the Central Bank at the heart of Colombo's central business district. The bomb exploded and the effects were appalling, with nearly 100 people killed and 1,400 injured. Many key buildings were destroyed or severely damaged, including the bank itself, the Celinko Insurance Building, the Colombo World Trade Center, the Air Lanka offices, the Ceylon Hotels Corporation building, the Bank of Ceylon and several hotels. While vigorously denied by the government of Sri Lanka, the bombing had a considerable effect on business confidence, made worse by a further bombing of the World Trade Center nearly two years later.[9]

French experience of paramilitary activity by Algerian radicals is also relevant. This arises from the bitter and protracted internal conflict in Algeria and the belief among radical anti-government groups, such as the GIA, that the French authorities have offered support to the Algerian government. A result has been a series of bomb attacks in France, especially the targeting of the Metro. A more extreme incident involved an attempted large-scale attack on Paris which, if it had succeeded, would have caused massive loss of life.

On 24 December, 1994, an Air France Airbus A300 bound for Paris was hi-jacked by four members of a radical Algerian militant group. 239 passengers and crew were on board, three of whom were subsequently killed by the hi-jackers. After two days of negotiation, the plane was allowed to leave Algiers and landed at Marseilles, ostensibly to refuel. The aim of the hi-jackers was reported to be to destroy the aircraft in mid-air over Paris, killing themselves and all the remaining passengers and crew, as well as causing heavy casualties on the ground. If the plan had succeeded, the death toll could have been many hundreds. In the event, the aircraft was stormed by a French commando unit at Marseilles and all of the hi-jackers were killed.

The Tokyo subway incident in 1995 is notable as the first large-scale incident by a non-state group employing chemical weapons with the intention of causing mass loss of life. In the attack, on 20 March 1995, members of the Aum Shinrikyo religious sect released sarin nerve gas at numerous points on the subway system, affecting three subway lines and 15 stations over a distance of more than eight miles, mostly located in downtown Tokyo. Twelve people died and 5,500 were made ill, some of them seriously. The intention was to damage the core of the Tokyo urban transport system, primarily by causing maximum casualties running into thousands of deaths. As well as the terrible human costs, the effect on business confidence would have been extreme had the nerve gas worked as intended.[10]

The attack, though, was bungled; the nerve agent was impure, its dispersal inefficient and the ventilation system of the subway seems to have diluted the gas far more rapidly than anticipated. Relatively few people were killed, even though thousands suffered harmful effects. Even so, police investigations later suggested that the sect was also working on other potential weapons of mass destruction including anthrax.

The World Trade Center bomb

One of the most revealing incidents in terms of current trends was the attack on the New York World Trade Center in 1993. In this seven-building complex, the two largest components are the North and South Towers, each of 110 storeys, separated by the 26-storey Vista Hotel and sharing a six-storey basement with it. During a normal working day the whole complex is occupied by 50,000 people, mostly in the twin towers.

Shortly after mid-day on 26 February 1993, a large van bomb, estimated to contain 1.5 tons of explosive, detonated in an underground car park on Basement Level 2, close to the south wall of the North Tower and underneath one end of the Vista Hotel. The bomb was made up of a substantial quantity of home-manufactured explosive and is believed to have been surrounded by hydrogen gas cylinders to amplify the explosion by creating a fuel-air effect. This is a process which had been employed in the bombing of a barracks in Beirut in October 1983 when 241 US Marines were killed.

The bomb failed to collapse either the North Tower or the hotel, but damage was severe and casualties were high. Six people were killed and over 1,000 injured. The explosion hit the communications centre on Basement Level 1, above the point of detonation, knocking out most power and emergency facilities and leaving a crater nearly 100 feet wide and 200 feet deep. It deposited many hundreds of tons of debris on to lower basement levels, severely damaging the complex's air conditioning and emergency generating systems, and ruptured pipes, releasing over two million gallons of water into the lower levels.

Structural damage to the North Tower was relatively minor, but the Vista Hotel was severely affected and required emergency bracing to control the risk of collapse, a very difficult process undertaken with great skill in the hours and days immediately following the bomb. It was later concluded that a catastrophic failure of either the hotel or the North Tower had been avoided, in part because the bomb was incorrectly positioned and insufficiently powerful, but primarily because the complex had been built to standards in excess of those required at the time of construction.

If the bomb had succeeded in its purpose, the North Tower would have collapsed on to the Vista Hotel and the South Tower. Casualties would have been around 30,000 killed and it would have been the most devastating single attack since the atom bombing of Nagasaki nearly 50 years earlier. A number of people, widely described as Islamic fundamentalists acting from broadly anti-American motives, were later charged, tried and imprisoned for the bomb attack, although there were also unconfirmed reports of an Iraqi connection. Because the bomb failed in its primary purpose, the attack attracted relatively little attention from international security specialists, although it had a considerable impact within domestic security circles and caused a review of security in high-rise buildings throughout the United States.[11]

The Tamil Tiger attack in Colombo succeeded in its aim, although its significance was not widely recognised, but the Tokyo, Paris and New York incidents all failed to achieve their aims. This 'run of luck' may be hugely welcome, but it has served to obscure a trend – that it is becoming more likely that sub-state actors, whether aided by states or not, can cause massive casualties and disruption in confrontations that do not follow the usual patterns of war. The Air France hi-jack was intended to kill many hundreds, the Tokyo subway nerve gas attack was intended to kill thousands and the World Trade Center bomb might have killed 30,000.

In the coming decades, counter-state and counter-society abilities are likely to become progressively more available to radical groups. In part, this will be due to acquired knowledge and experience of economic targeting using conventional forms of destruction, in part it will be due to the availability of biological and chemical systems and possibly crude radiological and nuclear systems. Overall, these trends suggest that seemingly invulnerable states, however powerful and wealthy they may be, have innate weaknesses that can be readily exploited in an era of asymmetric warfare, weaknesses that were demonstrated to some effect by a protracted period of economic targeting by the Provisional IRA in Britain during the 1990s.

The Provisional IRA campaign of economic targeting[12]

On 9 April 1992, the Conservative Party led by John Major won an unexpected victory in the British general election, an election in which the protracted conflict in Northern Ireland played only a marginal role. The conflict had developed in the late 1960s and for most of the previous 25 years had primarily been fought between the Provisional IRA and British security forces, although by the early 1990s loyalist paramilitaries were becoming particularly active in their violence against republicans. The Provisionals had engaged in many forms of conflict involving bombings, the use of home-made mortars and numerous shootings and assassinations, including the British Ambassador to Ireland in 1976, Earl Mountbatten in 1979 and an attempt on the then Prime Minister, Margaret Thatcher, in 1984. Throughout the 25 years, over 2,500 people had died and over 7,500 had been injured.[13]

By the early 1990s the conflict was at a stalemate – the British security forces were unable to defeat the Provisionals, but they, in turn, could clearly not achieve a united Ireland by violence. Furthermore, their supporters were suffering badly as a result of loyalist paramilitary violence. Throughout the conflict there had been Provisional actions that had had an economic effect, but the day after the general election saw the start of a protracted and focused campaign of economic targeting against city business districts, the transport network and energy resources.

On 10 April a large van bomb detonated outside the Baltic Exchange in the heart of the City of London, killing three people, injuring 91 and causing about £1 billion of damage. Almost at the same time, another large bomb was exploded on a flyover at one of London's busiest road junctions where the M1 motorway intersects with the North Circular Road. No one was killed but transport disruption was considerable. Two further bomb attempts were made later that year. One targeted the Canary Wharf business complex in the former docks area of London, a prestigious development second only to the City of London as a business centre in South East England. The bomb was defused, as was a massive three-ton bomb intercepted in North London on the night before the Lord Mayor's show.[14]

The following April, the Provisionals planted a bomb in the City of London again, this time in Bishopsgate. One person was killed, many were injured and damage was similar to the Baltic Exchange bomb. Three months later, a large bomb was intercepted at a ferry port hidden in a truck that had come from Ireland. Over the two year period, six attempts were thus made to explode large bombs in Britain, three of which succeeded causing considerable damage.[15]

Later in 1994, a cease-fire was started, following difficult negotiations with the Provisionals that had been instigated by a courageous nationalist politician, John Hume, but which involved unofficial British government contacts. After the start of the ceasefire, negotiations on a long-term settlement to the Northern Ireland conflict made little progress, partly because of intransigence in Northern Ireland and partly because the Major government was intensively preoccupied with internal party divisions over Europe and other issues.

In February 1996, the cease-fire broke down and the Provisionals bombed London's Canary Wharf business district, killing two people and causing substantial damage. In the following five months there were several further attempts to target locations in Britain, including an unsuccessful attempt to demolish Hammersmith Bridge over the Thames in London, and a number of bomb alerts on UK motorways causing substantial disruption. In July, a very large bomb was detonated in the retail heart of Manchester. Although no-one was killed, 200 people were injured and it took over three years to rebuild the damaged properties and fully re-open that part of the city centre to the public. At different times from 1992 to 1996 attempts were made to target gas supplies and oil refineries, and there were also numerous disruptions to transport, mainly through false alarms and primarily affecting London.

In the early autumn of 1996, British security forces intercepted two separate Provisional IRA operations in the London area. One was aimed at bombing the main electricity grid serving the whole of London, an attack that would have caused protracted disruption and severe economic consequences. The second operation was concerned with assembling five or six large van bombs and all of the materials were recovered. These security operations appear to have damaged the Provisional IRA's capabilities, but there was repeated disruption to the UK transport system throughout the 1997 general election campaign, including the closure of the main North-South motorway, rail routes and a number of airports. Following the 1997 election and persistent attempts to find new approaches to solving the Northern Ireland conflict, an agreement was reached that resulted in a further cease-fire.

Throughout the several years of economic targeting, the British government persistently claimed that the tactics of the Provisional IRA were having little or no impact. There are, though, many indications that this was very far from the truth. In London, in the wake of the 1992–3 bombs, the City authorities went to great lengths to reassure the international business community that stringent precautions were being taken, including permanent road blocks around the central business district. There was real concern that the bombing campaign would damage London's position as Europe's main financial centre, allowing Frankfurt to gain an advantage. It was also notable that, after the cease-fire collapsed in February 1996 with the Canary Wharf bombing, the British and Irish governments commenced a new drive for peace within hours of the incident.[16]

Two other features of the Provisional IRA campaign of economic targeting are of note. One is that the impact was achieved even though only a minority of the attempts succeeded. The second is that the organisation was operating in conditions of considerable difficulty. The bombs were assembled primarily in relatively secure parts of the Irish Republic and had to be brought into Britain through carefully monitored ferry ports, they had to be placed at their targets in districts that were commonly monitored by closed-circuit television and the Provisionals were not operating within a supportive community in Britain. More generally, the entire Provisional IRA organisation, mostly active in Northern Ireland, had fewer than 1,000 active members and its numbers in Britain were probably well under 100.

In spite of all of these limitations, the organisation managed to research and target a number of key aspects of the British economy over several years, thereby having a substantial effect on the political process. In short, it demonstrated that a modern urban-industrial state was certainly vulnerable to political violence, even though most of the explosive devices used were home-made fertiliser bombs.

The Khobar Towers bombing

The examples of asymmetric warfare discussed so far all relate to paramilitary organisations operating from political or religious motivations against civilian targets. There are, in addition, many examples of paramilitary groups operating effectively against military forces. Many such operations verge on guerrilla warfare, a form of conflict experienced repeatedly in the wars of de-colonisation and elsewhere, and paramilitary responses are relatively common features of conflicts that involve occupation.

The protracted conflicts in Lebanon after 1975 yield a number of examples, two of which are significant in the present context. One is the considerable difficulty experienced by Israel, initially in 1982–85 and again more recently, in attempting to control parts of Lebanon, especially those of majority Shi'ite populations, with the occurrence of suicide actions being very difficult to counter. A dramatic example affected not Israel but the United States, when a Marines barracks was targeted by a powerful truck bomb in October 1983, killing 241 people, with another attack the same day on the French military headquarters killing 74 people. Although this was one of the worst single incidents affecting the US armed forces in recent years, it had relatively little impact outside military circles, largely because it was overshadowed by the US invasion of Grenada.

A more recent and substantial example of a paramilitary attack on US forces was carried out in a state allied to the United States. After the Gulf War, the United States retained substantial forces in Saudi Arabia, largely to contain Iraq, and many of these forces were centred on the bases at Dhahran. On 25 June 1996 a truck bomb was detonated outside the Khobar Towers block of flats, part of a complex used to house US troops. The devastation was considerable, leaving a huge crater in front of the flats and tearing the front of the complex down. There were over 500 casualties, including the deaths of 19 Americans who were in the flats at the time.

For the United States it was a security nightmare, to be matched by the embassy bombings in Nairobi and Dar es Salaam two years later. While it had long been US practice to deploy troops, aircraft and ships to bases throughout the world, there was always the difficulty of maintaining security, although the paramilitary attack on the Khobar Towers and the consequent loss of life had not been anticipated. For US forces in Saudi Arabia, the solution to the problem was expensive in the extreme – if some of the existing bases were insecure, then new facilities had to be built. Dhahran was run down as a base and many of the forces were moved to a new base, constructed at a cost of $500 million, at a secure and remote site in the heart of Saudi Arabia. US forces, ostensibly in Saudi Arabia to protect that country, were themselves under such threat from paramilitaries that they were virtually in a state of siege.[17]

Coupled with the problems faced by US forces in Somalia in 1993–94 and the embassy bombings in 1998, the protection of US forces and government offices overseas has become a priority. In particular, US ground forces, whether in Saudi Arabia, Kosovo, Bosnia or elsewhere, have increasingly operated as secure garrisons, with the emphasis on self-protection limiting conventional military operations, even if these are primarily peacekeeping in nature. This culture, in turn, is a further factor in the US military requirement to place emphasis on military operations using stand-off weapons presenting little or no danger to US personnel.

Business – and thinking – as usual

The developments in paramilitary action and asymmetric warfare discussed here would appear, at first sight, to suggest that elite control of international security is already becoming problematic. If we add to this the likely effects of the developments analysed in the previous chapter, then it is fair to argue that they will exacerbate these trends, making control even more difficult. Some military analysts are aware of these trends, they are finding it difficult to come to terms with them and, for the most part, they are seriously worried people. Most senior military, though, along with most students of international security, are failing to recognise what is happening, and have yet to escape from an almost quaint reliance on military superiority. A graphic illustration of this was the *Global 95 Wargame* at the US Naval War College in July 1995, a 'twin crisis' wargame centred on Korea and the Persian Gulf. In both cases, chemical weapons were used, but in the Gulf the crisis escalated and a resurgent Iraq used biological weapons to devastating effect against US forces and Saudi civilians. The US responded with a nuclear attack on Baghdad, ending the war. As *Defense News* reported, the wargame raised a number of critical issues:

> The United States has virtually no response to the use of such potentially devastating weapons other than threatening to use nuclear weapons, a Joint Staff official said Aug. 22. But it is unclear whether even nuclear weapons would provide a deterrent, unless the US was willing to take the difficult moral step of destroying a city, he said.
>
> On the other hand, if the United States did launch a nuclear attack in response, 'no country would use those weapons for the next 100 years,' the official said.[18]

Would that really have been the result of such an action? In all probability there would have been retaliation to at least the same level of destruction. The nuclear bombing of Baghdad in this scenario would no doubt have ended the war, and perhaps destroyed the Iraqi leadership, but the destruction of one of the historic cities of the Arab world, and the first use of nuclear weapons since 1945, would have occasioned retaliation directly against the United States.

The most probable pattern would have been the acquisition by paramilitary groups of appropriate weapons of mass destruction for use against targets in the United States. In 1995, the Pentagon conducted a planning exercise which posited one such attack. In this scenario, a paramilitary group introduced anthrax into the ventilation system of the New York Stock Exchange, aiming to infect and kill the people who run the world's largest stock exchange.

Many forms of retaliation would be possible, including radiological, nerve gas or anthrax attacks on centres of population, commerce or government in New York, Chicago, Washington or a dozen other cities. They might have taken place many months or even years after the war, but there is every probability that they would have happened. The idea of 'scaring off' states or paramilitaries, as suggested by the commentator on the *Global 95 Wargame*, is an extreme example of 'liddism', a dangerous approach that demonstrates a potentially fatal misunderstanding of the ways of the post-Cold War world.

There are other recent examples. Shortly after the embassy bombings in Nairobi and Dar es Salaam in August 1998, US forces launched retaliatory raids against targets in two countries, Afghanistan and Sudan. The first raid targeted a paramilitary training camp reportedly controlled by Osama bin Laden who had, more than a decade earlier, been part of the US-supported opposition to Soviet rule in Afghanistan. His group was supposedly responsible for the embassy bombings, but there was little direct evidence of this. The attack on the Sudanese factory apparently producing chemical weapons was even more questionable. Both responses had an aura of revenge – hitting out like a wounded bear against anything perceived to be remotely connected to the embassy bombings.

These actions were reminiscent of repeated actions by successive Israeli governments to attacks by Palestinian and Hizbullah militias over many years. The reaction has been very much the iron fist, usually causing deaths and injuries many times greater than those inflicted on Israeli troops and civilians. Yet the net effect of all these attempts to keep the lid on opposition to Israeli control has been further instability. Israel has not yet been able to address the fundamental problems that lie behind the actions of the militants. Worse still, every time Israeli forces retaliate against militant actions, they induce more people to join those very same militias.

Take, once again, the case of the World Trade Center bombing. If that attack had had its intended effect, the results would have been calamitous, not just for the City of New York but for the United States as a whole. But would it have resulted in any rethinking of security? Probably not. A more likely result would have been a massive and violent military reaction against any groups anywhere in the Middle East that were thought to have had even the slightest connection with the attack.

The overall problem is that the Western security community has not yet been able to come to terms with the changing causes of insecurity, still less with the very considerable vulnerabilities of Western urban-industrial societies to political violence and paramilitary action. With biological, chemical and radiological weapons likely to become available, these vulnerabilities will deepen, and 'liddism' will become untenable, quite possibly within the next decade.

It therefore makes great sense to look at the developing problems of international instability in a much more fundamental way. This means going back to the basic causes of the problems, the reasons for the widening rich-poor divide, environmental constraints and weapons pro-liferation, and proposing policies that may stand some chance of controlling those problems at source.

Shifting the Paradigm

So far, this book has argued three points. The first is that the factors most likely to influence the development of conflict in the coming decades are the socioeconomic divide, environmental constraints and the spread of military technologies, not least weapons of mass destruction. Second, this is likely to lead to conflicts involving anti-elite action from within the marginalised majority, rapidly increasing migratory pressures and conflict concerning environmental factors, especially strategic resources and climate change, all within the context of middle-ranking states unwilling to accept a Western hegemony. Finally, the Western perception that the status quo can be maintained in such circumstances, by military means if need be, is not sustainable given the vulnerabilities of advanced wealthy states to paramilitary action and asymmetric warfare.

It follows that it is necessary to develop a new paradigm around the policies likely to enhance peace and limit conflict. At the centre must be a process of enhancing common global security based on action to be taken to reverse the socioeconomic polarisation, enhance sustainable economic development and control processes of proliferation and militarisation.

The aim of this chapter is to provide an outline sketch of the features of such an approach as they might apply in broad terms. It will then go on to discuss the potential role of middle-ranking states, such as Britain, operating within the existing international community, together with the potential for non-government organisations of many different kinds to peddle influence in the direction of a more just and sustainable world order.

Arms control

Any discussion of the requirements for arms control and disarmament has to start by recognising that such activities are not, in themselves, going to provide a complete answer to the control of weapons of mass destruction and other forms of militarisation. At the same time, the international arms control agenda suffered several setbacks in the late 1990s and there are many areas where progress is both necessary and urgent.

Concerning nuclear weapons, it is urgently necessary to resurrect the Comprehensive Test Ban Treaty, linking it to the promotion of the responsibilities of existing nuclear powers under the terms of the Non-Proliferation Treaty. Put bluntly, such states have to engage in serious and progressive nuclear disarmament as required under Article 6 of the treaty. This may be done by unilateral, bilateral or multilateral actions. Preventing the loss of the Anti-Ballistic Missile Treaty is essential, as is rapid progress on the START I and START II agreements between the United States and Russia, accompanied by further aid to Russia to facilitate de-nuclearisation.

Further transparency on nuclear stockpiles is required for all nuclear weapons states, including Israel, along with no-first-use pledges, voluntary decreases in nuclear arsenals and the extension of nuclear-free zones. In particular, there should be an immediate and transparent commitment to forgo all further nuclear weapons developments. Ultimately, but still in the near future, work should commence on a Nuclear Weapons Convention that would be intended to oversee the abolition of nuclear weapons.

There already exists a Chemical Weapons Convention (CWC), developed during the 1990s and including some quite severe verification procedures. Given the potential for developing a wide range of new chemical agents, not least psychotropic (mind-altering) chemicals, there is a compelling need for support for the treaty and its implementation to be much higher up on the international political agenda.

A Biological and Toxin Weapons Convention (BTWC) was agreed in Geneva as long ago as 1972, but it is a singularly weak treaty as it lacks any proper verification measures. Negotiations for a strengthened treaty have been in progress in Geneva for some time, but a revitalised treaty will require stringent verification procedures and a well-resourced inter-national inspection organisation. Of all the arms control negotiations of the current era, the improvement of the BTWC may turn out to be the most important. The many developments in genetic engineering and biotechnology are greatly adding to the potential for producing hugely dangerous biological warfare agents. It is no exaggeration to say that if these cannot be brought under control, then the coming decades will involve dangers that could be as great as those from nuclear weapons.[1]

During the late 1990s there was remarkable and welcome progress on the banning of anti-personnel land mines, due primarily to intensive campaigning in many countries. From this significant base it is necessary to move on to control many of the area-impact munitions that are now proliferating. The bomblets dispersed by cluster bombs and artillery missiles are every bit as dangerous as land mines but are subject to no kind of control. Neither are the new generations of fuel-air explosives which have proved so devastating in a number of recent conflicts.

There have been hesitant but welcome developments in the efforts to control the trade in light arms, but these are still in their early stages. They are not helped by the emphasis placed in so many countries on maintaining a vigorous and usually very profitable arms trade. None of the major arms exporting countries has seriously addressed the issue of defence diversification, involving the conversion of defence industries to civil production. Until this begins to get under way, efforts to erect ethical foreign policies towards arms sales will have little effect.[2]

The arms control agenda suggested here goes well beyond what is now contemplated, even on a very optimistic assessment of prospects. If it is attempted, though, it will be limited in its chances of success if it does not form part of a wider agenda of actions to ensure a persistent programme of co-operative and sustainable development. Otherwise, it will be seen by many countries as a method for elite states to limit military security in the South while they continue to dominate the world economic and political system.

Closing the wealth – poverty divide

The gap between rich and poor is grotesquely excessive, is getting worse and, as well as being a threat to security, is an affront to justice. Reversing the trend requires a number of key changes in the policies of the main Northern states. Most important of all is to develop a process of trade reform that reverses several decades of trading obstacles to international development. Such reform has been advocated by UNCTAD for nearly 40 years, but there has been a consistent unwillingness on the part of wealthy Northern states to accept it.

Nevertheless, there remains an urgent requirement for a structuring of world trade that provides economic advantage rather than handicap to Southern states, not least through a comprehensive integrated commodities programme, but also through a broad pattern of trade preferences, including invisibles, that stimulate Southern economic development. Such ideas run directly counter to free market orthodoxy and hardly figure at all in the deliberations of the World Trade Organisation or the IMF and World Bank. UNCTAD has been side-lined for most of the past 30 years, even though its constant calls for trade reform would, if implemented, have already transformed the economic prospects of most Third World states.[3]

A second policy development, of immediate importance and potentially able to lead to rapid improvements in socioeconomic well-being, is a radical programme of debt cancellation, going far beyond the welcome but limited advances of the latter part of 1999.

Comprehensive debt relief would transform the economic prospects of countries right across the South, removing the biggest immediate obstacle to development progress. While trade reform and debt cancellation can be linked to good governance and socially fair internal development policies, it hardly behoves Western states to impose such governance, given their role in limiting the development potential of Southern states in recent decades.[4]

One of the greatest problems facing Third World states is the risk of economic downturns occasioned by bond and currency market speculation, a process akin to gambling on a gigantic scale, and revolving around markets trading at the rate of up to $1.5 trillion a day. One method of exerting some kind of control on short-term speculative activity is a very minor tariff levied by major countries on foreign-exchange dealings. Commonly termed the Tobin Tax, after one of its most significant advocates, the Nobel Laureate James Tobin, the tax would both dampen down excessive speculation and would liberate enormous sums of money that could be diverted to poverty relief, as well as emergency help for sudden economic problems. Even a tax of 0.25 per cent could raise revenues of well over $100 billion annually.[5]

Allied to a degree of control of bond and currency markets would be the abandoning of efforts to extend the IMF's control over capital account liberalisation (CAL), a process that would otherwise allow it to force member states to remove restrictions on capital flows. This increased power, at least on past performance, would most likely be used to limit the power of Third World states, and would certainly provide the IMF with a powerful lever to counter attempts to limit market liberalisation. A related issue is the pressure to redevelop the idea of a Multilateral Agreement on Investment (MAI). The MAI would greatly aid trans-national corporations (TNCs), not least by limiting the capacity of member states to control their activities. Earlier attempts to develop an MAI foundered, but this is unlikely to deter its supporters, including many powerful financial institutions and TNCs, from trying again.[6]

Another damaging and persistent effect of globalisation has been the ability of trans-national corporations to sub-contract manufacturing to local producers, constantly seeking the lowest-wage markets as product sources. One reason why this has become such a feature of the world economy is, paradoxically, the improvement in basic educational levels in many Third World countries in the past 40 years. This, coupled with rural-urban migration, has provided labour pools that are far greater than the employment opportunities available. As a result, labour costs can be kept down to levels which would be far below any poverty line recognised in elite states.

Although there are enormous difficulties involved, some way has to be found to inject a degree of justice into international labour markets. This could be done, not least, through the rehabilitation of the International Labour Office as an organisation with a legitimate role to play in fostering labour rights. Some consumer groups in elite states have begun to play a significant role in this issue, but it remains at the root of much poverty throughout the South.

On wider issues of development, there is also a role for direct official and non-governmental assistance, especially in areas of extreme need. Even the meeting of the official UN target of 0.7 per cent of GNP as official development assistance would represent real progress, although the requirement is for assistance that far exceeds such a target and involves a radical improvement in quality. The reality is that official development assistance has, with a very few exceptions, been in decline for the past decade. Furthermore, a very large proportion of that assistance has been in the form of loans, or is specifically tied to the expertise and exports of donor countries in such a manner that its principal effect is to open up new markets rather than have a direct effect on development.

If development assistance was quadrupled from present levels and was substantially 'untied', then it could serve as a basis for a range of improvements, especially if two specific functions were embraced. The first would be a persistent concentration on the poorest sectors of populations, especially in the form of gendered programmes designed to enhance self-reliance rather than dependency. The second function would be to place a core emphasis on the need for processes of development in the South that are, unlike those past and present processes in the North, environmentally sustainable.

This would comprise a wide range of programmes and technical exchanges. These would include substantial assistance in developing renewable energy sources, including hydro, wind and solar energy, the development of efficient and safe integrated transport networks, sustainable agricultural systems that build on extensive local knowledge and experience and cheap and widely available communications systems. A major feature of trans-national corporation behaviour is the production of goods with minimal concern for environmental and health impacts. This trend has to be reversed so that Third World states are aided to develop industries that are as environmentally efficient as the most advanced industries of the North, as well as being able to adapt them to their own circumstances.

Responding to environmental constraints

While such a key function of international aid should be to promote sustainable development in the South, responses to environmental constraints need to focus much more strongly on the activities of wealthy industrialised states. Global effects of human activity such as ozone depletion and climate change are very largely due to the activities of industrial states and associated elites elsewhere. In other words, by far the greatest responsibility for these effects lies with perhaps one-fifth of the global population. Unless that elite minority is able drastically to cut back its current environmental impact, then the embracing of sustainable development policies in Third World states will be largely irrelevant. Furthermore, governments of such states will simply not allow their own development priorities to be dominated by global environmental issues if the elite states are unwilling to transform their own economies in the direction of sustainability.

The most urgent requirement is for rapid progress on the control of greenhouse gases, probably the most important single issue on the security agenda for the next half century. Beyond that, there is a need for a wide range of actions directed towards environmentally sustainable economic activity, especially in the areas of energy conservation, use of renewable energy resources, low-impact transport and materials recycling.[7] The overall impact of a cluster of sustainable economic policies, if integrated with trade reform, would be to cut back on environmental impacts and curb the rate of resource use, while accepting the necessity of a controlled increase in resource prices as part of a process of an international integrated commodities programme. In short, elite populations slow their rate of resource use while paying substantially higher prices for those resources and develop technologies that minimise the environmental impact of consumption.

Timescales and progression

The proposals outlined here address some of the main features of a common security approach, covering in very broad terms the changes required in the areas of sustainable environmental management, international development, arms control and disarmament. While no individual indications of timescales have been suggested, current global circumstances require a transformation in attitudes and approaches on all of these issues within a decade in order to avoid progressively greater problems of insecurity in the following two or three decades.

In parallel with these changes, it is essential to develop current capabilities for conflict prevention, peacekeeping, conflict resolution and post-conflict peacekeeping. Many of these requirements have been identified in the UN's Agenda for Peace and relate to activities within the United Nations Organisation. Others are regional and national responsibilities. The 1990s saw a considerable expansion in peace-keeping operations and some limited developments in conflict early warning and prevention, but all of these approaches are small in comparison with current levels of military resourcing.

A further substantial problem is that the ability to mount substantial peacekeeping operations is limited to relatively few countries, mostly Western states, and there is a continual perception that their commitment to peacekeeping relates to their narrow foreign policy requirements rather than wider international needs. This perception becomes even more dominant when intervention is undertaken without a specific UN mandate, as in Serbia in 1999.

There is consequently a need for a substantial strengthening of UN peacekeeping capabilities that would involve a readily available standing force with rapid-reaction elements committed specifically to UN operations and supplied by a number of countries representing the global community. While inevitably centred on components of armed forces that are highly mobile and versatile, these would need to be broadly multinational, and with integrated training in a wide range of skills.

There is also a need to put a far greater focus on conflict prevention through monitoring, observing and related functions. The current culture is very much against this, as demonstrated by the contrast between NATO and the Organisation for Security and Co-operation in Europe (OSCE) in Kosovo in 1998–99. In the autumn of 1998, a fragile agreement was reached that enabled the OSCE to put together a small force of just over 1,000 observers in an attempt to curb the violence and ethnic cleansing already under way in Kosovo. Although these efforts subsequently failed, to be followed by sustained military action, for several months a group of under-resourced observers, acting in difficult circumstances, was able to have a positive effect in many parts of Kosovo.

What if the OSCE had been able to put in a fully trained and experienced force of 20,000 or 30,000 observers? The very idea seems laughable. Where would they come from? Would they be drawn from a permanent force? What would they do when they weren't 'observing'? But NATO subsequently put far more than 20,000 troops into the region, at far greater cost, and it is likely that they will be there for many years.[8] NATO collectively has more than two million troops under arms yet this is accepted as an essential part of maintaining international security. Compared with this, a permanent force of observers numbering perhaps one-hundredth of this seems small by comparison. It is, in essence, a matter of culture, and just one more example of the manner in which the security paradigm needs to change.

Policies for a middle power

Overall, this brief review entails a radically different approach to international peace and security than that currently on offer. It advocates major changes in trade, development and environmental responses but sees these as essential features of common security – policies that are necessary in the interests of human justice but are also in the real long-term interests of the current wealthier sectors of the human community.

The changes in policy being suggested represent a very substantial change of direction, especially for the more powerful industrialised states of the North. Yet there are sufficient signs of insecurity, instability and conflict to indicate that they are necessary changes. They are more likely to be implemented as the current paradigm of 'top down' international security control is challenged in a number of quarters. Significant among these will be leaders and thinkers in Southern countries, and non-government organisations and campaigning groups in the North and South. They could be aided by even minor changes in policies in individual elite countries and in interstate organisations such as the European Union. Most of all, though, they would be stimulated if one or more Northern states began to take substantial domestic initiatives, combined with agenda-setting on the international scene.

Britain is in an interesting and potentially influential position in this regard on at least three counts. It is a member of the European Union, the second most important trading group in the world, it retains unusually close links with the United States and, through the Commonwealth, it is part of an organisation that spans continents and cultures and represents more than a quarter of the world's people. A role for Britain in promoting peace with justice in the early twenty-first century would have two components – changes in domestic and foreign policy that demonstrated a commitment to an equitable world order, and a sustained programme of agenda-setting among the international community.

There are many potential policy initiatives, some of them building on recent developments. One example is the UK position on debt relief, including some relatively positive changes of policy in relation to the most heavily indebted countries. This position could be extended to a wider range of countries, while such policies are advocated forcefully within the European Union, the OECD, the Group of Eight and other bodies. A range of fiscal and other measures could be adopted to encourage much more positive policies from the private financial sector, especially if done as part of EU policy.

Although it runs counter to the current culture within the UK Department for Trade and Industry, it is necessary for Britain to develop international trade policies designed specifically to help the poorest states, while arguing for them within the EU, the WTO, UNCTAD and other bodies. In doing so, it will be desirable to make common cause with the few other member states of these organisations with broadly similar outlooks.

Although Britain has, in recent years, begun to increase its official development assistance budget, there is scope for very substantial further enhancement. This would involve moving rapidly towards the UN target of 0.7 per cent GNP, and then increasing it above 1 per cent. That budget could be directed primarily to poverty relief and sustainable self-reliance, while similar approaches are urged within multilateral agencies.

On issues of the global environment, there are three areas for action. The first and most important is to encourage and accelerate the take-up of new technologies to counter greenhouse gas emissions, investing vigorously in greatly improved energy efficiency and developing a major national programme on renewable energy resources. This would extend into substantial investment in a radical programme of integrated transport systems. In the process, this would result in Britain being the leading state in these areas of activity, developing a substantial technology base that would, among other things, be in demand overseas.

Second, it would be essential to ensure that issues of climate change, especially in relation to development, are consistently high on the international political agenda, especially in groups such as the G8, EU and OECD. If Britain was developing a domestic policy agenda along the lines outlined, it would be in a strong position to engage in persistent agenda-setting, again working with other states that were working along similar lines.

Finally it would be highly desirable to invest substantially in two areas of research. One would be to expand substantially climate change research, giving Britain a world leadership role in this crucial area of scientific research. Within this research area, much emphasis is currently placed on assessing the impact of climate change on Britain. While this is understandable, it would be of great value if wider research agendas could be developed that concentrated on the impact of climate change on Third World states, not least through collaborative programmes with climatologists and others in these countries.

The other area for additional work would be to institute a high-powered programme of research into countering the effects of climate change in poor countries. Even if it is possible to get control of greenhouse gases over the next decade, the effects are already there and are likely to increase. To aid the states that are likely to be most seriously affected, it is necessary to identify the major problems and direct research agendas towards coping with them. Two of the most significant areas are in health and agriculture. Climate change will have a substantial effect on disease distribution and intensity and will affect agriculture through the anticipated 'drying out' of some of the most productive parts of the world. In terms of impact, research and development programmes intended to enhance the ability of agricultural ecosystems to cope with such climate change could be remarkably cost effective.

A separate policy area would be the development of Britain's role in peacekeeping training, conflict prevention, conflict resolution and post-conflict peace-building. This would make it an acknowledged world leader in this field, while working to enhance the role of the Organisation for Security and Co-operation in Europe and to improve the capabilities of the United Nations in pursuing the Agenda for Peace.

There would also be a sustained programme of enhancing UK policies on arms control, especially the critical and urgent need to improve the control of biological weapons and the need to re-invigorate the Non-Proliferation Treaty and the Comprehensive Test Ban Treaty. A further aim would be to maintain the Strategic Arms Reduction Treaty process while seeking to extend it to middle-ranking nuclear powers and to avoid the loss of the Anti-Ballistic Missile Treaty. A lead should be taken in beginning negotiations for a Nuclear Weapons Convention, especially through a willingness to withdraw and dismantle all UK nuclear forces.

Britain could also enhance and aid the development of the EU Code on arms transfers as a basis for domestic policy and Anglo-American co-operation. This would be accompanied by a national programme for arms diversification aimed, not least, at reducing reliance on arms exports and re-directing industries into areas with a long-term relevance to the new security agenda, especially those areas involving sophisticated technologies applied to sustainability.

While there are many other potential developments, these indicate major examples of policy initiatives that would systematically demonstrate best practice while giving Britain the political authority to propose numerous international initiatives.

It has to be recognised, though, that the developing problems of international security cannot be considered specific to individual government departments. In the British case, the Ministry of Defence has a key role in several areas, not least peacekeeping and arms control, and the Foreign and Commonwealth Office relates also to arms control, conflict resolution, arms exports control, the work of the United Nations and many other areas. The Department for International Development is centrally involved in development, and environmental issues concern it and several other departments, not least the Department of Environment, Transport and the Regions and the Department of Trade and Industry. Debt relief concerns DfID and the FCO, yet is clearly a Treasury issue.

All this indicates an urgent need for co-ordination across departments of state and also an integrated capacity to think through issues that simply cut across current areas of government. There is certainly a need for a central strategic policy organisation focusing specifically on the coming issues of international security.

If, over the next five years, Britain was to develop its domestic policies and international advocacy, it might well end up providing the country with a coherent role in international affairs that would make it a singularly influential state. It could give Britain the role for which it has been searching for half a century. The development of such a role might even prove electorally popular.

International responses

Proposing policies for a state such as Britain does have a value, especially if it enables such a state to develop more influence in major intergovernmental bodies. However, on its own, this will not have the effect required in developing an effective new security paradigm. In broader terms, radical policy changes are required across all the major elite states. In this context, the future evolution of the European Union is particularly significant. On present trends it will develop over the next decade to embrace a number of countries in Eastern Europe, while developing a substantially higher degree of economic integration.

The outlook for the European Union is of an enlarged community of states that concentrates on its own economic well-being and develops a greater concern for its own security. Such a security concern is already embodied in the evolution of a so-called European defence identity, and this could very easily lead to a 'Fortress Europe' outlook in which an increasingly wealthy Europe anxiously protects its wealth from external pressures.

What is desirable, instead, is the evolution of a European Union that is much more outward looking and recognises the need to follow, at an EU level, the range of policies advocated above. While effecting such a transformation in EU outlook is no mean task, there are elements of such policies present in the activities of a number of individual EU member states. If coalitions of states can be formed around particular issues, whether they be aid, debt relief, energy conservation, climate change responses or other areas, then there is potential for changing the outlook of the entire union.

As the world's sole superpower, and also as a state with a profound impact on the global economy, the United States remains central to any process of transforming the security paradigm. For the present, the trend within the United States is in the opposite direction, and is best characterised by the term 'aggressive isolationism'. It is summed up in James Woolsey's phrase mentioned in Chapter 4, that the United States had slain the dragon but now lived in a jungle full of poisonous snakes.

If a state is impregnable in its insecurity, then it might appear unlikely to be able to embrace policies that serve the common security interests of the wider international community. This may be true for the United States, but there are a number of reasons for optimism. The first is that there is a rich intellectual and activist tradition within the United States that is vigorously concerned with many of the problems outlined in this book, not least in areas of human rights, sustainable economies and defence alternatives.

Furthermore, the very creation of NAFTA, involving the United States, Canada and Mexico, brings together two industrial states that have differing cultures and attitudes to world affairs with a Southern state that is already experiencing substantial problems of anti-elite insurgency. There are prospects for NGOs developing a wide range of links between these states, not least through revitalised unions, that can begin to explore the changed human rights and economic relationships that are required across the wider world community.

Finally, while the dominant security paradigm within the United States is one of 'keeping the violent peace' there is the beginning of a recognition that this might prove increasingly difficult, not least as trends in asymmetric warfare make it exceptionally difficult to maintain control by conventional means. While this is currently limited to just a few far-sighted individuals in the military, academic and policy communities, there is potential for this to develop into a substantial intellectual movement that assists in effecting a paradigm shift.

Conclusion

Writers on international security in the early post-Cold War days were liable to moan about the complexity of the new global security environment, contrasting it with the much simpler 'them and us' structure of the Cold War era. This present analysis suggests that the new security agenda is, in reality, no more complex – a deeply divided world faces environmental constraints and, unless the divisions are healed and sustainable development is at the core of that process, we face an unstable and potentially conflict-ridden world in the early decades of the new century.

There are two main obstacles to facing up to this challenge. The first, and by far the most substantial, is that the necessary response will involve considerable limits being placed on the wealth and power of the elite global minority, requiring radical economic and political changes that are substantially greater than anything experienced in the last half century. The second is that most Western thinking and writing on international security is deeply ethnocentric and conservative. With few exceptions it seems incapable of rising above a narrow concern with Western elite security and well-being, yet this paradigm shift has to take place if the new thinking on security is to be embraced and developed.

If there is no change in thinking, Western security policy will continue to be based on the narrow and misguided assumption that the status quo can be maintained, an elite minority can maintain its position, environmental problems can be marginalised and the lid can be kept on dissent and instability. Little or no attempt will be made to address the core causes of insecurity, even if failure to do so threatens the elite minority as well as the marginalised majority.

We are left with a challenge that may seem insuperable, yet there are many signs of a change in thinking. Some of the leading figures of the

Cold War now accept that it was a highly dangerous era, and some now advocate policies of nuclear disarmament that would formerly have been regarded as wildly radical. A substantial public campaign across many Western countries on the debt crisis has begun to translate into government action. Environmental issues are continually being raised by numerous campaigning and policy groups, and there is already a recognition that climate change induced by human activity is a reality and will require radical responses.

Furthermore, issues of fair trade, particularly around the much-criticised policies of the World Trade Organisation, are coming to the fore. The experience of mass public protests and violence at the WTO meeting in Seattle in 1999 was traumatic, not just for that organisation but for the IMF, the World Bank and other intergovern-mental agencies. Bitterly criticised by citizen groups and by Third World delegations, the assumption of dominance of the WTO by elite states was seriously damaged – a crack began to appear in the edifice of Western economic control.

Whether these collective signs indicate the beginnings of a substantial change in attitudes is difficult to predict, but it is reasonable to conclude that the coming years represent a period of fundamental challenge and potential transformation. The early decades of the twenty-first century could be an era in which deep divisions in the world community lead to instability and violence that will transcend boundaries and affect rich and poor alike. They could also be an era of substantial progress in developing a more socially just and environmentally sustainable world order.

11 September and the New American Century

The first edition of this book, written during the period up to March 2000, argued that the Western security paradigm was, in essence, that international security could best be maintained by the continuation of a globalised liberal market economy, supported by a range of institutional and security organisations. The paradigm recognised the increasing volatility and unpredictability of a global security system in which the near-certainties of the Cold War confrontation had been replaced by a 'violent peace', with conflicts continuing across most regions of the world. Even so, it was thought that military postures were adequate to handle this uncertain world and that Western society would continue to benefit from its dominance of the international economic and financial systems.

This paradigm was questioned, both in terms of the changing causes of conflict and the ability to maintain control. In essence, the argument was presented that an elite world, focused mainly on the states of the North Atlantic community, was essentially unstable. Two 'drivers' of insecurity were developing – the widening socio-economic divide and the problem of global environmental constraints. These would be likely to lead, in different ways, to much greater problems relating to issues of migration, to a greater likelihood of different forms of environmental conflict and, above all, to the development of anti-elite insurgencies and paramilitary actions, some of them trans-national in their effect.

In particular, attention was drawn to the increasing capacity of relatively weak groups, whether in the form of states or sub-state actors, to take action against the perceived vulnerabilities of advanced industrial states. In examining this capacity, two types of example were cited (Chapter 6). One was the manner in which Iraq sought to develop a deterrent system based on weapons of mass destruction, and was able to do so in the case of biological weapons in a remarkably short space of time. The other was the development of a range of paramilitary actions resulting in political violence such as the bombing of the Colombo central business district by the LTTE (Tamil Tigers), the Tokyo subway nerve agent attack, the use of economic targeting by the Provisional IRA, the attack on US military and diplomatic interests in the Middle East and East Africa, and the attempt to destroy the World Trade Center in New York in 1993.

The argument was made that the full impact of these events had not been properly appreciated and that they demonstrated a potential vulnerability of Western elite systems to 'revolts from the margins'. Furthermore, they showed that it might prove impossible to maintain control of a potentially unstable world system, that keeping the lid on dissent, 'liddism', might be singularly inappropriate, contriving to increase violence and insecurity rather than diminish them.

If this analysis was correct, then it suggested that the Western security paradigm should best evolve into a posture that encouraged the addressing of the core problems, seeking to aid economic co-operation for sustainable development, coupled with global environmental management and decreased reliance on military approaches to international security. In the final chapter, a number of indications were given as to an appropriate agenda, and a hopeful note was sounded that a combination of citizen groups in Northern and Southern countries, coupled with effective leadership in some Northern states, might ensure that the old security paradigm could be replaced by one that was more in the interests of the global community as a whole.

In making this case, it was argued that such an approach was ethically more acceptable than current patterns that tend to increase socioeconomic divisions and environmental instability. However, it was also argued that this should not, in any way, be regarded as a solely idealistic approach – if the existing security paradigm was inadequate then it was also a matter of self-interest to Western elites that they engage in approaches that would yield a more just and stable world.

Although the analysis presented a number of examples where such thinking was beginning to encroach on Western political cultures, it also expressed the fear that there were exceptionally powerful arguments against such optimism. In particular, it was suggested that perceptions of Western vulnerability might well re-inforce the existing paradigm, making it appear even more necessary to maintain control rather than addressing core issues of instability and conflict.

The attempt to destroy the New York World Trade Center in 1993 was cited as an example in this context, and it was suggested that if the attempt had succeeded, then it might not have resulted in any fundamental questioning of the paradigm:

Take, once again, the case of the World Trade Center bombing. If that attack had had its intended effect, the results would have been calamitous, not just for the City of New York but for the United States as a whole. But would it have resulted in any rethinking of security? Probably not. A more likely result would have been a massive and violent military reaction against any groups anywhere in the Middle East that were thought to have even the slightest connection with the attack. (Chapter 6)

That 1993 attack was intended to collapse the North Tower across the Vista Hotel and into the South Tower, bringing about the destruction of the entire complex, and causing the deaths of perhaps 30,000 people. The 2001 attack used two passenger jets instead of bombs, and while the effects were less devastating, both towers collapsed and 3,000 people died.

In presenting the analysis in the first edition of *Losing Control*, it was anticipated that problems of marginalisation, environmental constraints and anti-elite action would develop over a number of years, perhaps over one or two decades, and that there was not necessarily likely to be any immediacy of events that would bring the issues more rapidly to the fore. That is not how things have worked out in the past two years, and the purpose of this chapter is to review the rapid pace of events, especially in relation to the attacks in New York and Washington on 11 September 2001 and the subsequent 'war on terrorism', and to assess whether these make it more likely that the existing Western security paradigm will be strengthened or whether they will encourage a substantial change in Western approaches to international security.

Although the focus in this chapter will be primarily on these events, it is appropriate to mention that other developments do relate to the argument of the book. Mention was made of the anti-globalisation actions at the World Trade Organisation meeting in Seattle in 1999, with the suggestion that 'a crack began to appear in the edifice of Western economic control' (Chapter 7). A combination of nonviolent demonstrations and a small element of violent activists had substantial effects on later meetings of international financial institutions in Washington and Prague, culminating in substantial demonstrations, and rioting, at the meeting of the Group of Eight in Genoa, Italy, in 2001.

Behind these public demonstrations of opposition there was a far greater perception that a North/South rift was developing. There was, for example, continued opposition to the planned Multilateral Agreement on Investments, and a wider concern that trade in intellectual property rights would act against the interests of Southern states. Even after the traumatic events of 11 September, there were some Western commentators who were able to say in public that it would be necessary to address the root causes of political violence and that configuring the response to the attacks as a 'war on terrorism' would prove inadequate.

Beyond this lay an unease, even permeating through to some of the elements of Western political leadership, a recognition that liberal market globalisation might not be delivering economic justice. It was not expressed in such blunt terms, but it was recognised that the expected improvements in international development were simply not happening. Moreover, there was a clear recognition in Europe, at least, that the issues of the global environment were rising up the political agenda, especially in terms of climate change.

Similarly, on the issue of migration, a range of events suggested that this, too, was being seen as a major international issue. In Europe this took the form of a greatly increased concern over migratory pressures into Western Europe, not least in relation to asylum seekers desperate for entry into Britain.

In South East Asia there was a dramatic illustration of such pressures, late in 2001, when the Australian Navy intercepted a cargo vessel bound for an Australian port after it had rescued several hundred refugees from a sinking ferry. Despite considerable international pressure, the Australian government, facing a general election, refused even to allow the refugees to land on Christmas Island and they were eventually transferred to the tiny state of Nauru in the West Pacific.

While these and other events in 1999–2001 serve broadly to strengthen the arguments presented here, it is the attacks in New York and Washington that are greatly more significant. Their impact, not least in the context of the pre-existing defence and foreign policies of the Bush administration, is likely to be profound over the next decade or more, having a considerable effect on the prospects for changes to the Western security paradigm.

The impact of 11 September

On 11 September 2001, four large passenger aircraft were hi-jacked after taking off on internal flights from airports in the Eastern United States. Two of the planes were flown into the twin towers of the New York World Trade Center, one crashed into the headquarters of the US Department of Defense, the Pentagon building in Washington, and a fourth crashed in open country, apparently after a struggle between some of the passengers and the hi-jackers.

The fires that followed the crashes in New York caused the collapse of both towers of the World Trade Center, as well as the almost complete destruction of the other five buildings in the complex together with neighbouring tower blocks. The aircraft that hit the Pentagon crashed into part of the building where a renovation was being completed. It was not yet fully re-occupied, but nearly 200 people were killed in addition to all of those on the plane.

Although the great majority of the building survived, fires continued for several days, and reconstruction costs were subsequently estimated at $500 million. Within the US military, though, the impact was much greater, especially in the Navy, whose personnel had been occupying that part of the Pentagon. More generally, the fact that such an attack could be staged on the centre of US military power, and in such a manner, caused both shock and consternation.

Over the previous 20 years, US military forces deployed overseas had experienced numerous security problems. From the bombing of the marines barracks at Beirut airport in 1983 through the disastrous experience in Somalia in 1993 to the Khobar Towers and *USS Cole* attacks in more recent years, there had been an experience of antagonism to overseas deployments, but none of these compared to the attack on the Pentagon. That this building could be subject to such devastation through the actions of hi-jackers equipped only with knives showed a security weakness that was deeply worrying.

While this had its impact on the US military, and also demonstrated the innate vulnerability of federal buildings in Washington, it was over-shadowed by the sheer destruction in New York, the impact of which was to have a profound effect on American perceptions of their own security. This, in turn, was to lend exceptionally strong support to the Bush administration in its chosen response to the atrocities.

When the World Trade Center was completed in the early 1970s, it represented a remarkably concrete and visible symbol of US business prowess and capabilities. The twin towers were then the tallest buildings in the world, but they represented much more than this. Most US and foreign tourists visiting New York would go to the top of one of the towers, the seven-building complex housed a remarkable array of commercial and financial enterprises, and the towers themselves dominated the whole of downtown Manhattan. They were, for Americans, the most significant buildings of the post-war era.

The impact of the attacks was heightened by their nature, and by the subsequent sequence of events. After the first plane hit the North Tower, network television covered the attack on the South Tower and, by the time the towers collapsed, the disaster was being watched across the country by scores of millions of Americans. The impact was profound and is still not fully appreciated outside of the United States. Initial estimates spoke of a likely death toll exceeding 10,000. That it turned out to be much less was little consolation as it still represented the most sudden and unexpected attack since Pearl Harbor in 1941.

The reaction was inevitable and predictable. America was under terrorist attack, initially by unknown paramilitaries, and a strong response was expected. But this response would be undertaken by an administration that had only been in office for eight months and was markedly different from its predecessor. The Bush administration had won an extraordinarily narrow victory at the polls, dependent on questionable results in the state of Florida, and had been expected, as a result, to adopt a rather consensual approach to policy formulation.

Within a very few months of taking office, this had been shown not to be the case – a range of policies were demonstrating a markedly right-wing orientation, both domestically and in terms of international relations. That this was the case owed much to the manner in which such policies had been under development prior to the 2000 election, and these, in turn, were to have a substantial impact on the response to 11 September.

The Republican security agenda at the turn of the century

During the late 1990s, with the Republican control of both Houses of Congress, aspects of US foreign and security policy demonstrated an increasingly conservative agenda. On issues within the responsibility of the presidency, there were notable exceptions, not least the persistent attempts to get a settlement between the Israelis and the Palestinians. On other issues, the changing agenda was clear cut. The Senate was not prepared to ratify the Comprehensive Test Ban Treaty for nuclear weapons, even though an impressive array of states, including close allies of the United States, were in favour.

On several other issues there were indications of the developing agenda. They included opposition to aspects of the proposed international ban on land mines and marked opposition to the establishment of an independent international criminal court. Another issue, climate change, was potentially divisive between the United States and a number of European governments, where the latter were in favour of adopting the Kyoto protocols on the release of greenhouse gases, in marked contrast to the majority view in Congress.

More generally, there was a foreign and security policy agenda being developed by a number of right-wing think tanks and interest groups that indicated that an incoming Bush administration would take a strongly conservative line on many issues. In relation to this, there was a significant parallel with the situation in the United States some 20 years previously.

In the late 1970s, during the latter stages of the presidency of Jimmy Carter, there developed a strong view in Republican circles that it was essential to equip the United States much more strongly in its confrontation with the Soviet Union. Such circles were broadly antagonistic to the arms control agenda and took the view that the Soviet Union was involved in attempts to gain military superiority.

This general analysis was concentrated and publicised by groups such as the Committee on the Present Danger, the Heritage Foundation and High Frontier, and was boosted massively by the Soviet intervention in Afghanistan – proof positive, if any were needed, of the expansionist intentions of the Soviet Union. The Iranian revolution and subsequent hostage crisis were also seen as clear evidence of a weakening of the United States, and Ronald Reagan's election to the presidency was accompanied by a strong rhetoric of 're-arming America'. Many of those involved in the think tanks and interest groups went on to occupy significant positions in the Reagan administration, and formed part of the political process that resulted in substantial increases in defence spending accompanied by more assertive military postures.

The comparison with the period 20 years later is significant. Although President Clinton won a second term in 1996, he was bitterly unpopular in Republican circles to an extent which is rare in US politics. One aspect of this unpopularity was the belief that he was not prepared to enable the United States to act sufficiently in its own security interests overseas. In part, the disaster in Somalia was one example of this. Another was the continuing and apparently insoluble confrontation with Iraq and another was the belief that the US could find itself dragged into a long-term conflict in the Balkans.

More generally, there was a perception that the proliferation of missiles and weapons of mass destruction in 'rogue states' represented a threat to the continental United States. Furthermore, there was clear-cut evidence that terrorists and their state sponsors were working against US interests, as shown by bomb attacks against US facilities in Saudi Arabia and the embassy bombings in Kenya and Tanzania.

But there was a wider and less clearly defined view that the United States was abrogating international leadership of a form that was in its own security interests. With the Cold War nearly ten years distant and Russia greatly weakened, there was still a potential challenge from China, as well as diverse threats from states and sub-state actors.

Furthermore, even the success of the global free market was being called into question, both by anti-globalisation protestors and even by some Southern states. In short, where the world desperately needed US leadership to demonstrate the innate value of the Western style of economy and polity, what was on offer was a weak presidency prone to compromise.

The view of the liberal market economy was fundamental to this outlook. At root, this comes from a deep-seated conviction that there is only one economic system, itself set in one political context. The system is the globalised free market and the context is liberal democracy. That this is the only way is demonstrated by the collapse of the Soviet bloc and most other examples of centrally planned systems. There is, put simply, an implicit belief that there is no other way.

Furthermore, there was a significant element within conservative thinking that shared the belief that the United States has an historic mission to be a civilising force in world affairs. History is at an end in that, with the ending of the Cold War, the American way of life is predominant. This does not imply a direct neo-colonial control of the world, but more a shaping, through governmental, business and other processes, of a world economy and polity that is broadly in the US image. In other words, we can rightly look forward to the twenty-first century as an American century.

One of the most significant standard-bearers of the Republican Right, founded in 1997, is the Project for the New American Century. Its statement of principles asks: 'Does the United States have the resolve to shape a new century favourable to American principles and interests?' It believes that this is essential and that it is necessary 'to accept responsibility for America's unique role in preserving and extending an international order friendly to our security, our prosperity and our principles'.[1]

But this underlying thinking goes further than this, with a refusal, in the more forceful business and political circles, to accept that there *can* be any legitimate alternative. It is simply unthinkable, not least since to accept the possibility of alternatives implies that the dominant model might not be fully valid. There is thus, in this world view, a cultural assumption that no other approach is acceptable, and that any other approach must at least be deeply wrong-headed if not malign.

It is for this reason, in particular, that the attacks of 11 September are so significant, especially the destruction of the World Trade Center. It is not just that there was an appalling loss of life, that a key part of the US financial structure was damaged and that Wall Street itself was forced to close for four days. The effects spread across a whole raft of US industries, causing economic damage sufficient to precipitate a major economic downturn. The attacks, in short, represented a real assault on the whole political, economic and security paradigm that had become central to the Bush administration.

The early months of the Bush administration

This move to a unilateralist stance in international relations became clear very early in the life of the administration, and came as something of a surprise to many observers. The nature of the Bush victory in November/December 2001 had been so close, dependent on a few hundred votes in a single state, that there had been an expectation that the administration would tend towards conciliation – developing its polices more in terms of a coalition across the mainstream of the political spectrum.

In the first few months, this notion was rapidly disabused, and it is worth noting that, as in 1980, the incoming administration included prominent members of those groups on the Republican Right that had been so committed to an assertive international stance. Supporters of the Project for the New American Century included incoming

Vice-President Dick Cheney and the new Secretary of Defense Donald Rumsfeld.

During the course of the early part of 2001, there were numerous examples of foreign policy and security decisions that exhibited a strongly unilateralist stance, often in marked contrast to the attitudes of European allies. President Bush made it clear that the United States would pursue the development of a national missile defence programme, even if it meant withdrawing from the Anti-Ballistic Missile Treaty, that decision eventually being taken later in the year. There was opposition to UN conventions on the prevention of terrorism, and to the initiation of negotiations on the control of the weaponisation of space, and a markedly critical stance on the UN discussions on the control of light weapons.[2]

There were also clear changes of policy on two issues, the status of North Korea and the attempts to build an accord between the Israelis and Palestinians. In the case of North Korea, careful work by the Clinton administration, together with the historic summit between the leaders of North and South Korea, had suggested that North Korea might ultimately lose its status as a putative 'rogue state', but the attitude of the Bush administration, early in 2001, was to disengage from further negotiations. In relation to the Israeli–Palestinian confrontation, there was palpable disinterest, contrasted strongly with the efforts of the previous administration.

Perhaps most indicative of the new mood was the attitude to two key international agreements, the Kyoto accords on climate change and the negotiations in Geneva seeking to strengthen the Biological and Toxin Weapons Convention (BTWC), a treaty negotiated back in 1972 but lacking any real power of inspection or verification.

The decision to withdraw from the Kyoto Protocols was a considerable surprise to European allies, who eventually went on to continue the process without the United States. The effect, though, was deep-seated, and was the clearest sign that the new administration looked narrowly to its own domestic circumstances.

The developing opposition to the proposed protocol to strengthen the BTWC was much less in the public eye in Europe, but opinion leaders across Europe were thoroughly dismayed at the US attitude, especially as there had been more than six years of careful negotiation on one of the most difficult arms control issues of the late twentieth century.

All these indications of US unilateralism do not imply that such an approach is inevitable, but it does mean that the approach adopted in Washington was essentially based on a security outlook that sees many such treaties and proposals as ones that limit the capacity of the United States to ensure its security, imposing an international regime in which cheats may well prosper but the good guys are constrained.

This may not be seen as a conspiracy as such but, in an obviously unipolar world, lesser states seem intent on tying it down with a series of treaties that persistently limit its capacity to defend itself and its wider interests. This self-view goes even further. Much as Gulliver was tied down by the Lilliputians, so a mixed group of states seeks to limit a benevolent superpower in its efforts to ensure a peaceful world developing substantially in the American image. As one leading Republican writer, Charles Krauthammer, put it three months before the 11 September attacks:

> Multipolarity, yes, when there is no alternative. But not when there is. Not when we have the unique imbalance of power that we enjoy today – and that has given the international system a stability and essential tranquility it had not known for at least a century.
>
> The international environment is far more likely to enjoy peace under a single hegemon. Moreover, we are not just any hegemon. We run a uniquely benign imperium.[3]

This view, which lies at the heart of Republican thinking on international affairs, contrasts markedly with the multilateralist outlook, widely held among America's European allies and by much opinion in the United States itself. This believes that co-operative international behaviour, codified in treaties, is the cornerstone of a more stable and peaceful world order.

This is not to say that the United States, under the Bush administration, has become unilateralist in all things. As Krauthammer argues, where it is in US interests to have agreements, then they are acceptable. Thus, NATO may expand eastwards, the North American Free Trade Area is welcomed, and many aspects of world trade negotiations serve US interests. But the policy is highly selective and it fits a paradigm in which US security interests are paramount and where the only way to ensure peace and prosperity is for the United States to have freedom of action, whatever the effects on the world in general and its allies in particular. Criticisms are unwarranted and short-sighted, for what is good for the United States is necessarily good for the world.

A transatlantic divide

The attitudes and policies that had become evident in the first few months of the Bush administration began, almost at once, to create discernible strains in transatlantic relations, even if most of the concerns felt by European political leaders have been expressed in private. Opinion formers and commentators across Europe expressed much more open dismay and consternation, and their views were exemplified in many areas of security and foreign policy where clear transatlantic differences began to emerge.

This was particularly noticeable in relation to the Kyoto Protocols, where European governments have remained in favour of continued negotiations, and in the support in Europe for the negotiations on biological weapons, but it came through in numerous other ways. As the United States withdrew its interest in negotiations with North Korea, the European Union dispatched a high-level group to the region in May 2000. In Europe, especially in Germany, there was a much greater sensitivity to Russian concerns over NATO enlargement, and to Chinese fears over national missile defence, and the European Union retained a stronger, if still inadequate, commitment to the Middle East peace process.

More generally, one of the effects of European enlargement has been to bring in countries such as Sweden, joining the Netherlands, Ireland and others that take a more progressive stance on a number of core international issues, not least climate change, the world debt crisis and conflict prevention and resolution. This adds to a longer-term European culture of co-operation that has developed over more than five decades and results in a far greater salience for multilateral co-operation, even where agreements may not be to the short-term advantage of individual participants.

The response to 11 September

Across much of the world, the immediate response to the atrocities of 11 September was of strong sympathy for the United States. The full impact of the attacks caused considerable shock, not least because the twin towers were widely recognisable across the world.

Within days, there was an appreciation among many opinion formers, especially in Europe, that one effect of the attacks might be to encourage the United States to be highly co-operative in its response. It was immediately recognised that there would be comprehensive collaboration between security and intelligence agencies. It was also thought likely that the Bush administration would recognise that any successful attempts to bring the planners of the attacks to justice would best be undertaken as part of a global process of co-operation. Such a process would also need to recognise that there were underlying reasons for the level of anti-Western and anti-American attitudes present, not least in the Middle East and South West Asia.

In the event, the US response to 11 September was singularly independent. A number of states co-operated in the war in Afghanistan, but they were surprisingly few in number and there was no doubt whatsoever that this was not a broadly-based coalition of partners but a substantial military operation organised and commanded by the United States.

In the immediate aftermath of the attacks, attention focused on the al-Qaida network and its putative leader Osama bin Laden, but the refusal of the Taliban regime in Afghanistan to offer up the leadership to the United States, following several years of harbouring elements of the network, resulted in the United States developing two war aims – the destruction of the regime and of the al-Qaida network in Afghanistan.

The first phase of the war in Afghanistan lasted three months and resulted in the destruction of the Taliban regime and the dispersal of al-Qaida operatives then present in the country. There was an initial supposition that the United States would put substantial ground forces into the country, but the military tactics used took a very different root with three components. The first was the use of special forces to undertake reconnaissance and to identify targets for bombing, and the second was the use of a range of strike aircraft, especially strategic bombers, to destroy Taliban facilities and militia.

The third element, and the key to the whole war, was the use of anti-Taliban forces, especially the Northern Alliance, as ground troops to evict Taliban militia from all of their centres of power. In essence, this meant that the United States took sides in a long-running civil war, supporting a range of groups that themselves had had an appalling human rights record before the Taliban had progressively taken power in the mid- and late 1990s. In the process, large quantities of arms were provided to anti-Taliban forces, most of them coming from Russia although it appears that these transactions were largely financed by the United States.

By the end of 2001, most of the al-Qaida centres and almost all of the concentrations of Taliban military power had been dispersed or destroyed, but the manner in which this happened has implications for the future. In a number of isolated cases there was severe ground fighting between Northern Alliance and other forces, on the one hand, and Taliban and al-Qaida militia on the other. But in the great majority of the cases, the Taliban and al-Qaida did not engage in fighting at all, preferring to withdraw, usually with their weapons intact, and to melt away into their home areas or communities in which they could rely on support, including those in Pakistan.

Such a withdrawal was undertaken most remarkably from Kabul itself, where an overnight retreat was accomplished with hardly any casualties, but there were similar processes in many other parts of the country. One obvious result is that the Taliban regime lost control of Afghanistan, and an interim administration was established in Kabul. But the longer-term implications were much less clear. The public perception was of a war won with minimal casualties for the United States, but the US military view was that a much longer-term if lower-level confrontation in Afghanistan was likely. This is due to the recognition that the Taliban militia were rarely defeated but chose not to fight on terms massively favourable to the Northern Alliance and to US air power.

This view is supported by two other factors. One is that it proved exceptionally difficult to take into custody senior commanders of the Taliban and al-Qaida, including the leadership of both organisations. The second is a prevailing view that much of the al-Qaida organisation moved from Afghanistan into Pakistan during the course of the conflict.

The reporting of the war in the US media tended to concentrate heavily on the rapid collapse of the Taliban, as might be expected in the circumstances. In Europe, and especially in the Middle East, there was rather more reporting of other aspects of the war and its immediate aftermath. One element was the extent and ferocity of the US bombing campaign, including the use of cluster bombs and other area-impact munitions. Lack of accurate intelligence resulted in numerous mistakes in targeting. Moreover, Taliban militia, on the occasions when they faced Northern Alliance forces, were frequently interspersed with local farmers and villagers – these were not concentrated front lines in the normal military sense.

The overall effect of this, and of the mis-targeting, was to cause numerous civilian casualties, possibly exceeding 3,000 during the last three months of 2001, similar to the number of people killed on 11 September. There were also pernicious after-effects. Cluster bomb units were used against Taliban militia around the city of Herat in western Afghanistan in November 2001, and in the following two months more than 40 local people were killed and as many injured as a result of the accidental detonation of unexploded cluster bomblets.

The second element was the overall community effect of the war on Afghan society. The rapid advances of the Northern Alliance and the retreat of the Taliban was coupled with a massive flow of light arms into Afghanistan, a country in which there was already a vigorous arms market and a heavily armed male population. The absence of central control resulted in an immediate return to the disorder of the early 1990s, characterised by competing warlords, banditry and further movement of refugees. It is also likely that the need of local factions to ensure a source of income will result in increased opium production.

In cities that came under some degree of central control, especially Kabul, the situation was very much better than under the Taliban regime. In much of the rest of the country, there was an uncomfortable paradox. The Taliban regime had been a particularly brutal and repressive regime, even if it had originally been welcomed in the mid-1990s because of the degree of order it brought to a chaotic and anarchic country. Even so, when it collapsed, there was a return to precisely that disorder. There were notable efforts by some external powers and non-government bodies to provide aid through the winter of 2001–02, and the International Security Assistance Force was established to provide stability in Kabul. This provided no more than 5,000 personnel, whereas a UN estimate of the size of a stabilisation force required to bring security to the country as a whole was 30,000. Unfortunately, there was not the international commitment to such aid, especially from the United States, and the result is that the achievement of a peaceful society in Afghanistan will take very much longer.

Although the Pentagon view in early 2002 was that the war would continue, in some form, for some months to come, an initial independent analysis of the war pointed to four military outcomes for the United States and its local Afghan allies through to January 2002:[4] between 3,000 and 4,000 Taliban coalition troops had been killed, including 600–800 'Afghan Arabs' out of up to 3,000 affiliated to al-Qaida; approximately 7,000 were prisoners, the great majority still in Afghanistan; most of the senior Taliban leadership survived the war and avoided capture, many moving into Pakistan; and perhaps half of the senior al-Qaida leadership in Afghanistan was killed or captured, and many camps or other facilities were over-run or destroyed.

More generally, the analysis came to two significant conclusions. One was that while the Taliban regime had been forced from power and widely discredited as an ideological movement, many members would be likely to resume a role in the Afghan polity. The other was that while the capacity of the al-Qaida network had been greatly disrupted, this might only be temporary. Such a view was supported by that of the acting assistant director of the FBI's counter-terrorism division, J.T. Caruso, reported in mid-December 2001, who expressed the view that, as a result of the military action, the al-Qaida network's capacity to commit 'horrific acts' had been reduced by 30 per cent.[5]

There are two other aspects of the war that are relevant to a longer-term analysis of its effects on the Western security paradigm. The first is that the United States has been able to extend its military presence substantially into Central Asia. As well as bases in Afghanistan itself, and facilities in Pakistan, the US has developed a sizeable military presence in Uzbekistan and a new base is being developed at Bishkek in Kyrgyzstan as well as facilities in Tajikistan.

While such a presence may not be widely popular in these states, and certainly not in Moscow, the regimes will be supportive, not least because of the economic rewards that follow such deployments but also because a foreign military presence can, in some circumstances, ensure the survival of an unpopular regime. The impact on China is likely to be far less favourable as the United States consolidates its influence in Central Asia. Iran, too, will view this presence, along with the substantial US forces in western Gulf states, as unconducive to its own security.

This, in turn, is part of a wider effect of the war, and of the increasing US presence in the region and its effect on political and public opinion. Within the United States, the common view of the atrocities of 11 September is that they were carried out by a terrorist organisation motivated principally by an irrational and visceral anti-American attitude. Thoughtful opinion within the United States does not take this view, but there is little general recognition of the political context in which the al-Qaida network has developed.

This relates principally to two factors, the US military presence in the Persian Gulf in general and Saudi Arabia in particular, and a belief that the House of Saud has lost its legitimacy as the Guardian of the Two Holy Places. Across the Middle East there is a wider Arab perception of a United States that is deeply implicated in the treatment of Palestinians by Israel, but this has been a secondary issue for the al-Qaida network, with the US presence in Saudi Arabia being seen as a follow-on to the Soviet presence in Afghanistan in the 1990s.

What is particularly significant is that there is extensive support within Saudi Arabia for the al-Qaida demand that the United States' military forces leave the country, with that support represented by financial aid from many sources as well as tacit recognition of the aim within some elements of the House of Saud.

There is a second aspect of the 11 September attacks and the US response that must be considered. The destruction of the World Trade Center and the attack on the Pentagon were carefully planned operations, conceived and implemented over a long period of time. Furthermore, they formed part of a long-term strategy, probably developed in concert with other paramilitary coalitions in South West Asia, with previous acts including small-scale attacks against US personnel in Saudi Arabia, the more devastating Khobar Towers and USS Cole bombings, and the destructive attacks on the US embassies in East Africa.

It should therefore be assumed that those ultimately responsible for 11 September had planned those attacks as part of a strategy that would expect a very strong US counter-reaction, especially from the new Bush administration. It should therefore be assumed that the war in Afghanistan was not only anticipated but was part of the strategy itself. From the point of view of an al-Qaida strategy measured in decades rather than years, a strong and sustained US military offensive, including the substantial build-up of US forces in the region, would be exactly what is required to further encourage and enhance the developing anti-US mood, providing long-term support for al-Qaida and other networks opposed to the presence of the United States in the Gulf as well as its ongoing support for Israel.

Indeed, any extension of the 'war on terrorism' to other Islamic centres, not least the Philippines, Somalia and possibly even Iraq and Iran, would be considered, in the long term, to be in the considerable interests of al-Qaida and associated groups. To this extent, the 11 September attacks not only succeeded in their aims of attacking core symbols of US economic and military power, they incited a reaction that will, in turn, ultimately ensure further action against the United States, as well as aiding the development of a more general line of fracture between the West and the Islamic world.

The view from the majority world

In the United States there has been overwhelming support for the 'war on terror'. In Europe, sympathy over the attacks remains, but the support for the war has been much more mixed, with a widespread concern that it might ultimately lead to more tensions and violence. In much of the Middle East and South West Asia there has been considerable opposition to the war in Afghanistan. What, then, of the rest of the world – in particular the 'majority world' of three-quarters of the global population.

While there is no common view, there is a persistent and deep-seated thread of opinion that sees the US response to 11 September as part of a continuum of action over some decades. One analysis, published soon after the attacks on New York and Washington, condemns them as horrific, despicable and unpardonable, but cautions against an automatic 'iron fist' response that ignores the underlying context. It points to the frequent use of indiscriminate force by the United States, not least in Korea and Vietnam, and to the bitter mood throughout much of the Middle East and South West Asia, directed partly at the United States because of its perceived dominance of the region but also against autocratic states dependent on continuing US support. The analysis concludes:

> The only response that will really contribute to global security and peace is for Washington to address not the symptoms but the roots of terrorism. It is for the United States to re-examine and substantially change its policies in the Middle East and the Third World, supporting for a change arrangements that will not stand in the way of the achievement of equity, justice and genuine national sovereignty for currently marginalized peoples. Any other way leads to endless war.[6]

A report from the South Centre, published three months after the 11 September attacks, and with the war in Afghanistan continuing, summed up the mood among many Southern opinion formers. The 'war against terror' is seen alongside Northern dominance of the international financial institutions such as the IMF, the World Bank and the WTO, as well as attitudes to climate change and the tardy and thoroughly limited progress on debt relief.

> Increasing numbers in the South perceive the evolving situation as no less than modern imperialism, using the full panoply of mechanisms to bend the will and shape the global order to suit the preferences and need of the major advanced industrial nations. Moreover, this new

imperialism is largely unhindered, in fact it is even aided and abetted, by the multilateral mechanisms developed over the past five decades.

Growing resentment in the South at the sense of powerlessness in the face of Northern arrogance and impunity breeds frustration, which hardly provides fertile ground for development or peace or building the international community. Now, the fear of speaking up in defence of one's own interests has been further exacerbated by the new dictum 'You are either with us or against us'.[7]

Such views will find virtually no favour in Washington, representing, as they do, quite fundamental contradictions to the current world view. Yet they represent views that are widespread right across the majority world away from the North Atlantic states, even if they will have little or no effect on current US policy.

Conclusions

The analysis originally developed in this book was essentially looking to the longer-term condition of international security. The view was that socio-economic divisions and environmental constraints would lead to considerable problems of conflict and insecurity over a 10- to 30-year timescale, that the Western security paradigm of maintaining control would prove illusory as the innate vulnerabilities of advanced urban industrial societies became evident. On this analysis it was assumed that there would be an opportunity, perhaps over the next ten years, to rethink the security paradigm and develop a far more rounded approach to common security. Issues such as co-operation for sustainable development and environmental management might therefore come to the fore. As a consequence, the socio-economic divide could narrow, excesses of environmental conflict might be avoided, and a more global agenda for peace could evolve. In short, there was time to make a difference before the existing paradigm ran into severe difficulties, making it apparent that it might not be sustainable.

What, then, is the relevance of 11 September and its aftermath to this analysis, and will it make a re-examination of the paradigm more or less likely? The first point to emphasise is that the al-Qaida attacks on New York and Washington did not come from a desperate underclass of marginalised people across the globe, driven to violence by an utter frustration at the possibilities of peaceful change. Even so, the context of the development of the network does show a relevance to the present analysis in three respects.

One, inevitably, is that the atrocities of 11 September have demon- strated all too clearly the manner in which a remarkably powerful state has been shown to be vulnerable to paramilitary attack, and a second does relate closely to the theme of environmental constraints. The al-Qaida motivation against the United States arises only marginally from US support for Israel and much more fundamentally because of opposition to the US military presence in Saudi Arabia. This, in turn, is due to the huge geo-strategic importance of the Persian Gulf region, and its oil supplies, to the United States and its allies.

Finally, al-Qaida and similar networks draw much of their support from the 'demographic bulge' of young people growing up in the Middle East and South West Asia who see themselves as marginalised and with diminishing prospects. This is not to deny the substantial support that such networks receive from wealthy individuals – itself a reflection of the antagonism towards Western influence. Furthermore, many of those directly involved at the higher levels of the organisation are well educated. In one sense, the attacks of 11 September really are an illustration of that uncomfortable 'revolution of frustrated expectations'.

Perhaps the real significance is that 11 September brought forward the question of 'losing control' by some years, perhaps even a decade, and the result appears to be an utterly determined endeavour to regain control. This came through most clearly in President Bush's State of the Nation address to Congress in January 2002, where he made it clear that the United States was now engaged in a long-term war on terror that would take in opposition to the United States wherever it was perceived, naming three countries in particular – Iraq, North Korea and Iran – as an 'axis of evil'. The attitude is 'if you are not with us, you are against us' and the United States requires its allies to work with it in ensuring a stable world in the Western image, with the ready and persistent use of force available to ensure such stability, as and when required.

Put bluntly, from the perception of the Bush administration, majority opinion in the United States, and some opinion in Europe, 11 September has strongly re-inforced the paradigm and made it far less likely that a wider analysis will be considered. This is, in particular, in marked contrast to the more common view in the rest of the world, where sympathy for the United States over the losses of 11 September is still there, but there is a real fear of a new vision for the twenty-first century in which an unjust and unstable *status quo* is rigorously maintained.

For the future, then, what is a reasonable prognosis? Although it is a rather crude device to present it in terms of just two choices, it is a helpful simplification. One possibility is that 11 September re-inforces all of the core elements of the security paradigm, and that the major effort is concentrated on maintaining control of an unstable and evidently violent world. Defence budgets will rise, counter-insurgency and anti-terrorism action will come centre stage, bases will be maintained in 'regions of potential threat' and long-range force projection will be enhanced. There will be little deference to international law or multilateral agreements, and root causes of violence will be largely ignored.

Given the international trends towards greater divisions, and the increasing frustrations of a marginalised majority, this will most probably lead to the development of more radical and extreme social movements, leading to further events, possibly much more devastating than the massacres of 11 September. These, in turn, will be likely to lead to a redoubling of efforts to maintain control, a never-ending war indeed.

The other possibility is that the trauma of 11 September encourages individuals, citizen groups, intellectuals and indeed political leaders to recognise the long-term security significance of what happened and to re-double efforts to move to a more equitable and stable world. This should not be dismissed as idealism as there are very many signs of this, as indicated in the previous chapter. Indeed, one of the more hopeful features of the post-11 September analysis, understandably much more common outside of the United States, was concern to address root causes of political violence instead of concentrating on control of the symptoms.

In the final analysis, it is a matter of choice, and the next decade is likely to prove pivotal in determining the degree of international instability that could prevail for much of the new century. The early effects of 11 September suggest a hardening of the old paradigm, but there is every chance that it may become possible to further analyse and demonstrate the futility of that approach. The responsibility for those in a position to do so, whether activists, academics, politicians or many others, is considerable.

War on Terror and Axis of Evil

The previous chapter, '11 September and the New American Century', was written shortly after President Bush had given his State of the Union address to Congress on 29 January 2002, four months after the 9/11 attacks. The address was akin to a victory celebration, interrupted by over 70 bursts of applause, and given at a time when the Taliban regime in Afghanistan had just been terminated, the al-Qaida movement had been dispersed, and the Bush administration was already beginning to set its sights on regime termination in Iraq. In addition to its emphasis on early victories in the wake of the 9/11 atrocities, the speech was most notable for extending the war on terror to embrace a clutch of rogue states termed an 'axis of evil'. The most significant of these were North Korea, Iran and Iraq:

> States like these, and their terrorist allies, constitute an axis of evil, arming to threaten the peace of the world. By seeking weapons of mass destruction, these regimes pose a grave and growing danger. They could provide these arms to terrorists, giving them the means to match their hatred. They could attack our allies or attempt to blackmail the United States. In any of these cases, the price of indifference would be catastrophic.[1]

Later in the speech, he placed particular emphasis on the need for decisive action if cooperation to limit the risk of proliferation was to fail:

> We'll be deliberate, yet time is not on our side. I will not wait on events, while dangers gather. I will not stand by, as perils draw closer and closer. The United States of America will not permit the world's most dangerous regimes to threaten us with the world's most destructive weapons.[2]

Four months later, President Bush addressed a graduation ceremony at the West Point Military Academy, using the opportunity to place further emphasis on the need for pre-emptive action against perceived threats.

Concentrating first on the dangerous developments in irregular warfare he pointed out that:

> Enemies in the past needed great armies and great industrial capabilities to endanger the American people and our nation. The attacks of September the 11th required a few hundred thousand dollars in the hands of a few dozen evil and deluded men. All of the chaos and suffering they caused came at much less than the cost of a single tank. The dangers have not passed. This government and the American people are on watch, we are ready, because we know the terrorists have more money and more men and more plans.[3]

It was not enough to seek to defend the homeland – the response would have to go well beyond that:

> ...the war on terror will not be won on the defensive. We must take the battle to the enemy, disrupt his plans, and confront the worst threats before they emerge. In the world we have entered, the only path to safety is the path of action. And this nation will act.[4]

The key issue was that such action could not just be against presumed sites of terrorist preparation but would also apply to states accused of harbouring terrorists:

> All nations that decide for aggression and terror will pay a price. We will not leave the safety of America and the peace of the planet at the mercy of a few mad terrorists and tyrants. We will lift this dark threat from our country and from the world.[5]

In the months that followed, the emphasis in Washington moved markedly towards regime termination in Iraq, and as this posture evolved, so the mood in Western Europe started to move against the Bush administration. This was in marked contrast to the widespread support for the United States in the immediate wake of the 9/11 attacks, although three key states remained committed to the US approach – Italy, Spain and Britain. Germany, France and several other states had governments that were beginning privately to express concern at what was seen as the increased belligerence of the US attitude, but this was much more strongly expressed in the development of a strong anti-war movement, including in those countries such as Britain whose governments were willing to offer support.

Al-Qaida in 2002

During the course of 2002, two issues stood out in contrast to the move towards war with Iraq, both of them making it difficult to understand the preoccupation of the Bush administration with that country. These were the increased activity of the supposedly dispersed al-Qaida movement, and the early indications of problems ahead in Afghanistan.

Although there was a sustained tendency during the eight years of the Bush administration to see the al-Qaida movement as a narrowly hierarchical and precisely organised entity, this was always a distortion, in that it variously had elements of a consortium, a franchise, a generalised and dispersed movement or even an idea.[6] Even so, the many groups loosely connected with al-Qaida had engaged in a range of anti-American attacks prior to 9/11. These included attacks on US service personnel in Riyadh in the early 1990s, the first World Trade Center attack in 1993, the bombing of a US Air Force barracks block at the Dhahran base in Saudi Arabia in 1996, the attacks on US embassies in Nairobi and Dar es Salaam in 1998 and the bombing of the *USS Cole* in Aden harbour in 2000.

In comparison with these actions over an eight year period, the movement was far more active in the months following its apparent dispersal and demise in Afghanistan. In March 2002, an attack on worshippers at a church in Islamabad killed 5 people and injured 46, and a month later a party of German tourists visiting a synagogue at Djerba in Tunisia was attacked, killing 14 Germans and 7 local people as well as injuring 24 people. One month later, 11 French naval technicians and 3 Pakistanis were killed in a bomb attack outside a hotel in Karachi and 23 other people were injured. The French technicians were working on a contract with the Pakistani Navy. In June there was an attack on the US consulate in the same city, which killed 11 people and injured at least 45. Later that year there were four major attacks in three countries. In October, an attempt was made to sink a French oil tanker, the *Limburg*, off the coast of Yemen, and later that month 202 people were killed and 300 injured in an attack on the Sari nightclub in Bali. Although most of those killed were Balinese or Australians, the nightclub was often frequented by US service personnel. The following month an attempt was made to shoot down an Israeli tourist jet taking off from Mombassa Airport in Kenya, and a nearby hotel at Kikambala that was regularly used by Israeli tourists was bombed, killing 11 people and injuring 50.

While these attacks were widely reported and seen as evidence of expanded al-Qaida capabilities, the emphasis in Washington remained on Iraq, with frequent claims that the Saddam Hussein regime was in some manner linked with the movement. There was also an assumption that the war in Afghanistan was over and that the country would make a peaceful transition to a pro-western state, albeit with a long-term US military presence at two large bases near Kabul and Kandahar. A further advantage to the United States was that the process of terminating the Taliban regime had involved a series of military agreements with Central Asian republics that collectively gave the United States greater influence in a region rich in oil and gas reserves which would otherwise be more under the influence of Russia and China.

The al-Qaida movement and its motives

The further activities of the al-Qaida movement after the 9/11 attacks did not mean that it was purely operating on a short-term timescale, consolidating its status after the initial impact. Instead, the movement was and is a phenomenon with a very long timescale for achieving its aims.[7] Originating mainly in the immediate aftermath of the collapse of Soviet control of Afghanistan at the end of the 1980s, the movement looked to Islamist thinkers such as Sayyid Qutb for its motivation and purpose. Having achieved, from its own perspective, the collapse of the Soviet Union following its defeat at the hands of the mujahideen, al-Qaida's ideologues were stunned at the willingness of the Royal House of Saud to accept US aid in evicting Iraqi forces from Kuwait in 1991, and even more bitterly opposed to the subsequent and potentially long-term presence of US military forces in Saudi Arabia – the Kingdom of the Two Holy Places.

Following his forced departure from Saudi Arabia, where he was seen as a security threat, Osama bin Laden moved during the 1990s to Sudan and then returned to Afghanistan where he and his associates developed the al-Qaida movement. It was, at this stage, primarily a movement that was bringing in volunteers from across the region and training them to fight alongside the Taliban movement as it sought to wrest control of Afghanistan from the Northern Alliance of warlords. This was still largely the situation in early 2001, when the 9/11 attacks were being planned by the Hamburg group, but al-Qaida was already a movement with short-term aims and a long-term goal, all of which went well beyond supporting the Taliban.

Those short-term aims comprise the eviction of 'crusader' forces from the Middle East, with Saudi Arabia being the most important together with the termination of the House of Saud as being pro-western, elitist and corrupt, and entirely unacceptable as the Keeper of the Two Holy Places. Other regimes in the region also have to be replaced with proper Islamist rule, with the Mubarak regime in Egypt being a prime candidate, and there is visceral opposition to the 'Zionist occupation of Palestine'. There is also support for other Islamist movements including the Chechen rebels, the southern Thailand separatists and the Kashmiris. All of the apostate regional governments, as well as foreign forces present in the region constitute the 'near enemy', and the movement has even been able to claim some success when US military forces were required by the Saudi authorities to leave the kingdom in the early 2000s. There is little expectation that the other aims can be achieved rapidly, with timescales measured in decades rather than years.

Beyond these relatively short-term aims is the longer-term desire to establish a new Islamist Caliphate, initially embracing the Sunni Arab Middle East, with ultimate prospects for a global entity, but not within many decades. Because of its substantial involvement in the Middle East and especially with its fundamental support for the Zionist state of Israel, the United States is regarded as the fundamental obstacle to the Islamist cause and is therefore seen as the 'far enemy'.

It is realistic to see al-Qaida as a transnational revolutionary movement with clearly defined political aims, instead of an illogical and even nihilist movement. What does differentiate it from revolutionary movements rooted in ideological foundations that may be political or ethnic, is that its religious context provides an eschatological sense of timelessness. Unlike most revolutionary movements, al-Qaida has a divine foundation which means its leadership does not see success as inevitable in its lifetime.

In this context, though, supporting and encouraging the 9/11 attackers still had defined aims. One of these was undoubtedly to demonstrate the capacity of the movement to strike at the very heart of the far enemy, therefore signalling the power of the movement and encouraging an outpouring of support from the *umma*. More specifically, though, there was the enticing prospect that such an extraordinary blow to a superpower would be certain to result in a crushing military reaction, most likely rooted in the termination of the Taliban regime and a full-scale military occupation of Afghanistan.[8]

Afghanistan – aftermath of regime termination

The decision to terminate the Taliban regime was taken immediately after the 9/11 attacks and was hugely popular in the United States. An opinion poll in the US taken in early November when the war was still under way showed more than half of those polled would support the war even if it cost the US forces 10,000 casualties and lasted more than two years.[9] In practice, though, a full-scale ground war in Afghanistan was not practicable in the immediate aftermath of 9/11 since it would take many months to bring the troops and supplies in from Pakistan and winter would meanwhile intervene. From the start the US military therefore opted for a different approach which involved using its airpower advantage, the actions of Special Forces and, in particular, the re-arming of the Northern Alliance.

Within three weeks of the start of the war, the US Air Force was operating F-15 strike aircraft from a base in Uzbekistan, and supplies were reaching Northern Alliance militias in large quantities, principally from Russia but financed by the United States. In the first six weeks of the war, 13,500 tons of bombs were dropped on the country, but one US analysis indicated that there had already been at least 1,000 Afghan civilians killed and several thousand more died through hunger, disease or exposure. By the end of November, the war appeared to be over as the Northern Alliance moved south, but throughout the country Taliban militias melted away with most of their weapons intact. Of greater concern were reports that al-Qaida paramilitaries had begun to leave Afghanistan as early as two weeks into the war. Indeed, when US Special Forces were able to probe the al-Qaida training camps later in the year, they were deserted.

One analysis, written at the start of December, suggested that a long war was already in prospect:

> Put bluntly, an apparent US victory achieved before the end of this year may, in reality, be just a further stage in a longer-term civil war in Afghanistan. This is supported by the likelihood that many Taliban and al-Qaida units have already crossed the border into north-west Pakistan, where there is substantial local support for their position, support no doubt fuelled by recent treatment of Taliban prisoners.[10]

The dispersal of Taliban and al-Qaida units, along with the attacks described above, did little to focus US attention on Afghanistan, partly because the Bush administration expected other countries to play a major post-war recovery role. UN diplomats and other analysts pointed to the risk of a security vacuum developing in the absence of a large peacekeeping and stabilisation force, with an estimated 30,000 such personnel being required as a matter of urgency. In the event, European states were not willing to make such a commitment. The International Security Assistance Force that was established had barely 5,000 troops assigned to it and placed most of its emphasis on providing security in Kabul and some of the northern regions, away from the Pashtun provinces in the south which had been the main areas of Taliban strength.

On reflection, what is more surprising is that the Bush administration was unwilling to acknowledge that an insurgency was developing in Afghanistan as early as the spring of 2002, with combat troops from the US Army and Marine Corps having to be deployed in a series of operations. While these attracted little media coverage in the United States and Western Europe, they were, on occasions, substantial and violent engagements.

One example was an extensive series of operations near Gardez, just 100 miles south of Kabul and a long way from the traditional areas of Taliban strength around Kandahar in the south. As the *Washington Post* reported at the time:

> An opening advance on Saturday by Afghan and US Special Forces, intended to flush out suspected al Qaeda fighters in the town of Sirkanel, was thwarted when enemy gunfire kept coalition troops pinned down

for hours. Elements of the 10th Mountain Division also were reported stopped in their tracks Saturday in a 12-hour battle outside the town of Marzak. Mortar rounds and rocket-propelled grenades landed as close as 15 yards to their position, and 13 American soldiers were wounded. 'I don't think we knew what we were getting into this time, but I think we're beginning to adjust', said Sgt. Mark Neilsen, 48, from Indianapolis.[11]

A number of US helicopters were damaged in the operation and five Cobra attack helicopters and two UH-53 transport helicopters had to be flown in from the amphibious support ship *USS Bon Homme Richard* in the Indian Ocean. US and French strike aircraft dropped 450 bombs in the first four days of the conflict.

As the insurgency began to develop, it became apparent that counter-insurgency operations were being compromised. In August 2002, US forces launched Operation Mountain Sweep, which involved 2,000 US and coalition troops in a large-scale attempt to clear guerrilla units from a series of towns and villages. The operation lasted eight days but was a failure – yielding just ten prisoners, two caches of documents and a van load of weapons. There was a suspicion that while there had indeed been guerrilla forces in the area, they had advanced warning of what became a thoroughly compromised operation and had largely dispersed. An analysis published in early September 2002 reported:

> Al-Qaida claims that it has penetrated the major coalition operating bases such as Bagram Air Base north of Kabul, and that it has support in much of the country, but especially in the Pashtun areas. These claims are quietly accepted by senior US military in the country, as is the fact that guerrilla units have active supply lines and ample logistical support, both made easier through operating in parts of Afghanistan where there is a deep-seated antagonism to US forces.[12]

This assessment was paralleled by an analysis from the independent Houston-based security company STRATFOR:

> Sources say that there are nightly attacks on U.S. troops, which is confirmed by non-governmental organizations in the country, who add that increased restrictions have been placed on the movement of off-duty U.S. forces. U.S. troops reportedly control only the towns where they have bases, and then only in daylight, while Karzai's government reportedly controls only parts of Kabul.[13]

Thus, al-Qaida's aim of trapping the United States in Afghanistan, much as the Soviet Union had been crippled in the 1980s, may have been unsuccessful in the short term, but within eight months of the termination of the Taliban regime, there were early signs of a Taliban resurgence.

Meanwhile the al-Qaida movement was aided by three other factors during the course of 2002. One was the effect of detailed media coverage of civilian casualties in Afghanistan, especially through satellite TV news channels such as Al Jazeera. This was a continual source of anger across the Islamic world, but was heightened by the extensive Israeli military assaults in the West Bank during April and May, leading to much loss of life and material destruction. Transcending these, though, was the extraordinary manner in which the United States now extended its war on terror to encompass regime termination in Iraq. This was a process that was expected to be quick and easy but ended up providing an unexpected and sustained advantage to the al-Qaida movement.

Motives for war

Within three weeks of the start of the Iraq War in March 2003, the Saddam Hussein regime had been terminated. A Coalition Provisional Authority (CPA) was subsequently established, under the management of the Pentagon rather than the US State Department. Although many analysts later considered that the roots of the subsequent war lay in a total lack of post-conflict planning, the CPA under Paul Bremer was clear as to what was planned and expected. Iraqis would welcome the coalition as a liberating force, a highly efficient free-market economy would rapidly be established that would include a low level flat-rate tax system, there would be wholesale privatisation of state enterprises with investment opened up to international companies and a minimum of financial regulation. The new Iraq would function as a democracy which, it was assumed, would be pro-American and would have its security ensured by the long-term presence of substantial US military bases. The rapid development of a post-Saddam Iraq would be guaranteed by the revitalisation of the country's oil industry. With one tenth of the world's oil, Iraq would quickly develop into an economically powerful free-market liberal democracy, demonstrating the values of the New American Century and serving as a model for a democratic transition across the region.

From a neoconservative perspective, the value of removing this particular rogue regime lay in two geopolitical aspects. The first was its proximity to Iran, the one state in the region that was regarded as even more of a threat to US interests than Iraq. With over 70 million people, large oil and gas reserves, a presumed nuclear weapons programme and a regime antagonistic to the United States, Iran was regarded as a stronger and more long-term part of the axis of evil than even Iraq. Moreover, the perception of Iran as an implacable enemy stretched well beyond neoconservative circles. This was partly because there was still the legacy of the shock of the unexpected Iranian Revolution when a key ally of the United States, the Shah's regime, had so unexpectedly been terminated. It was also due to the enduring memory of the humiliation of the United States when diplomats and members of their families were held hostage for 444 days during the revolution. This had a particular resonance with the US diplomatic community.

The second aspect was the significance of Persian Gulf oil reserves, making up more than 60 per cent of the world's total. Although Saudi Arabia had by far the largest reserves – some 25 per cent – Iran, Iraq, Kuwait and the United Arab Emirates each had around 10 per cent, with the region as a whole being extraordinarily significant. Furthermore, another 20 per cent of world reserves were held by Russia, Kazakhstan and Venezuela. Because of the depletion of domestic reserves in China, the UK and the US, combined with the existing oil import dependency of almost all of Europe as well as India and Japan, most of the industrialised world and the new emerging economies were becoming more and more dependent on imported oil. While parts of sub-Saharan Africa and South America were significant, they were relatively unimportant compared with the states of the Persian Gulf.

This was the situation in 2002, in the run-up to the Iraq War, and formed part of a much more long-term 'resource shift' (see pages 90–2) as industrialised economies were becoming more dependent on primary commodity imports, and it remains the case now. Moreover, Persian Gulf oil reserves have been recognised as a security issue for the United States since as far back as the early 1940s. They were given a substantial boost by the oil price increases of 1973–74 which led to the establishment of the Rapid Deployment Force in 1980 and its later expansion into US Central Command by the Reagan administration in 1984.[14]

The concern of neoconservatives and others in Washington in the early 2000s was that too many of the countries in the Persian Gulf region were either opposed to United States interests or were of dubious reliability. Iraq under Saddam Hussein was unacceptable, with a strong lobby in Washington having argued for his removal in the closing years of the Clinton administration,[15] and Iran was even more reviled. There was also concern over the reliability of Saudi Arabia, especially in the aftermath of the Saudi reaction to Desert Fox in 1998. This military operation had involved a major programme of air raids into Iraq, possibly coinciding with an intended internal coup against the Saddam Hussein regime. Its success depended partly on the use of the US Air Force's long-range F-15E strike aircraft based in Saudi Arabia, but the Saudi authorities refused to countenance the use of their territory as a base for combat operations. What was of even greater concern was their refusal to allow the USAF to re-deploy the F-15Es to bases in other countries in the region.

Thus in a region containing most of the world's oil, two of the five key states were opposed to the United States and one was of doubtful reliability. Terminating the Saddam Hussein regime would not only give the United States the strongest of allies in the heart of the region, but it would also put considerable pressure on Iran. Indeed, with Afghanistan to the east and Iraq to the west, both with a major US military presence, and with the US Navy's Fifth Fleet dominant in the Persian Gulf and the Arabian Sea, the Tehran regime would surely be cautious – the road to Tehran really did run through Baghdad.

A war too far?

From the very start of the 2003 war to terminate the Saddam Hussein regime, events took an unexpected turn. There was confidence that an initial 'shock and awe' air assault using cruise missiles and F-117A 'stealth' strike aircraft might cause the collapse of the regime, and there was even greater confidence that coalition troops would be welcomed in southern Iraq by the Shi'a communities that had suffered so much under Saddam Hussein. In the event, regime termination required an invasion with ground troops, some of them meeting opposition immediately they crossed the border from Kuwait towards Basra in the south. Within three weeks, US troops had moved right up to Baghdad and had taken the city, with the regime collapsing, but this apparent victory concealed three issues.

The first was that while the massive coalition firepower advantage resulted in the decimation of the regular troops of the Iraqi Republican Guard in the open country south of Baghdad, these were no longer the elite troops of the Iraqi Army of the early 1990s. Regime concern over their loyalty had resulted in the formation of an inner core of four brigades of the Special Republican Guard. These, together with troops linked to the five intelligence and security organisations, were far more important and there is little evidence that they took any substantive part in the resistance. Instead they largely melted away, many of them forming a core part of the insurgency that subsequently evolved.

The second development was the rapidity with which supply lines came under attack. Within days of the start of the rapid advance towards Baghdad, the US Army and Marine Corps found themselves having to divert considerable resources to the protection of these supply lines in the face of repeated attack from irregular forces, some of them even prepared to use suicide attacks. By the second week of the war, the equivalent of three infantry brigades were involved in logistics protection, roughly half of all the combat US troops in the country. This was an unexpected development, largely missed by most analysts at the time, but a powerful marker of what was to come.

The final issue was the almost immediate failure of public order, especially in Baghdad, with widespread looting and the collapse of public services. A regime weakened by years of sanctions disappeared underground almost overnight and the occupying power was incapable of maintaining control. Moreover, within weeks of the outbreak of the war, a substantial insurgency was developing. Even as President Bush made his 'mission accomplished' speech on the flight deck of the *USS Abraham Lincoln* there were persistent attacks on coalition troops and, within four months, attacks in Iraq on the Jordanian consulate, the Red Cross building and the United Nations headquarters had all demonstrated that the coalition was losing control.

Aftermath

In the first six years of the Iraq War, independent assessments pointed to at least 98,000 civilians killed, with perhaps as many as 200,000 wounded, many of them maimed for life.[16] In seeking to curtail and control the insurgency, coalition forces detained 120,000 people without trial, some of them for several years. At any one time during most of this period, at least 20,000 people were in prison. Across Iraq there were huge movements of refugees with around 4 million people forced to leave their homes. Although over half of them were displaced within Iraq, many sought refuge in other countries, including over a million in Syria. During the six years the US leadership faced opposition to its use of torture, prisoner abuse and rendition, losing much support across the world. By early 2009, there was relative peace in Iraq, but this was not without frequent bombings and assassination attempts.

Of the many aspects of what became a complex conflict, three stand out in helping to explain what happened – the collapse of a full international coalition, the impact of US casualties, and the regional impact of the involvement of Israel.

The failure of coalition

By August 2003, the US forces in Iraq were facing major security problems and were in urgent need of support. Given the unpopularity of the war in many Western countries, there was little likelihood of European allies committing more troops and there were few other countries that had armed forces sufficiently versatile to be able to send large numbers of troops to Iraq. To commit a full division of combat troops – more than 15,000 personnel – while allowing for troop rotations, a country would have to have the ability to spare some 40,000 fully trained and disciplined troops in addition to meeting its own security requirements. The only country that was politically acceptable to the United States and was in a position to do this was India, and the Bush administration therefore sought such support. The intention was for India to commit a division to north-eastern Iraq, replacing US troops that could then be moved to the more dangerous insurgency areas in the centre of the country, especially around Baghdad.

The Indian Prime Minister, Atal Behari Vajpayee, led the nationalist BJP party and would have gained three advantages from this move. One was that it would consolidate India's position as a close ally of the United States at a time when Pakistan was gaining support from Washington through aiding US military dispositions in Afghanistan. Secondly, India's increasing dependence on Persian Gulf oil would be aided by an Indian military commitment to the region and, finally, it would be a powerful demonstration to China of India's ability to project military force.

In the event, though, there was substantial domestic opposition to such an involvement, with opinion polls showing powerful opposition to the Iraq War. Moreover, the Vajpayee government was facing elections in five of India's states later that year, and a general election was due in 2004.[17] In spite of powerful urging from Washington, the Indian government was unable to oblige. The effect of this was profound because it meant that there was no way in which the United States could expand its 'coalition of the willing'. Instead, in the years that followed a number of countries quietly withdrew from Iraq, turning the whole operation from what could be claimed as a thorough-going international coalition into a war fought very largely by the United States. A few states retained a presence, but only Britain kept a brigade-sized deployment through towards the end of the decade, with the British contingent at Basra finally being withdrawn in 2009.

Casualties and firepower

As the war developed, US Army and Marine Corps units assigned to Iraq found themselves facing a rapidly developing urban guerrilla war against opponents who had ready access to a wide range of weapons and munitions. Prior to the occupation there had been an assumption that the Saddam Hussein regime kept very strict control over its own armaments, maintaining them in a few securely guarded depots and restricting access to trusted units. In the chaos of the first few weeks after regime termination, many of those depots were inadequately guarded by US troops and were looted, but it also became clear that the regime had spread the arms much more widely than had been realised. It was, in effect, more secure in its support among Sunni communities than Western intelligence agencies had believed, with this loyalty doing much to explain the level of opposition to occupation.

As US forces engaged in counter-insurgency warfare, they began to experience serious casualties. Moreover, the nature of these casualties was different from previous wars such as Vietnam. In late twentieth century conventional warfare, the ratio of those seriously injured to those killed was typically about 3:1. By the time of the Iraq War that had changed, at least for US forces. Sustained improvements in combat medicine included new anti-clotting agents, better training for front-line troops, early stabilisation of wounded soldiers, rapid casualty evacuation by helicopter and early air-lifting of critically injured soldiers to Ramstein military hospital in Germany all resulted in a much higher survival rate. This was further enhanced by the development and use of body armour.

The overall effect of this was that the ratio of those seriously injured to those killed moved to at least 6:1 and even 7:1. This was very positive in that far more people were surviving, but their injuries were often appalling, especially in terms of loss of limbs and injuries to the face, neck and groin. The relatively low death toll therefore disguised a substantial human cost, and this had a profound impact on the attitudes and combat tactics of those on the front line. To put it bluntly, their major advantage lay in the extraordinary firepower they could bring to bear on their opponents, but this was an enemy immersed in a civilian population, often in crowded urban areas. The issue of civilian casualties was there from the start – the Pentagon had expected an easy victory, yet almost from Day One it found otherwise.

Three examples illustrate this and they are, in a real sense, fully understandable given the predicament of the young American soldiers and Marines. Right at the start of the war, as Marines entered Baghdad, they came up against irregular opposition. The *International Herald Tribune* reported one incident:

> Caught in the crossfire, according to a chilling account by an Associated Press reporter, were a number of pedestrians, including an old man with a cane, looking confused. When he failed to heed three warning shots by the Marines, they killed him. A red van and an orange-and-white taxi were also riddled with bullets when they failed to heed warning shots.[18]

A year later the city of Fallujah west of Baghdad was regarded as a seat of the insurgency and on 13 April 2004 there was a very violent incident in which a Marine Corps convoy was ambushed in the city, with some vehicles getting isolated from the main group and forcing 17 Marines to take refuge from intensive attack in nearby buildings. A substantial force, supported by air power, was sent in to extricate them and what followed was a three-hour battle in which the 17 Marines were rescued, some of them wounded. A *Washington Post* journalist was embedded with the Marine forces outside the city and reported what happened next. Before dawn the next day:

AC-130 Spectre gunships launched a devastating punitive raid over a six-block area around the spot where the convoy was attacked, firing dozens of artillery shells that shook the city and lit up the sky. Marine officials said that the area was virtually destroyed and that no further insurgent activity has been seen there.[19]

Note that this was a punitive raid, launched some hours after the incident, in which scores of houses were destroyed in a densely populated city, almost certainly with large numbers of civilians killed and injured in the process.

Another incident indicates the pressures that US troops were under. Later in 2004, a US army unit on patrol in the city of Baquba was involved in a violent confrontation with insurgents. It had earlier taken casualties but on this occasion killed some of the insurgents. According to a journalist embedded with the soldiers, the bodies of the insurgents were then tied to the bonnets of the unit's trucks and paraded through the city. This extraordinary action was born out of the intense frustration felt by the soldiers and by a determination to show to the local people that insurgency would not be tolerated. The actual impact was to produce a sullen and resentful crowd that watched as the bodies of local young men were paraded like animals shot by a hunting party.

All of these incidents are grim reminders of what actually happens in any war but is rarely reported. They are not in any way typical of the United States alone, and Iraqi insurgents used even more extreme tactics, but to many Iraqis what made the behaviour of the US forces different was that the United States was seen as an occupying power. Moreover, evidence eventually emerged that over the first five years of the war, the use of air power was the one tactic that caused the highest level of civilian casualties.

In April 2009, a detailed analysis of civilian casualties was published in one of the world's premier journals, *The New England Journal of Medicine*, based on the extensive civilian casualty database developed by the Iraq Body Count (IBC) nongovernmental organisation. The authors analysed 14,196 incidents in which 60,481 civilians were killed violently, and, according to the lead author, Dr Madelyn Hicks of King's College, London, 'By linking a large number of deaths to the particular weapons used in specific events, the IBC database offers a unique opportunity for detailed analysis of the public health impact of different forms of armed violence on Iraqi civilians.'[20]

Examining all the different kinds of incidents, including small arms, roadside bombs, suicide bomb, mortars and air strikes, one of the worst rates of killing was achieved by suicide bombers, with 16 civilian deaths per incident. This might be expected given the frequent deliberate intention to kill as many people as possible, often in crowded market places. What is surprising, though, is that the analysis showed that air strikes were even worse with 17 civilian deaths per incident. Furthermore, and because of the detailed nature of the IBC primary research, data on many of the incidents included the gender and age of the victims. According to the report, 46 per cent of victims of known gender were female and 39 per cent of victims of known age were children.

The Israel factor

One further factor in the evolving Iraq War had a major impact across the Middle East, even if it was almost entirely unrecognised in Western Europe and the United States. This was the need for the US military to engage with Israel as they struggled to contain the insurgency. There has long been a close relationship between the Pentagon and the Israeli Defence Forces (IDF). By the early 2000s, the Israeli Air Force was largely equipped with US F-15 and F-16 strike aircraft and there was close collaboration over Israel's Arrow ballistic missile defence system. There was somewhat less collaboration between the US Army and Israeli ground forces but the problems in Iraq during the course of 2003 convinced many in the Pentagon that Israeli experience of controlling Palestinian paramilitary opposition had to be fully utilised.

A series of meetings took place in Israel in early December, 2003, when the head of the Israeli Ground Forces Command, Major-General Yiftah Ron-Tal hosted a number of meetings with key US military personnel. These included the Commander of the US Army's Training and Doctrine Command (TRADOC), General Kevin Byrnes, the deputy commander of TRADOC's Futures Center, Major-General Robert Mixon Jr, and the commander of the US Army's Infantry School at Fort Benning, Georgia, Brigadier-General Benjamin Freakley. The well-informed US military journal, *Defense News*, reported that

> the goals were twofold: to strengthen cooperation among US and Israeli ground forces in future warfighting and military modernization planning, and to evaluate ways in which the US military can benefit from operational lessons Israel has accrued during the past 38 months in its ongoing urban, low-intensity conflict with Palestinian militants.[21]

According to an unnamed US military source:

> Israel has much to offer in the technological realm, while operationally, there are obvious parallels between Israel's experiences over the past three years in the West Bank and Gaza and our own post-offensive operations in Iraq. We'd be remiss if we didn't make a supreme effort to seek out commonalities and see how we might be able to incorporate some of that Israeli knowledge into our plans.[22]

From a US perspective it would indeed have been 'remiss' if that experience was not utilised, and following this engagement, US forces used many items of Israeli equipment. In consolidating the relationship the US Army Corps of Engineers went on to construct a large mock Arab town in Israel's Negev Desert, complete with mosque and markets, which was subsequently used by Israeli and US ground troops in training for urban warfare.[23]

The close connection between the United States and Israel, which also involved Israeli training missions in Kurdish areas of Iraq, was of great value to the al-Qaida movement. Although al-Qaida has had little direct connection with the Palestinian cause, Israeli actions in Gaza and the West Bank, and the closeness of the Israeli/American relationship, have been of great propaganda value. With US forces collaborating closely with Israel in their operations in Iraq, the al-Qaida propagandists have been persistent in representing the entire Iraq War as a Crusader/Zionist plot to occupy Iraq and take control of Arab oil. Furthermore, they have been able to remind their supporters that the city of Baghdad was at the centre of the greatest Islamic Caliphate, the Abbasid Caliphate of a thousand years ago. For al-Qaida, the Iraq War was an extraordinary and unexpected gift.

Iraq and al-Qaida

On 7 July 2005, four suicide bombers killed 52 people in London. Given the domestic unpopularity of the Iraq War, the Blair government went to great lengths to insist that the '7/7' attacks were about the global war on terror and had no connection with Iraq. The insistence was not helped by a video recording by one of the bombers, pointing to the carnage in Iraq as one of his motives. Nor was it helped by the repeated insistence of the Bush administration that the war in Iraq was at the epicentre of the war on terror. If al-Qaida supporters could be drawn into Iraq and then defeated, the movement as a whole would suffer a crippling blow.

The actual significance of the Iraq War for the al-Qaida movement is more complicated. The war itself developed into a complex insurgency that had strong elements of anti-occupation resistance, but also evolved into a bitter inter-confessional struggle between militias linked to Sunni and Shi'a communities. Within this was an element of al-Qaida involvement, centred for several years on the Jordanian-born Abu musab al-Zarqawi, who was leader of insurgent groups that merged with al-Qaida para-militaries in late 2004. He was killed two years later but not before the brutality of his leadership lost the al-Qaida movement support across the wider region.

In spite of this, the first six years of the Iraq War was of great benefit to the al-Qaida movement on two main counts. One was the persistent regional reporting of the civilian losses, with the Al Jazeera and Al Arabiya satellite TV channels being particularly effective. These channels tended to be far more graphic in providing TV footage of casualties that would be routinely self-censored in Western countries. This had an impact well beyond the Middle East, not least among South Asian Moslem diasporas in Western Europe.

The other is likely to be of much greater significance in the long term – the development of Iraq into a paramilitary combat training zone. In the 1980s, one of the consequences of the protracted conflict with the Soviet Union in Afghanistan was the creation of a cohort of thousands of paramilitaries with extensive combat experience. While the great majority were Afghans, many of them came from other countries, particularly in the late 1980s. They were drawn from right across south and west Asia and North Africa, and many of those that survived linked up with Osama bin Laden and the evolving al-Qaida movement. Their experience was gained mainly against heavily armed but relatively low morale Soviet forces, most of them conscripts.

Iraq, more recently, served a similar purpose, as many thousands joined the insurgency from other countries. Many of them died, but others survived and moved back to their own countries or on to other conflicts, especially in Afghanistan but also Somalia. What has therefore been created is a new cohort of young paramilitaries, but unlike the previous generation from 1980s Afghanistan, these people have combat experience against professional soldiers and Marines with a huge array of weapons and sensors. Moreover, the experience has been gained primarily in an urban environment. Even if the Iraq War does slowly ease, and a degree of peace is achieved, this cohort of people now exists. What its long-term impact will be is impossible to say, but if the Afghanistan experience is relevant it may take a decade of more to take effect. It may even be the defining legacy of the Iraq War.

Iraqi futures

By the end of 2008, the very high levels of violence in Iraq had started to diminish. In the United States, the Bush administration and the McCain campaign team developed a narrative of victory in which the surge of US troops into Iraq was primarily responsible for the improving situation. Iraq could therefore be represented as a success story with two effects. One was to limit the advantage to the Obama campaign of an unpopular war, and the other was to imply that an Obama administration would prematurely withdraw troops from Iraq, snatching defeat from the jaws of victory.

The conflict in Iraq was, in practice, far more complex than a war in which a surge of US troops was making all the difference. The funding of the Awakening Movement of Sunni militias opposed to the excesses of the al-Qaida paramilitaries was also significant, as was the decision of Moqtada al-Sadr's Mehdi Army to institute a ceasefire. Yet another factor was the break-up of inter-confessional communities into more narrowly based Sunni or Shi'a neighbourhoods. The human cost of the dislocation was high, but one effect was to decrease the potential for inter-group conflict.

Once Barack Obama had won the election in November 2008, his administration proceeded to plan for a US troop withdrawal, the intention being to reduce forces from around 150,000 troops to under 50,000 within two years. An early part of this process would be the withdrawal of US combat troops from Iraqi cities, but this would depend greatly on the violence being controlled. This was by no means assured as, early in 2009, there was an upsurge in violence. More generally, there remained a question as to how long tens of thousands of US troops would remain in Iraq. While the intention appeared to be complete withdrawal by 2011, the establishment of the world's largest embassy in Baghdad combined with major construction projects at several US bases suggested that US forces would remain in considerable numbers for much longer. They might be defined as trainers for Iraqi units, or reserve forces to protect US diplomats and other civilian personnel, but they would still be there.

In spite of the Obama administration's diplomatic overtures to Iran, the region remains of singular importance for the United States because of the massive oil reserves. A complete withdrawal from Iraq, combined with uncertainties over the future of relations with Iran and Saudi Arabia is hardly an attractive outcome. Even if US troops are largely in barracks, they can still be readily represented by al-Qaida propagandists and others as 'ghost' occupiers of a major Islamic state. Given the decades-long timescale of the al-Qaida movement's aims, and the potentially decades-long significance of Persian Gulf oil, the value of Iraq to the al-Qaida movement may be far from over.

Afghanistan and Pakistan

From early 2003 through to the end of 2005, the Bush administration was almost entirely pre-occupied with the war in Iraq. Relatively little attention was paid to Afghanistan where some US troops remained engaged in counter-insurgency operations close to the border with Pakistan. Elsewhere in the country, NATO slowly increased the size of the International Security Assistance Force (ISAF) from its original cohort of around 5,000 troops, but over the three-year period, the security situation in the country deteriorated markedly. In part this was due to the failure of the Karzai administration to reach reasonable standards of governance, widespread corruption and maladministration becoming the norm. It was also due to a slow but steady comeback by Taliban militias, sometimes working with local warlords for mutual benefit. These militias gained considerable benefit from being able to move back and forth between Afghanistan and two areas of Pakistan, the province of Baluchistan to the south and the Federally Administered Tribal Areas (FATA) to the south-east. The FATA districts, especially North and South Waziristan, became safe zones for Taliban militias and also al-Qaida paramilitaries, with occasional military incursions by Pakistani Army units having little effect.

A further factor was the growth in opium poppy cultivation in Afghanistan, especially in the southern Helmand Province, but even more significant was a subtle yet important change in the production of heroin. In the 1990s and early 2000s, a substantial majority of all the opium produced in Afghanistan was exported as raw paste, but by 2005 this had changed dramatically, with perhaps three-quarters refined within the country and exported as the very much higher value heroin. This meant that far more illicit currency was coming into the country, much of it being controlled by Taliban militias and thereby giving them a welcome source of income to finance their operations.

From early 2006 through to the end of the Bush administration, Taliban and other paramilitary groups grew in strength on both sides of the Afghanistan/Pakistan border. In response, NATO forces were increased in number, with Britain eventually committing close to 8,000 troops, mainly into Helmand Province in the south, and Canadian and Dutch troops also heavily involved. Other NATO member states deployed troops in the north and west of Afghanistan but these were primarily in a stabilisation role, with rules of engagement that greatly limited involvement in combat. By the end of 2008, the levels of violence had increased, with US and other forces engaged in a bitter counter-insurgency conflict, especially towards the border with Pakistan.

As Taliban, al-Qaida and other paramilitaries made more general use of western Pakistan as a safe haven, so US forces began to use powerful armed drones such as the Predator and the Reaper, to conduct air raids into Pakistan. The use of these weapons increased substantially by the end of 2008, with reports of some paramilitary leaders being killed, but at the cost of hundreds of civilians dying as well. While there may have been some tacit approval from the Pakistani government, the drone attacks became a source of considerable anger in Pakistan, with a further increase in the anti-American mood. Even so, the Bush administration took the view that this was an essential action for the US military and also developed proposals for a substantial increase in troop levels. The plan that might well have been implemented if John McCain won the 2008 Presidential Election, was for at least 30,000 more US troops to be moved into Afghanistan, with the expectation that other NATO states would increase their deployments. By the time

Barack Obama had been elected, an initial force of 4,000 was about to deploy to Afghanistan and this went ahead with the knowledge of the incoming administration.

The attitude of the Bush administration, which would almost certainly have been embraced by McCain, was that there was no alternative to achieving a military victory in Afghanistan. 30,000 additional troops might help ensure this, but if not, then further reinforcements would be necessary, especially if a progressive withdrawal from Iraq reduced the pressure on the otherwise overstretched US military. In the event, the incoming Obama administration faced three choices. One was to maintain forces at the 2008 levels, thereby suppressing any further gains by the Taliban and any return of the al-Qaida movement into Afghanistan. This might lead to a level of engagement lasting many years, if not decades, but would at least ensure that Afghanistan would not become the seat of a renewed focus of terror. The second choice would be to follow the Bush administration's plans and seek a military victory. A fundamental problem with both of these approaches was that it did not take into account the abilities of opposing forces to operate out of western Pakistan. If either approach was to work, it required continuing military operations in Pakistan, with all the destabilising potential of such a policy.

The third option would be to accept that the presence of Western forces in Afghanistan was one of the major factors actually stimulating the conflict since these were seen essentially as foreign occupiers. This option, in effect, was based on the view that the experiences in Iraq and Afghanistan actually demonstrated that it was no longer politically possible for Western forces to occupy Islamic countries. Just as the colonial era effectively ended with Indian independence and partition in 1947, even if it took some colonial powers at least two more decades to accept this, so the early twenty-first century is an era in which occupation is not tenable. If this view is correct, then withdrawal from Afghanistan becomes the only viable option.

The initial view from the Obama administration was that a reinforced military was necessary. In March 2009, an additional 17,000 troops were earmarked for deployment, with a further 4,000 to work in training the Afghan National Army. With the 4,000 already there, this would add 25,000 troops, and with much smaller additions from other NATO states, this would take the total Western forces in the country towards 90,000. Furthermore, air strikes into western Pakistan continued to be approved, and by April 2009 there were reports that some 700 Pakistanis had been killed in these raids. The one difference between the Bush and Obama policies was that the new administration accepted that there would have to be a negotiated solution that could well involve moderate Taliban elements being incorporated into the Kabul government. For the Obama administration, the belief was that this would only happen from a position of NATO superiority, this running counter to the view that an increased military presence would only incite further opposition, making a negotiated settlement less feasible. If this latter analysis was accurate, then the Afghanistan/Pakistan conflict showed every possibility of outlasting the Obama administration, even if it served two terms.

Old and New Thinking

The central argument in the first edition of *Losing Control* was that there were trans-national trends that would largely determine the nature of conflict over the following thirty years. These trends were the widening socio-economic divide resisted by an increasingly knowledgeable but marginalised majority of the world's people, environmental constraints set largely by the impact of human activity on the global environment, and a marked trend by elite communities to address these issues by seeking to maintain the status quo, through military force if necessary.

Chapter 5 pointed to the manner in which the socio-economic divide had grown from 1960 to the early 1990s. The richest fifth of the world's people saw their share of world wealth grow from 70 per cent in 1960 to 85 per cent in 1991, while over the same period the poorest fifth's share declined from 2.3 per cent to 1.7 per cent (p. 85). It analysed the manner in which the world's trading system had evolved in the colonial era, largely determining the role of the majority world in trade after the end of that era. While recognising the vitality of an increasingly globalised economy it also pointed out that the great majority of new investment in developing countries went into just ten countries, with much of the economic growth concentrated in such countries.

The chapter argued further that while there were many examples of economic growth, not least in what were termed the newly emerging economies, there was a very strong tendency for much of that growth to be concentrated in the hands of a relatively small elite. Overall, the globalised free market that evolved rapidly in the 1980s was fairly successful in delivering economic growth, albeit at a slower rate than in the previous more Keynesian era. What it singularly failed to do was to deliver socio-economic justice and emancipation. A consequence was a greater risk of a 'revolt from the margins', an early example being Sendero Luminoso (Shining Path) in Peru (pp. 86–7).

The human impact on the global environment was analysed in relation to two issues. One was the increasing concentration of physical resources in Southern states. This was a consequence of the 'resource shift', where most of the readily available fuel and non-fuel minerals of the industrialised world were closer to depletion than those of Southern states. Continuing directly from the colonial era, where the principal function of most colonies was the provision of primary commodities for their colonial masters, the resource shift now meant that most industrialised states were increasingly dependent on the South for many key resources.

While this could be a significant source of conflict, especially in singularly resource-rich regions such as the Persian Gulf and Central Africa, of much greater concern is the long-term consequence of climate change. In the late 1990s, climate change was being recognised as a major issue and a possible source of insecurity, but the argument in the first edition of this book was more specific. Pointing to evidence that the tropical and sub-tropical regions would be far more affected by climate change than had been initially realised (pp. 92–3), the argument was made that the most pressing security issue in the coming decades would be the impact of trends such as climate change on a global human community in which most of the people affected were already marginalised, leading to suffering, desperation and the ever-present risk of radical responses.

In this context, the existing security paradigm was challenged as being essentially about maintaining the status quo, but that this was both wrong and unsustainable. Thus, a bitterly divided world would be one in which elite attempts to 'close the castle gates' would be untenable – this could not be done in a globalised world. Specifically, developments in irregular or asymmetric warfare and the innate vulnerability of advanced industrialised states, not least in relation to their critical infrastructure meant that 'liddism' – keeping the lid on conflicts – would prove impossible. A much more emancipating security paradigm had to evolve.

Consequences of 9/11

Shortly after the first edition was published in 2000, there were the 9/11 attacks on New York and Washington, and the George W. Bush administration reacted with massive military force in seeking to regain control. Chapter 8, in a revised edition of the book, was written in the months immediately after 9/11 and pointed to the particular nature of the Bush administration. The view of the twenty-first century as a New American Century was embraced not just by neoconservatives but by many assertive realists in the administration. The 9/11 atrocities were of appalling concern to almost all Americans and to much of the rest of the world, but to the Bush administration they were more than this – they were indicators of the totally unexpected fragility of what had been assumed to be the overwhelming dominance of the world's only superpower as it moved to create the New American Century.

There was thus an urgent need to regain control and the subsequent evolution of the Bush administration's 'war on terror' can best be understood in this context. The previous chapter explored this evolution and pointed to three core problems, all stemming from this need. The first was that the decision to terminate the Taliban regime by force was deeply mistaken. The response to 9/11 should have been to see the atrocities as appalling acts of massive trans-national criminality, with an emphasis on bringing those supporting the perpetrators to justice. This would not have been either quick or easy, but it would have removed, from the start, any idea that the al-Qaida movement was a major force that should be regarded as a global enemy. Instead it would have been seen for what it was, an extreme but essentially criminal movement motivated by an obscure minority interpretation of one of the world's major belief systems.

Once that mistake had been made and the Taliban regime terminated, the al-Qaida movement could represent itself as speaking for the Islamic world in standing up to 'crusader aggression'. The second grievous error followed directly on from the first; this was the ignoring of the security vacuum developing in Afghanistan after regime termination as the Bush administration became utterly preoccupied with Iraq. This eventually allowed the Taliban to re-emerge within Afghanistan and western Pakistan, maintain and further develop links with the al-Qaida movement and other jihadist groups, and begin the process of wearing down foreign forces in Afghanistan.

Finally, the third and most costly mistake was the decision to extend the 'war on terror' to an axis of evil and terminate the Saddam Hussein regime in Iraq. Of all the costs of this terrible conflict – hundreds of thousands of innocent people killed and maimed, millions of refugees, torture and prisoner abuse – there is the additional result that a cadre of combat-trained paramilitaries now exists that has gained its experience against the world's best equipped armed forces. The consequences of that could turn out to be the worst aspect of the war.

The first eight years of the war on terror represent a quite extraordinary example of what might be termed 'old thinking' – a determination to maintain control through military force, with little effort made to determine the motivations of the al-Qaida movement or to seek to counter those conditions which have given it a continuing support. At the time of writing (mid-2009) that war is continuing, with the focus shifting eastwards – perhaps temporarily – to Afghanistan and Pakistan. Given the political changes in Israel, there is the prospect of further conflict in Gaza and Lebanon, and even some risk of a war with Iran. Viewed in a longer-term perspective, the war on terror has been deeply misguided and even disastrous. It has also a relevance to the more global issues analysed earlier in this book, and it is therefore appropriate to return to these and to look at the prospects for a more peaceful world in the coming years. Does the experience of the last eight years make peace more or less likely?

Resources and climate

Although there are substantial issues of conflict relating to specific resources such as diamonds, as well as ferroalloys and some other metallic ores, the most substantial aspect of the potential for resource conflict still lies with energy resources. The concentration of oil reserves in the countries around the Persian Gulf – close to two-thirds of the world's total reserves – makes this the dominant region, and all the indications are that it will become still more significant. Furthermore, the world's natural gas reserves are even more concentrated. Just three countries have 55 per cent of reserves – Russia with 26 per cent, Iran with 15 per cent and Qatar with over 14 per cent. As long as oil and gas make up the dominant internationally traded energy resources, the Persian Gulf will retain its strategic importance. As key industrial states such as the United States and China increase their dependence on oil imports, so the degree of competition for economic and political influence in the region will increase.

There is a long history of US concern with Gulf security. It can be traced from the Roosevelt administration in the early 1940s, the Rapid Deployment Force and then Central Command in the 1970s and 1980s, through to the 1991 Gulf War, the military presence in Saudi Arabia in the 1990s and regime termination in Iraq in 2003. It is highly unlikely to diminish unless there is a fundamental change in US demand for oil and gas. China, too, has a need to maintain energy supplies and takes a more nuanced approach rooted in long-term state-to-state economic agreements, but it also sees the security of the Persian Gulf, along with Central Asia, as essential for its own security.[1] All of this means that the Persian Gulf will remain the one region in the world where there will be intense concern with influence. Even the recession that began in 2008 is unlikely to diminish this for any length of time.

Even so, it is the phenomenon of climate change that is the much greater environmental issue and it is here that there have been numerous developments in the first decade of the twenty-first century. Two factors have been central to what has happened. The first is that for the first eight years the Bush administration was consistent in denying the risks from climate change, withdrawing from the Kyoto protocols and thereby making it well-nigh impossible for them to be further developed. The second factor, in parallel with the first, was the body of evidence that the rate of climate change was increasing.

The accelerating rate of climate change has three aspects. The first is that, as discussed earlier (p. 94), research communities working in areas related closely to public policy have a natural and understandable tendency to be cautious. If there is a requirement to convince political and business communities of action that needs to be taken in response to potential problems such as climate change, then researchers will tend to want wide-ranging and conclusive evidence to underpin their advice. This will be even more the case if that advice leans towards very costly short-term changes to prevent much greater long-term problems. This applies particularly to climate change but an added factor is the requirement for the Intergovernmental Panel on Climate Change (IPCC) to deliver reports that are essentially consensus statements. What has been remarkable in recent years is the way in which the IPCC has systematically increased its estimates of the rate of climate change, as well as the manner in which some of the key climate scientists involved in the IPCC have become so vocal in their warnings of its impact.

The second aspect is that this increasingly vocal concern has come at a time when there have been governmental and industrial interests that have been opposed to the concern over climate change, often to the point of denying any human involvement. The Bush administration was a prime example of this, but the governments of some leading oil-producing countries, and a number of the trans-national oil companies have also been involved, with some of the latter being assiduous in their support for the small minority of climate-change deniers within the scientific community. Given that the world's most powerful state, and some of the world's leading companies, have had an interest in playing down the significance of climate change, it is remarkable what little impact they have had.

This is largely due to the third aspect – that there is evidence of the acceleration of the rate of climate change, especially in the Arctic region, and there are strong indications that some positive feedback processes will increase the rate still further. Two of these concern Arctic sea ice and the status of Arctic permafrost. One of the trends of the past decade has been for an increase in the melting of Arctic sea ice during the summer months. This has already resulted in the opening up of new sea routes, and may lead to the increased availability of new sub-sea mineral resources. Where positive feedback comes in is that as the sea ice melts, the area of open water increases, less solar radiation is reflected back by the ice and more is absorbed by the open water. This speeds up the rate of warming of the sea and of melting of the ice. It is now probable that the Arctic Ocean will be almost completely free of summer sea ice by the middle of the century, and it could happen very much sooner.

The other instance of positive feedback is potentially much more substantial. The Earth's Arctic region is warming up faster than other regions and one effect of this is a thawing of the permafrost. As this happens, frozen vegetation that might have been locked up for many thousands of years thaws out and decomposes. In the process this releases methane gas, which is a much more potent cause of climate change than carbon dioxide. As a result, climate change accelerates, more permafrost melts and still more methane is released.

There may be other instances of positive feedback, including a drying out of tropical rainforests leading to more massive fires releasing more carbon dioxide, and a decrease in the capacity of the oceans to absorb carbon dioxide. There may possibly be examples of negative feedback, but there is little evidence so far that these are emerging. The net effect, therefore, is that climate change is accelerating, leading to the dangerous impacts discussed earlier.[2]

In the short term there is one phenomenon that might have a modest controlling impact. In addition to human-induced climate change there are natural solar and cyclical earth processes that affect climate. One of these is the El Nino effect in the southern hemisphere, especially the Pacific. During the early part of the 2010s there is a strong possibility that the El Nino effect will have a modest cooling impact, somewhat disguising the accelerating process of climate change. In one sense this might be positive in that it might give rather more time to respond to climate change. In another sense, though, there are two problems. One is that it might induce a false sense of security and even promote the denial of climate change. Secondly, as the forthcoming El Nino effect diminishes in the mid-2010s, the combination of the loss of its impact with ongoing human-induced climate change will mean that the process will accelerate greatly. That might finally lead to vigorous action, but only after several years of missed opportunity.

Ten years ago, the climate change scientific community pointed to the need for substantial cuts in carbon emissions, taking them down to 1990 levels and then to as much as 20 per cent below those. Now, the recommendations are far more severe. Bearing in mind that it will be very difficult for newly emerging economies and third world states to develop without some increase in carbon emissions, it follows that existing high level carbon emitters, such as the states of North America and Europe, will be required to make radical cuts. In some cases this is beginning to be recognised, and there is even an acceptance that targets of only three or four years ago were hopelessly inadequate. The UK government, for example, was suggesting an aim of a 60 per cent cut in carbon emissions by 2050, but has now accepted that this must be revised to 80 per cent. This is still hopelessly inadequate in relation to the real need to move to a low carbon economy – 40 per cent cuts by 2015 and 80 per cent cuts by 2025 are more likely to be necessary – but it does at least promote the idea that there will have to be transformative action.

Nearly forty years ago, one of the first studies of the global ecosystem, undertaken at the Massachusetts Institute of Technology, resulted in the publication of the Club of Rome's *Limits to Growth* in 1972.[3] It predicted major environmental and social problems for the world community if resource depletion, pollution and other trends were not changed (p. 88). At the time the study caused substantial debate during which many critics described it as far too pessimistic. In reality *Limits to Growth* was rather cautious in its prognosis and suggested that the major problems would not tend to arise for forty to sixty years. Its timing of dangerous impacts therefore related to the 2010–30 period. Bearing in mind that the world economy went through a difficult period of temporary stagnation in the mid and late 1970s, *Limits to Growth* therefore has a rather good track record of suggesting problems ahead. Indeed, in March 2009, the UK government's chief scientist, Professor John Beddington, warned of a 'perfect storm' in 2030 due to the combined impact of climate change and food, water and energy shortages.[4]

The social divide

In the past decade climate change has come to be recognised as a much more significant issue for human well-being, and there is also an improved understanding of its linkage with security. What needs to be examined is how this relates to the other major trend analysed in the original chapters of this book – the widening socio-economic divide. This is now more significant given the likely impact of the world-wide recession that developed during 2007–08, but even before then there were new indications of the extent of the divide.

One detailed study from the World Institute for Development Economics Research (WIDER) in Helsinki, a research and training centre of the United Nations University, was published in 2006. This was an analysis of the global distribution of household wealth in 2000 which indicated that the richest 10 per cent of the world owned 85 per cent of household wealth whereas the poorest 50 per cent owned barely 1 per cent of the wealth.[5]

Two illustrations of the impact of the divide are recent examples in China and India. In the past three decades China has experienced remarkable levels of economic growth, on occasions exceeding 10 per cent GDP increases per annum. However, much of this has been concentrated in the burgeoning coastal cities that have seen extraordinary construction booms and expanding factories, usually aided by tens of millions of migrant labourers mostly travelling in from the far less developed rural areas. One of the results of China's embracing of a market economy has been the rapid growth of the middle classes, probably now measuring over a hundred million people, but there has also been a widening gap between them and many hundreds of millions more, either living in the relatively underdeveloped rural areas or else working in low-waged employment in factories and on building sites.

Although rarely reported outside China, there are thousands of instances of social unrest, often in the form of unofficial strikes or riots, with these frequently being put down with considerable force. Because of the increase in such unrest the Chinese government introduced a new security force in 2006 to supplement the police and paramilitary groups that were already available to deal with unrest. The new force comprised elite squads of 600 personnel in each of 36 cities across China, equipped with a wide range of control systems, including helicopters.[6] These forces were inaugurated prior to the economic downturn that started the following year in which as many as 26 million migrant labourers were expected to lose their jobs out of a total of 130 million.[7]

A second example comes from India which, in the early years of the new century, has been seen as another potential economic powerhouse, but some of the effects of unbalanced growth have been both unexpected and severe. Over forty years ago there was a revolt in and around the village of Naxalbari in West Bengal. This resulted in the development of the neo-Maoist Naxalite movement but this subsequently fractured and was largely dispersed and defeated within five years. In the past ten years, and against widespread expectations, the Naxalites have come back with considerable violence and are now active in 185 districts located in 17 out of India's 28 states. The driving force behind the Naxalite revival is the relative marginalisation of people in India's poorer districts, and the rebellion became so intense in the early 2000s that the Indian Prime Minister, Manmohan Singh, described the Naxalites in April 2006 as 'the biggest internal security challenge ever faced by our country'.[8]

The Naxalite resurgence in India and the urban insecurity in China both pre-date the world-wide recession that began to develop with the US sub-prime mortgage crisis in 2007, but a more graphic illustration of the kind of impact that crisis might have became apparent in India in February 2009. One of the great successes of India's expanding retail sector was the development of the Subhiksha discount stores. Between 2007 and early 2009, the number of stores expanded tenfold to over 1,650 outlets across the country. In early 2009 the whole enterprise ran into serious financial difficulties, not least in its attempts to raise new bank loans. One early consequence was an inability to pay the companies that provided security guards for the company's stores and warehouses. By early February, many of the companies had withdrawn their personnel and over the weekend of 7–8 February, more than a third of the stores, about 600 in all, were looted.[9]

The Chinese public order control units, the Naxalites in India, and the specific example of the Subhiksha stores are all illustrations of the impact of socio-economic marginalisation, as are examples such as the Zapatistas cited earlier in this book (pp. 95–9). The first two pre-date the economic downturn of the late 2000s but the Subhiksha example is indicative of the reaction likely from the 'knowledgeable margins'. This was also in evidence during the period of sudden food price increases and shortages in 2007–08. These were more serious than any since the world food crisis of 1974, but one of the major differences this time round was the frequency of violent reactions. There were numerous riots and other civil disturbances in many countries, including Bangladesh, Cameroon, Egypt, Ethiopia, Haiti, Indonesia, Ivory Coast, Jordan, Mauritania, Mexico, Morocco and Senegal, whereas in the early 1970s there had been a far more passive response.[10]

These and similar developments are only the more visible indicators of a deeper resentment among marginalised communities that are more educated, more literate and have far greater access to communications technology than ever before. Moreover, over half of the world is now urbanised, making the divisions far more stark and less avoidable, not least in the growth of so many heavily-protected gated communities, some of them akin to medieval walled towns.[11]

What is particularly significant is that the alienated and often violent responses of recent years, and the even greater violence with which they have been repressed, have all evolved during a period of overall economic growth. For more than three decades, there has still been the possibility that there could be economic betterment in the midst of deep social divisions. The indications are that this has now come to an end as we enter a period of relative stagnation that may last up to a decade.

The impact of recession

The recession that took root in 2008 has three main characteristics. The first is that it is global. While most of the initial emphasis was on the sub-prime market crisis in the United States, the crisis spread rapidly through Europe and then across much of Asia, Latin America and Australasia. Secondly, it may have started as a crisis of liquidity and confidence in the financial sector, but the shortages of investment finance and other factors led rapidly to a substantial impact on industrial activity and commercial output. Finally, it is highly unlikely to be of a short duration. The immediate downturn may ease within two years but the very high levels of governmental borrowing in many Western economies is likely to lead to increased taxes and cutbacks in public spending that may last as long as a decade. While this may not be a specific issue for all states, its impact will be world-wide. In a globalised economic system, emerging economies such as China are highly dependent on markets remaining buoyant in the North, and many other Southern states still get the majority of their export earnings from sales of primary commodities such as minerals, fibres and foodstuffs to the North. In short, the impact will be world-wide and sustained.

While this impact will be felt in the old industrialised states of the North, many of these retain a social welfare system, even if it is less comprehensive than two or three decades ago. The impact on the South will be much greater, both because of the far larger numbers of people already on the economic margins, but also because of cuts in development assistance. A World Bank/IMF report released early in 2009 concluded that the financial downturn is creating a 'development emergency', making it even less likely that the 2015 Millennium Development Goals (MDGs) will be reached, modest though they are. Even though Southern countries may maintain growth rates averaging 1.5 per cent, these are insufficient to even match population growth, with some fifty poorer countries expected to see a per capita fall in income, and between 55 and 90 million more people expected to join several hundred million in absolute poverty. According to the *Global Monitoring Report 2009*,[12] the downturn will have a serious and persistent impact on health and education and may cause as many as 200,000 to 400,000 more infant deaths every year up to the MDG target year of 2015.[13]

The main intergovernmental response to the crisis has come from the G20 countries working with the IMF, World Bank and other intergovernmental financial and trade institutions. Some of the more progressive voices in the G20 forum look towards what is termed Global Social Democracy (GSD), responding to the perceived failures of the neo-liberal outlook of the past three decades. It is rooted in the belief that the globalised free market is essentially benign provided it is sufficiently regulated to avoid the grotesque excesses of recent years. A more ordered and controlled world economy is envisaged that prevents increasing inequality, promotes trade provided it does not exacerbate environmental and social problems, radically reduces the debt burden on poorer countries and recognises the need for increased development assistance as well as the world-wide requirement to curb climate change.

While such an approach is substantially different from the experience of recent decades, there are two main problems. The first is that, as Walden Bello has argued, Global Social Democracy is essentially about modifying the existing system, but it is a system that may be so flawed that it is incapable of being sufficiently controlled, let alone changed, to meet the challenges of a deeply divided and environmentally constrained world.[14] The second is that the trans-national elite minority that makes up a fifth of the world's people, and especially the super-elite at the top of the system, may be so determined to maintain their own position that even the proposed reforms will meet heavy resistance.

Furthermore, Global Social Democracy, as Bello argues:

> ...assumes that people really want to be part of a functionally integrated global economy where the barriers between the national and the international have disappeared. But would they not in fact prefer to be part of economies that are subject to local control and are buffered from the vagaries of the international economy? Indeed, today's swift downward trajectory of interconnected economies underscores the validity of one of anti-globalization movement's key criticisms of the globalization process...[15]

If GSD still sees the market as the basic economic mechanism in what is a technocratic project that seeks to reform from above, then Bello argues that it is essentially about social management not social liberation. Moreover, even if we might argue that GSD could result in some modest improvements in a deeply flawed model, it is unlikely in the extreme to be able to cope also with the deep environmental constraints that we now face.

Ten years on

Looking back over the ten years since the first edition of this book, the original prognosis remains relevant – an economically divided world subject to increasing environmental constraints yet with elite communities determined to maintain their position rather than address the underlying problems. Tentative prescriptions for change were suggested (Chapter 7), but it was also accepted that what would be required would be transformational. Even so, there was some cause for optimism as environmental issues were rising up the political agenda and even the disjointed anti-globalisation protests were essentially about a deep critique of the economic status quo. There was, it seemed, some possibility that the first decade of the twenty-first century would see some real re-thinking of the old control paradigm and that 'liddism' might be seen to have had its day. It might indeed be possible to avoid Edwin Brooks's dystopic vision of 'a crowded, glowering planet of massive inequalities of wealth buttressed by stark force yet endlessly threatened by desperate people in the global ghettos...'

It hardly bears saying that the decade has turned out very differently, yet we may come to see that its real significance is the manner in which we have witnessed the failure of old thinking. In all three respects – the war on terror, the environment and the market economy – the status quo has been found wanting. We now face a much greater challenge than a decade ago but we also have much more evidence of the need for new thinking and transformative action. In one sense we have lost a decade in the task of moving towards a more emancipated, sustainable and peaceful world, but the urgency is now more clearly recognised and the inadequacies of previous approaches more apparent.

The war on terror resulted in radically different outcomes to those expected. What was meant to happen was that al-Qaida would be destroyed and Afghanistan would become a centre of US influence close to resource-rich Central Asia. Iraq would not just be a shining example of a truly free-market economy but would greatly expand US influence in the Middle East, constrain Iran and begin to effect a political transformation to uniformly pro-western democracies. All this would be initiated by a vigorous process of military action that would demonstrate the underlying power of the New American Century. This new Century would be modelled on the neoconservative vision – what was good for America would unquestionably be good for the world.

Instead, al-Qaida remains potent and Afghanistan has succumbed to deep insecurity – an unstable narco-state with the Taliban, warlords and other paramilitaries running much of the country even as the 80,000 foreign troops try to impose control. Its much more powerful nuclear-armed neighbour, Pakistan, is facing a worsening security environment and there seems a real prospect that the two states will together witness endemic insecurity for many years if not decades. In Iraq, the first six years of war saw hundreds of thousands of civilians killed or seriously injured and 4 million refugees. As the Israeli government moved to the right, prospects for an Israel/Palestine settlement diminished and anti-Americanism increased across the region. The Bush administration ended in early 2009, leaving its successor with a multitude of security problems in the Middle East and across into Southern Asia. Barack Obama soon demonstrated a different approach, at least in relation to the US approach to Islam and the Middle East, as well as his recognition of the need to move towards a nuclear-free world. Even so, the global problems now in prospect are far greater than can be handled by one change of administration in a single country, however powerful it may be.

More generally, while there remains a belief that the al-Qaida movement must still be seen as an enemy in the style of the old military mindset, this is a receding perspective and there is a more widespread recognition that the much-vaunted war on terror has been deeply counter-productive. It is, in short, a classic example of 'liddism', with the pot boiling over amidst a chronic inability to turn down the heat. What is most remarkable is the demonstration of the power of irregular warfare. The conflicts in Iraq and Afghanistan have each involved no more than a few thousand active paramilitary forces yet they have cost the United States and its allies trillions of dollars and have tied down over 200,000 troops from the world's best equipped and trained armed forces.[16]

It was also a lost decade for action on climate change, but here there have been real changes of mood. Ten years ago climate change was a phenomenon of concern to a small part of the scientific community, a relatively small group of activists and an even smaller group of security analysts. There was little effort to link climate change to the problems facing the majority world of the South. That has changed in almost all respects. Climate scientists are now far more determined in their insistence on radical action, calling for moves to a low carbon economy that would have been unthinkable a decade ago. There may recently have been a tendency to 'securitise' climate change, seeing it as a matter primarily for action that will preserve the security of the richer and more powerful states. That attitude, though, comes up directly against the many people who link climate change with a globalised world in which those metaphorical castle gates cannot be closed.

Finally, the sudden, unexpected and severe economic crisis that unfolded in 2007–08 greatly undermined the veracity of the idea of the globalised free market. One characterisation of that idea, written in early 2007, put it as follows:

> All might not be entirely well with the world but for most people, including the intellectual, political and economic leaderships, the liberal model is the essence of what we are about and that is how things will continue. The Washington consensus holds good and there is no alternative, even if modest adjustments may have to be made. There really is only one game in town.[17]

It took only a few months to disabuse 'most people' of that illusion, yet there remain huge dangers. The responses to the economic crisis may involve something a bit more than 'modest adjustments' yet could fall far short of transforming the globalised economy into a system that places economic justice ahead of greed. Climate change and other environmental issues may well be put to one side in the interests of quick responses to the economic downturn – the chance of a green new deal will be lost. Lessons will not have been learnt from the failed war on terror.

And yet...

What could also happen is that the fundamental inadequacies of our current systems will be recognised and, in the second decade of the twenty-first century we will see clearly the dismal failures of the first decade and begin the process of transformation. That will depend less on politicians and far more on civil society in its most innovative and prophetic modes. The opportunity is there for the taking.

Notes

Chapter 1

1. Chris McGreal, 'Fortress town to rise on Cape of low hopes', The *Guardian*, 22 January 1999.
2. Simon Romero, 'Above It All: Sao Paulo's Wealthy, Going Off-Road', *International Herald Tribune*, 16 February 2000.
3. Information concerning the development of the conventionally-armed air-launched cruise missile and the raid on Iraq in January 1991 did not enter the public domain until several years after the Gulf War. The most detailed account is to be found in: John Tirpal, 'The Secret Squirrels', *Air Force Magazine*, April 1994. *Air Force Magazine* has been one of the most consistent proponents of the development and use of long-range air power as a core facet of US security policy since the Cold War, with a series of articles throughout the 1990s exploring this theme.

Chapter 2

1. See, for example: Richard Ned Lebow and Janice Gross Stein, *We All Lost the Cold War* (Princeton: Princeton University Press, 1994).
2. Robert S. Norris and William M. Arkin, 'Global Nuclear Stockpiles, 1945–1997', *The Bulletin of the Atomic Scientists*, November/December 1997.
3. For a concise assessment of the early development of strategic nuclear weapons, see: Norman Polmar, *Strategic Weapons, an Introduction* (New York: Crane Russak, 1982). Other sources are: Thomas B. Cochran, William M. Arkin, Milton M. Hoenig, *U.S. Nuclear Forces and Capabilities* (Cambridge, Mass., Ballinger, 1984); Thomas B. Cochran, William M. Arkin, Robert S. Norris and Jeffrey I. Sands, *Soviet Nuclear Weapons* (New York: Harper and Row, 1989); Charles Hansen, *U.S. Nuclear Weapons – The Secret History* (New York: Orion Books, 1988).
4. A detailed description of the development and deployment of RAF nuclear forces was prepared in the early 1990s and subsequently declassified and published: Humphrey Wynn, *RAF Nuclear Deterrent Forces* (London: HMSO, 1994).
5. Malcolm Chalmers, *Paying for Defence* (London: Pluto Press, 1986).
6. Norris and Arkin, *Global Nuclear Stockpiles*.

7. Polmar, *Strategic Nuclear Weapons*.
8. For an analysis of the origins and development of the Nuclear Non-Proliferation Treaty, see: Paul Rogers and Malcolm Dando, *The Directory of Nuclear, Biological and Chemical Arms and Disarmament, 1990* (London: Tri-Service Press, 1990).
9. Examples were later variants of the SS-18 ICBM. The Mod 4 variant of this missile, operational during the mid-1980s, carried ten MIRV warheads, each rated at 500 kilotons.
10. Hearings on the *Military Implications of the Treaty on the Limitations of Strategic Offensive Arms and Protocol Thereto (SALT II Treaty)*, Committee on Armed Services, United States Senate, 95th Congress, 1st Session, 1979.
11. Quoted in: D.A.Rosenberg, 'A Smoking, Radiating Ruin at the end of Two Hours: Documents on American Plans for Nuclear War with the Soviet Union, 1954–55', *International Security*, 6, 1982, pp. 3–38.
12. D. Ball, *Targeting for Strategic Deterrence*, Adelphi Paper Number 185, IISS, London, 1983.
13. Ibid.
14. D. Ball, personal information.
15. Ball, *Targeting for Strategic Deterrence*.
16. A useful source on the Strategic Defense Initiative is: Paul B. Stares, *Space Weapons and U.S. Strategy* (London and Sydney: Croom Helm, 1985). A more critical assessment of SDI is: Rip Bulkeley and Graham Spinardi, *Space Weapons: Deterrence or Delusion* (London: Polity Press, 1986).
17. For a substantive analysis of Soviet strategy, see: David Holloway, *The Soviet Union and the Arms Race*, 2nd edition (New Haven and London: Yale University Press, 1984).
18. For a description of tactical nuclear weapons in Europe towards the end of the Cold War, see: Paul Rogers, *Guide to Nuclear Weapons* (Oxford: Berg Press, 1988).
19. A detailed analysis of NATO's nuclear posture is: Dan Charles, *Nuclear Planning in NATO* (Cambridge, Mass: Ballinger, 1987).
20. Walter Beinke, 'Flexible Response in Perspective', *Military Review*, November 1968, p. 48.
21. *Operations: FM 100-5*, US Dept of the Army, 1982.
22. See Rogers, *Nuclear Weapons*, for details of the terminal guidance system of the Pershing 2 missile and for a description of the deployment of the Pershing 2 and ground-launched cruise missiles in western Europe in the early 1980s, and of the Soviet SS-20 missile during the same period.
23. Interview with General Bernard Rogers, *International Defense Review*, February 1986. (Emphasis in the original.)
24. *Third Report of the Select Committee on Foreign Affairs*, House of Commons, London, 1987–88, p. 35.
25. A relevant contemporary analysis is: Ilana Kass and Michael J. Deane, 'The Role of Nuclear Weapons in the Modern Theatre Battlefield: The Current Soviet View', *Comparative Strategy*, Vol. 4, No. 3, 1984.
26. Unless otherwise stated, details of nuclear weapons accidents draw on three sources: M. Gaines, 'Nuclear Weapons: How Safe?', *Flight International*, 4 July 1981; Shaun Gregory and Alistair Edwards, 'A Handbook of Nuclear Weapons Accidents', *Peace Research Reports Number 20* (Bradford: University of Bradford, 1988); Jan S. Breemer, 'Soviet Submarine Accidents, Background and Chronology', *Navy International* May, 1986.

27. 'US Jet Crash Close to Nuclear Weapons Area', *Reuters News Reports* (RN01W,042695.466), 26 April 1995.
28. 'Vehicle Parked on Silo After Launch Signal', *Washington Post*, 29 October 1987.
29. Fred Charles Iklé, 'The Second Coming of the Nuclear Age', *Foreign Affairs*, Vol. 75, No. 1, January/February 1996.
30. Polmar, 'Strategic Nuclear Weapons'.
31. Quoted in Polmar, 'Strategic Nuclear Weapons'.
32. Polmar, 'Strategic Nuclear Weapons'.
33. Ibid.
34. Robert S. McNamara, 'The Conference on Disarmament Should Focus on Steps to Move Towards a 'Nuclear-Free World'', *Disarmament Diplomacy*, April 1996.
35. Scott D. Sagan, 'More Will be Worse', in: Scott D. Sagan and Kenneth N. Waltz, *The Spread of Nuclear Weapons, A Debate* (New York and London: W. W. Norton and Company, 1995).
36. Ibid.
37. Colonel William V. Kennedy et al., *The Intelligence War* (London: Salamander, 1987).
38. Robert Jackson, *Strike Force – The USAF in Britain Since 1948* (London: Robson, 1986).
39. A number of Task Force ships left Britain carrying stocks of anti-submarine nuclear depth bombs. There was a subsequent controversy within the Ministry of Defence, and most of the nuclear weapons were transferred to a fleet auxiliary, *RFA Regent*. While this ship went on to the South Atlantic to support the Task Force ships, it was subsequently kept away from the war zone, unlike its sister ship, *RFA Resource*. There remains uncertainty over whether ships that diverted from NATO exercise *Spring Train*, including *HMS Sheffield*, retained their nuclear weapons during the subsequent war. For a discussion of this and related issues, see: Paul Rogers, 'Sub-Strategic Trident: A Slow Burning Fuse', *London Defence Studies, No. 34*. (London: Brassey's, 1996).
40. For a detailed description of the *Able Archer* incident, see: Paul Rogers and Malcolm Dando, *A Violent Peace: Global Security After the Cold War* (London: Brassey's, 1992).
41. Gordon Brook-Shepherd, 'When the World Almost Went to War', *Sunday Telegraph*, 16 October 1988.
42. Ibid.
43. Bruce G. Blair, Harold A. Feiveson and Frank N. von Hippel, 'Taking Nuclear Weapons off Hair-Trigger Alert', *Scientific American*, November 1997, pp. 42–9.
44. David Hoffman, 'Doctrines of the Cold War Refuse to Die', *Washington Post*, 15 March 1998, p. A1.
45. Ibid.
46. Ruth Leger Sivard, *World Military and Social Expenditure, 1996* (Washington DC, World Priorities Inc.).
47. For an account of the 1974 world food crisis and the subsequent work of the UN World Food Congress, see: Paul Rogers, *Food in Our Time, But Not Yet* (London: World Development Movement, 1985).

48. Casualty figures for wars since 1945 are given in: Ruth Leger Sivard, *World Military and Social Expenditure* and *The Military Balance, 1999–2000* (London: International Institute of Strategic Studies, 1999).
49. For an account of the status of area-impact munitions at the end of the Cold War, see: Rogers and Dando, 'The Directory of Nuclear, Biological and Chemical Arms and Disarmament'. See also successive editions of *Jane's Weapons Systems* (London, Jane's Publishing Company).
50. One of the most informative essays on attitudes of nuclear planners during the Cold War was written by a former target selection analyst: Henry T. Nash, 'The Bureaucratization of Homicide', *The Bulletin of the Atomic Scientists*, April 1980.

Chapter 3

1. For a review of problems of nuclear proliferation, see: Rebecca Johnson, 'Nuclear Non-Proliferation at the Crossroads', *Special Briefings Series on UK Nuclear Weapons Policy, No. 3* (London, International Security Information Service, January 2000).
2. Robert S. Norris and William M. Arkin, 'Global Nuclear Stockpiles, 1945–1997', *The Bulletin of the Atomic Scientists*, November/December 1997.
3. Strategic Advisory Group of the Joint Strategic Target Planning Group, US Strategic Air Command: 'The Role of Nuclear Weapons in the New World Order', reported in *Navy News and Undersea Technology*, Washington DC, 13 January 1992.
4. Ibid.
5. Elaine Grossman, 'DOD Has "Significant" Ability to Alter Nuclear Weapons Targeting on Short Notice' *Inside the Air Force*, Vol. 3, No. 32, p. 1 (7 August 1994). Two years after the Reed Report, it was reported that staff at US Strategic Command (the successor to Strategic Air Command with the inclusion of control of US ballistic missile submarines) were 'in the early stages of building and testing computer models that could enable Mr Clinton to aim nuclear weapons at third world nations that threaten the interests of the United States and its allies.', see: Eric Schmitt, 'Head of Nuclear Forces Plans for a New World', *New York Times*, 25 February 1993.
6. Thomas W. Dowler and Joseph S. Howard III, 'Countering the Threat of the Well-Armed Tyrant': A Modest Proposal for Small Nuclear Weapons', *Strategic Review*, Fall 1991.
7. Les Aspin, 'Three Propositions for a New Nuclear Era', commencement address at MIT, 1 June 1992.
8. General Powell, then Chair of the Joint Chiefs of Staff, clearly stated his commitment that 'we will eventually see the time when the number of nuclear weapons is down to zero' (speech at Harvard University, 10 June, 1993). The Henry L. Stimson Center began its *Project on Eliminating Weapons of Mass Destruction* in January 1994. This was chaired by the former Supreme Allied Commander, Europe (SACEUR), General Andrew Goodpaster, and included three other retired generals and Robert McNamara. This involvement of the military, coupled with the work of a number of academic analysts, gave a new emphasis to ideas of a nuclear-

free world. See, for example: Barry M. Blechman and Cathleen S. Fisher, 'Phase Out the Bomb', *Foreign Policy*, No. 97, Winter 1994–95.

9. Also during this period, Congress blocked funds for some new nuclear warhead developments. For example, Project PLYWD, a post-Gulf War programme to produce a precision low-yield nuclear warhead was halted by legislation banning development of weapons below five kilotons. See, Robert S. Norris and William M. Arkin, 'Nuclear Notebook', *The Bulletin of the Atomic Scientists*, July/August 1994.

10. *Proliferation, Threat and Response*, Office of the Secretary of Defense, April 1996.

11. Carol Giacomo, 'U.S. May Use Nuclear Force Against Chemicals', *Reuters News Reports*, 28 March 1996.

12. Letter from Ralph Earle II, Deputy Director, US Arms Control and Disarmament Agency, 24 January 1996.

13. In 1995, the Department of Energy announced that Sandia National Laboratories would acquire a new supercomputer, ten times faster than the most powerful computer then available, which would enhance the ability to produce nuclear weapons without nuclear test explosions. See 'Industry Outlook', *Aviation Week and Space Technology*, 13 November 1995.

14. William B. Scott, 'National Labs Fill Gap in Weapons Stewardship', *Aviation Week and Space Technology*, 22 January 1996.

15. Ibid.

16. The Los Alamos facility was one of several options considered in order to preserve a nuclear weapons production capability. 'Another would be to develop a module that could be taken to other sites – such as the Savannah River weapons plant – to quickly increase production or rebuild capacities if need be.' Ibid.

17. 'US Nuclear Bomb Passes Final Drop Test', *Jane's Defence Weekly*, 1 April 1998. For a detailed assessment of the B61–11, see: Greg Mello, 'New Bomb, No Mission', *The Bulletin of the Atomic Scientists*, May/June 1997.

18. Mello, 'New Bomb, No Mission'.

19. William M. Arkin, 'What's New', *The Bulletin of the Atomic Scientists*, November/December 1997.

20. Arkin, 'What's New'. For an account of the move from Cold War nuclear targeting to nuclear war plans appropriate to limited threats, see: William M. Arkin and Hans Kristensen, 'Dangerous Directions', *The Bulletin of the Atomic Scientists*, March/April 1998.

21. For an analysis of the putative role of US nuclear weapons in counter-proliferation, see: Hans M. Kristensen and Joshua Handler, 'The US and Counter-Proliferation, a New and Dubious Role for US Nuclear Weapons', *Security Dialogue*, Vol. 27, No. 4, 1996. For an account of nuclear weapon research and development programmes, especially in relation to Third World targeting, see: Hans Christensen, 'Nuclear Futures: Proliferation of Weapons of Mass Destruction and US Nuclear Strategy', *BASIC Research Report 98.2* (London and Washington DC: British American Security Information Council, 1998).

22. Dunbar Lockwood, 'The Status of US, Russian and Chinese Nuclear Forces in Northeast Asia', *Arms Control Today*, November 1994.

23. Data from *The Military Balance 1989–90*, and *The Military Balance 1999–2000* (London: The International Institute of Strategic Studies, 1989 and 1999).

24. 'Russia Builds Up Nuclear Forces as Prospects for START II Fade', *Defense News*, 4 December 1995. See also, Barbara Starr, 'NATO Growth "Increases Russian Nuclear Threat"', *Jane's Defence Weekly*, 17 December 1997.
25. Lockwood, 'The Status of US, Russian and Chinese Nuclear Forces'.
26. 'Kremlin to Bolster Nuclear Stockpile', *Washington Post*, 30 April 1999. See also, *The Military Balance 1999–2000*.
27. *The Military Balance 1999–2000*.
28. Yuri Golotyuk, 'Russia Clenches its Nuclear Fist', *Izvestia*, 23 March 1999.
29. Paul Rogers, 'Sub-Strategic Trident: A Slow-Burning Fuse', *London Defence Studies No. 34* (London: Centre for Defence Studies, 1996).
30. David Miller, 'Britain Ponders Single Warhead Option' *International Defence Review*, September 1994.
31. David S. Yost, 'Nuclear Debates in France' *Survival*, Vol. 36, No. 4, Winter 1994–5.
32. Giovanni de Briganti, 'France to Replace Mirage IVP Bomber Fleet by 1997', *Defense News*, 8 January 1996.
33. *Strategic Concept*, paragraph 64, NATO, Brussels, April 1999.
34. *Summit Communique*, NATO, Washington DC, 26 April 1999.
35. *NATO Summit: The New Strategic Concept Fact Sheet*, The White House, Washington DC, 26 April 1999.
36. Paul Rogers and Malcolm Dando, *The Directory of Nuclear, Biological and Chemical Arms and Disarmament, 1990* (London: Tri-service Press, 1990).
37. Alistair Iain Johnston, 'China's New "Old Thinking"', *International Security*, Vol. 20, No. 3, Winter 1995/96.
38. Erik Eckholm, 'China to U.S.: Back Off Treaty Changes', *The New York Times*, 25 November 1999.
39. Ibid.
40. Robert S. Norris and William M. Arkin, 'Chinese Nuclear Forces, 1999', *The Bulletin of the Atomic Scientists*, May/June 1999.
41. James Risen and Judith Miller, 'CIA Now Says it is Less Sure That Iran Cannot Make Nuclear Bomb', *International Herald Tribune*, 18 January 2000.
42. Robert S. Norris and William M. Arkin, 'After the Tests: India and Pakistan Update', *The Bulletin of the Atomic Scientists*, September/October 1988.
43. Michael Evans, 'Kashmir "nearly led to nuclear clash"', *The Times*, London, 29 November 1999.

Chapter 4

1. Statement by James Woolsey at Senate Hearings, Washington DC, February 1993.
2. A specific area of competition has been between the US Navy's aircraft carriers and their strike aircraft, and the long-range strike capabilities of the US Air Force. Rivalries in the early 1990s led at one stage to a congressionally mandated Department of Defense Panel to combat duplication in service roles. See: Theresa Hitchens and Robert Holzer, 'Air Force, Navy Dispute Roles Amid DoD Study, *Defense News*, 7 March 1994.
3. This section draws on a number of sources published between 1995 and 1999: Hans Binnendijk, 'America's Military Priorities', *Strategic Forum Number 20*, Institute for National Strategic Studies, National Defense

University, February 1995; Thomas Hirschfeld and W. Seth Carus, 'We Need to Understand', *Proceedings of the United States Naval Institute*, February 1997; Paul Mann, 'Fathoming a Strategic World of "No Bear, But Many Snakes"', *Aviation Week and Space Technology*, 6 December 1999. Two sets of hearings in Washington DC in February 1999, involving the Directors of the Defense Intelligence Agency and the Central Intelligence Agency dealt with longer-term perspectives on security: Prepared Statement by Lieutenant General Patrick M. Hughes USA, Director, Defense Intelligence Agency before the Senate Armed Services Committee, 'Global Threats and Challenges: The Decades Ahead', Tuesday, 2 February 1999; Prepared Statement of George J. Tenet, Director of Central Intelligence, before the Senate Armed Services Committee, 'Current and Projected National Security Threats', Tuesday, 2 February 1999.

4. R. Adam Moody, 'Armageddon for Hire' *International Defense Review*, February 1997. The populist title of the paper disguises a detailed analysis of job losses in a number of significant Russian research establishments. Among other examples of unemployment, Moody cites estimates of 3,500 job losses at the Vektor Scientific Center for Virology and Biotechnology in Koltsovo, Russia, up to 1994, and 5,000 job losses at the Southern Machine Building Plant (Yuzhmash) producing SS-18 ICBMs, and space booster research, development and production, at Dnepropetrovsk, Ukraine, between 1991 and 1996.

5. The US Commission on National Security in the 21st Century was a Department of Defense-funded panel of experts set up in 1998, co-chaired by Senator Gary Hart (Democrat) and Senator Warren Rudman (Republican). Its initial report was published in September 1999, see: *Disarmament Diplomacy, No. 40, September/October 1999*.

6. Roger W. Barnett, 'Regional Conflict: Requires Naval Forces', *Proceedings of the United States Naval Institute*, June 1992.

7. James W. Canan, 'Expeditionary Force', *Air Force Magazine*, June 1993.

8. David Ochmanek and John Bordeaux, 'The Lion's Share of Power Projection', *Air Force Magazine*, June 1993. The arguments between the navy and the air force were rehearsed in print throughout the 1990s, with two journals, *Air Force Magazine* and *The Proceedings of the United States Naval Institute*, being the main protagonists for the air force and navy respectively.

9. During the course of the 1990s, the development of global engagement thinking was encompassed in the term the 'bomber road map', meaning the ability of long-range bombers to go anywhere. According to one assessment: 'In the future, capabilities based in the continental United States will likely become the primary means for crisis response and power projection as long-range air- and space-based assets increasingly fill the requirements of the Global Attack core competency.' John A. Tirpak, 'Global Engagement', *Air Force Magazine*, January 1997. For more general assessments of the future of US manned bombers, see: Robert Wall, 'U.S. Bomber Plans Focus in Upgrades', *Aviation Week and Space Technology*, 8 March 1999; John A. Tirpak, 'The Bomber Road Map', *Air Force Magazine*, June 1999; Bryan Bender, 'The Long Run, Planning the Future for US Strategic Bombers', *Jane's Defence Weekly*, 25 August 1999.

10. David Fulghum, 'USAF Embraces New, Fast-Moving Air Units', *Aviation Week and Space Technology*, 10 August 1998.

11. Following the depletion of stocks of the conventionally-armed air-launched cruise missile (CALCM) in the Kosovo War in 1999, Boeing was contracted to convert a further 322 of the nuclear-armed ALCM into the high explosive variant: Paul Proctor, 'CALCM Resupply Starts', *Aviation Week and Space Technology*, 6 December 1999.

12. William B. Scott, 'B-2 Drops GPS-Guided "Bunker-Buster"', *Aviation Week and Space Technology*, 21 April 1997.

13. David A. Fulghum, 'Secret U.S. Warhead Nearer to Fielding', *Aviation Week and Space Technology*, 3 April 1995.

14. *Economist Intelligence Unit*, 21 August 1999.

15. The development of CENTCOM and forward basing is analysed in: Paul Rogers and Malcolm Dando, *A Violent Peace, Global Security After the Cold War* (London: Brassey's, 1992).

16. Figures for the changes in the US Navy and Marine Corps between 1989 and 1999 from: *The Military Balance, 1989–1990*, and *The Military Balance, 1999–2000* (London: International Institute for Strategic Studies, 1989 and 1999). There was particularly heavy investment in navy sea-lift capabilities in the mid and late 1990s, see: Vincent Grimes, 'Sealift Steams Forward', *Navy International*, May/June 1995.

17. Quoted in: Jenny Pearce, *Under the Eagle* (London: Latin America Bureau, 1982).

18. The US Navy has also investigated the acquisition of ATACMS as a ship-based missile system for land-attack.

19. Mark Hewish and Rupert Pengelley, 'Special Solutions for Special Forces', *International Defense Review*, May 1995.

20. Douglas Farah, 'Shadowy U.S. Troop Training Operation Spreads Across Latin America', *International Herald Tribune*, 14 July 1998; Rachel Stohl, 'U.S. Plans Huge Colombian Aid Package', *Center for Defense Information Briefing*, Vol. 4, No. 3, 20 January 2000.

21. Charles Miller, 'U.K. Military: Take Offense', *Defense News*, 28 October 1996.

22. Admiral Jacques Lanxade, 'Stepping into the Breach – France's Global Role', *International Defense Review*, April 1995.

23. NATO's strategic concept, with its emphasis on outreach, is discussed in: Richard Hatfield, 'NATO's New Strategic Concept', *RUSI Journal*, December 1999.

24. A standard contemporary account of the SDI programme is: Paul B. Stares, *Space Weapons and US Strategy* (London and Sydney: Croom Helm, 1985). For a more critical analysis, see: Rip Bulkeley and Graham Spinardi, *Space Weapons: Deterrence or Delusion* (London: Polity Press, 1986).

25. Duncan Lennox, 'Ballistic Missiles', *Jane's Defence Weekly*, 17 April 1996; Bill Gertz, 'Missile Threats and Defenses', *Air Force Magazine*, October 1998.

26. John D. Gresham, 'Navy Area Ballistic Missile Defense Coming On Fast', *Proceedings of the United States Naval Institute*, January 1999.

27. For an overview of US ballistic missile defence plans, see: David E. Mosher, 'Ballistic Missile Defense – the Grand Plans', *IEEE Spectrum*, September 1997. See also: Michael A. Dornheim, 'Missile Defense Soon, But Will it Work', *Aviation Week and Space Technology*, 24 February 1997.

28. David A. Fulghum, 'Small Clustered Munitions May Carry Nuclear Wastes', *Aviation Week and Space Technology*, 10 October 1993.

29. Geoffrey E. Forden, 'The Airborne Laser', *IEEE Spectrum*, September 1997; 'YAL-1A Attack Laser', *Air Force Research Laboratory Office of Public Affairs Fact Sheet*, Kirtland Air Force Base, New Mexico, January 1998.
30. Ibid.
31. Robert Wall, 'Space-Based Missile Defense Program Crystallizing', *Aviation Week and Space Technology*, 16 August 1999; 'Space-Based Laser', *Ballistic Missile Defense Organisation Fact Sheet TO-98–01* (Washington: Department of Defense, July 1998).
32. 'Directed Energy Study Kicks Off', *Air Force Research Laboratory Office of Public Affairs DE Release No. 98–32*, Kirtland Air Force Base, New Mexico, 26 June 1998.
33. Paul Mann, 'Washington Watch – B-X in Space?', *Aviation Week and Space Technology*, 31 August 1998.
34. 'USSPACECOM Long Range Plan Summary', US Space Command Directorate of Public Affairs, 7 April 1998; Robert S. Dudney, 'The New Space Plan', *Air Force Magazine*, July 1998.

Chapter 5

1. Quoted in: James Stephenson, 'The 1994 Zapatista Rebellion in Southern Mexico – an Analysis and Assessment', *Occasional Paper Number 12* (Camberley: Strategic and Combat Studies Institute, The Army Staff College, 1995). Stephenson's paper is unusual as a military analysis of a conflict in that it pays particular attention to the social and economic conditions underlying the rebellion.
2. Stephenson, 'The 1994 Zapatista rebellion'. See also: Daniel Mato, 'The Indigenous Uprising in Chiapas: the Politics of Institutionalised Knowledge and Mexican Perspectives', *Identities*, Vol. 3, No. 1–2, 1996. Mato's paper is the first of a collection of five papers on aspects of the Zapatista rebellion in this issue of *Identities*, all by Mexican analysts.
3. Palmer Newbould, 'The Global Ecosystem', in Anthony Vann and Paul Rogers (eds), *Human Ecology and World Development* (London and New York: Plenum Press, 1974).
4. Edwin Brooks, 'The Implications of Ecological Limits to Growth in Terms of Expectations and Aspirations in Developed and Less Developed Countries', in Vann and Rogers (eds), *Human Ecology and World Development*.
5. Film interview in 1971, quoted in: Nance Lui Fyson, *The Development Puzzle* (London: Voluntary Committee in Overseas Aid and Development, 1972).
6. 'Problems of Raw Materials and Development' *UNCTAD Document TD/B/488* (Geneva: UNCTAD, 1974)
7. An informed history of the UNCTAD process is Nassau A. Adams, *Worlds Apart: The North-South Divide and the International System* (London and New Jersey: Zed Press, 1993).
8. There were, and are, several requirements for a group of commodity-producing states to be able to exercise 'producer power'. The states concerned must maintain a high degree of unity of action, they must control a large proportion of trade in that commodity and, if it is non-renewable, they must control most of the reserves. Large stockpiles must not be available in consuming countries, the commodity must not be capable of rapid substitution with an alternative and the group of states exercising producer power

must have sufficient commercial and financial resilience to be able to survive any action attempted by consuming countries. OPEC achieved all of these requirements in 1973/74, but its unity of purpose collapsed by the end of the decade, heralding a period of low oil prices from the mid-1980s. It regained some unity of purpose in the late 1990s, leading to production cuts and buoyant oil prices in the winter of 1999/2000. No other countries or groups have been able to emulate OPEC, though Morocco had a sufficient dominance in phosphate trade to double export prices in 1973/74. The Association of Natural Rubber Producers has, on occasions, been reasonably successful in maintaining export prices, not least because it is dominated by just three countries, Malaysia, Thailand and Indonesia, and copper and bauxite producers had occasional limited success in the 1970s. For a full discussion of the links between trade and poverty, see: Belinda Coote, *The Trade Trap: Poverty and the Global Commodity Markets* (Oxford: Oxfam Publications, 1996). See also: Kevin Watkins, *Fixing the Rules* (London: CIIR, 1992) dealing with more detailed North-South trade issues. A more general account of the links between resources, development and international relations is: Paul Rogers, 'Resource Issues', in Trevor C. Salmon (ed.), *Issues in International Relations* (London and New York: Routledge, 2000).

9. In the twelve months to 12 December 1973, prices of metals rose by an average of 133 per cent and of fibres by 59.5 per cent. For the most part this was not due to other resource producers following the OPEC model and prices declined markedly in the following 15 months. Angus Hone, 'Gainers and Losers in the 1973 Commodity Boom: Developing Countries' Prospects to 1980', *ODI Review No. 1* (London: Overseas Development Institute, 1974).

10. Instituto del Tercer Mundo, *The World Guide, 1999–2000* (Oxford: New Internationalist Publications, 1999).

11. Ibid.

12. Figures from Bimal Ghosh, 'Glaring Inequality is Growing Between and Inside Countries', *International Herald Tribune*, 24 January 1997.

13. John Cavanagh, 'Globalization: Fine for Some and Bad for Many', *International Herald Tribune*, 24 January 1997.

14. Anthony DePalma, 'Mexico's Economic Turnaround is Lost on the Poor', *International Herald Tribune*, 13 August 1997.

15. A widely held view is that the impressive successes of the 'tiger' economies of South East Asia illustrate the effectiveness of market liberalisation policies. There are two problems with this argument. The most successful states have been South Korea, Taiwan, Hong Kong and Singapore, but all have followed policies of comprehensive state intervention and central planning in many sectors of the economy. Furthermore, South Korea and Taiwan were massively aided by economic assistance stemming from their position in the Cold War confrontation, and Singapore and Hong Kong have had substantial geopolitical advantages as trading centres. The second point is that all are relatively small countries in terms of population, especially when contrasted with the Philippines, Indonesia or Vietnam. Of the other states of South East Asia, Brunei, with a population of 300,000, is immensely rich in oil, and Malaysia, with 22 million people and a per capita income of $3,700 per annum, has benefited from an unusually advantageous resource base of oil, natural rubber, tin and tropical hardwoods. Thailand, with 61 million people, has a per capita income of $2,000, and

in the Philippines, with 75 million people, it is $1,010. The 210 million people of Indonesia average $750 per capita, and the 95 million people in the Indo-China states average under $350 per capita (Figures from *The Economist*, 12 February 2000).

16. In the United States, over 40 million people cannot afford medical insurance, a recognised indicator of poverty. The US has also become a state with a particularly harsh culture of incarceration – early in 2000, the prison population exceeded 2 million, close to one in 100 of all its citizens. Prison construction has averaged $7 billion a year for the past decade; the prison industry costs $35 billion a year and employs 523,000 people. (Duncan Campbell, 'Anger grows as the US jails its two millionth inmate – 25% of world's prison population', *Guardian*, 15 February 2000).

17. For an impressive analysis of the context and development of the Shining Path, see: Carlos Ivan Degregori, 'The Maturation of a Cosmocrat and the Building of a Discourse Community: The Case of the Shining Path', in David E. Apter (ed.), *The Legitimization of Violence* (London: Macmillan, 1997).

18. Mark Huband and Roula Khalaf, 'Climate of violence overshadows Algerian peace hopes', *Financial Times*, 13 January 2000.

19. Donella H. Meadows, Dennis L. Meadows, Jorgen Randers and William H. Behrens III, *Limits to Growth* (London: Earth Island, 1972).

20. Rogers 'Resource Issues'.

21. Ibid.

22. William Wallis, 'Gem smuggling sparks call for diamond review', *Financial Times*, 14 January 2000.

23. *New Internationalist*, December 1999.

24. David Rind, 'Drying Out the Tropics', *New Scientist*, 6 May 1995.

25. Reported in: Susan Litherland, 'North-South: Global Security Elbows Out Development', *Inter Press Service International News*, London, 2 December 1993.

26. Ibid.

27. In a perceptive early analysis of trends towards a rich-poor confrontation, Ronald Higgins set a scenario of a 'Southern Army of the Poor' directing its actions against elite states of the North. Ronald Higgins, *The Seventh Enemy: the Human Factor in the Global Crisis* (London: Hodder and Stoughton, 1978).

Chapter 6

1. The main sources for the material on the Iraqi biological warfare programme, including the deployments at the time of the Gulf War in 1991, are a series of reports from the UN Special Commission on Iraq (UNSCOM) to the Secretary-General of the United Nations and thence to the UN Security Council. The key report in this series is from October 1995: *Report of the Secretary-General on the status of the implementation of the Special Commission's plan for ongoing monitoring and verification of Iraq's compliance with relevant parts of Section C of Security Council resolution 687 (1991)* (New York: UN Security Council report S/1995/864, 11 October 1995). See also two later reports, S/1996/848 of 11 October 1996 and S/1997/774 of 6 October 1997.

2. Paul Rogers, 'Security Consequences of the Osiraq Raid', *Contemporary Security Policy*, Vol. 19, No. 2, 1998.

3. Simon Whitby and Paul Rogers, 'Anti-Crop Biological Warfare – Implications of the Iraqi and U.S. programs', *Defense Analysis*, Vo. 13, No. 3, 1997. The use of biological weapons against crops has considerable potential and would be readily useable by paramilitary groups. A general discussion of this form of biological warfare is in: Paul Rogers, Simon Whitby and Malcolm Dando, 'Biological Warfare Against Crops', *Scientific American*, June 1999. The first comprehensive study of the subject in the open literature will be: Simon Whitby, *Anti-Crop Biological Warfare and its Control* (London: Palgrave, forthcoming).

4. In 1996, the US Department of Defense made available on the Internet a large number of reports and studies relating to the Gulf War. These included, by mistake, a classified report relating to the National Intelligence Estimate of November 1990. This report was quickly removed from the website but not before it had been read by a number of analysts.

5. Barbara Crossette, 'A Saddam Surprise? Evidence Points to Biological Weapons Project', *International Herald Tribune*, 9 February 2000.

6. For a discussion of asymmetric warfare options in relation to Western intervention see: Paul Rogers, 'Responding to Western Intervention – Conventional and Unconventional Options', *Defense Analysis*, Vol. 14, No. 1, 1998.

7. Bruce Hoffman, paper presented at the 'Seminar on Technology and Terrorism', University of St. Andrews, Scotland, 24–27 August 1992.

8. Sean Anderson and Stephen Sloan, *Historical Dictionary of Terrorism* (Metuchen, N.J. and London: The Scarecrow Press, 1995).

9. 'News Digest for January 1996', *Keesing's Record of World Events*, pp. 40906–7. The second bomb, in October 1997, was detonated in the Colombo CBD in the car park of the Galadari Hotel, close to the twin towers of the Sri Lanka World Trade Centre housing the Central Bank, the Stock Exchange and the telecommunications ministry. In addition to substantial damage, 18 people died and over 100 were injured, including at least 30 foreign tourists.

10. Andrew Hubback, 'Tokyo: Nerve Gas Attack', *Conflict International*, April/May 1995.

11. Paul Tarricone, 'After the Blast', *Civil Engineering*, May 1993, gives a general account of the WTC bombing, including some of the implications for the security of high-rise buildings. For a detailed account of the emergency measures taken to ensure the stability of the Vista Hotel, published in the immediate aftermath of the incident, see: Nadine M. Post *et al.*, 'Anatomy of a Building Disaster', *ENR News*, 8 March 1993.

12. A detailed analysis of the use of economic targeting by the Provisional IRA is in: Paul Rogers, 'Political Violence and Economic Targeting – Aspects of Provisional IRA Strategy, 1992–97', paper presented at the British International Studies Association Annual Conference, Manchester, December 1999.

13. An overall assessment of long term republican strategy up to the 1994 cease-fire is to be found in: M.L.R. Smith, *Fighting for Ireland: The Military Strategy of the Irish Republican Movement* (London and New York: Routledge, 1995).

14. The Baltic Exchange bomb targeted that part of the City of London that was home to many of the major insurance companies, although it is not clear that this was the intention of PIRA. For a detailed assessment of the immediate effects of the bomb and the disruption caused, see: Liz Fisher,

'Bloodied, but not beaten', *Accountancy*, August 1992. The title is indicative of the attitude of the business professions, and Taylor's article is also useful in giving a comprehensive account of the manner in which substantial efforts were made to minimise the commercial impact of the bomb in its immediate aftermath.

15. One of the buildings damaged by the bomb was the tallest office block in the City of London, the 200-metre NatWest Tower. After the attack, the tower underwent a comprehensive repair and renovation process lasting nearly three years. About half of the £100 million cost related to bomb damage and was likely to be covered by insurance. One part of the process was the installation of toughened laminated double-glazing to replace the original glass cladding that had been used in the construction of the building, prior to any concern about paramilitary action. See: Andrew Taylor, 'City Landmark's Towering Achievement', *Financial Times*, 2 December 1999.

16. Press reports during the period did focus on the problems being created by the PIRA campaign. According to *The Times*:

> The IRA, in deploying massive amounts of explosive against targets like the Baltic Exchange or Canary Wharf, is trying to demonstrate that it is not only the provincial towns of Ulster and Belfast that must pay the price for British rule in Northern Ireland. The London bombs are supposed to remind the British people that, in the IRA's view, a war is being fought in their name on the other side of the Irish Sea and there is an everyday cost for them in continuing... There appear to be two principal objectives to this kind of violence. If the IRA can sustain a campaign of this kind, albeit intermittently, over a number of years, it can substantially increase the already high price the British taxpayer pays for remaining in the province. The second objective is to try and push British public opinion into actively supporting a withdrawal from Ulster. The past twenty years have demonstrated that this will be difficult to achieve, given the indifference that has characterised public opinion on the Irish question. (*The Times*, 17 November 1992)

Business trade journals at this time, especially those published overseas, were quick to point to the impact of the London bombs on British confidence. For example:

> The explosion which ripped into the City on a quiet Saturday earlier this spring, killed one person and injured four, but the strategic damage the IRA seems to have wanted to inflict – and succeeded – is seriously sapping the world financial community's confidence in the Brits' ability to keep the financial district safe for business. The fact that the blast occurred on the first anniversary of another such outrage is being interpreted as a message to foreign banks that the IRA can come and go in England with impunity. (Theodore Iacuzio, 'IRA Bomb Blasts Confidence in London as Safe Financial Hub', *Bank Systems and Technology*, June 1993)

See also: Keith Wheatley, 'Economic Warfare', *Australian Business Monthly*, Vol. 13, No. 9, July 1993. In relation to the insurance implications of the PIRA campaign, see: Ralph Atkins, 'The Cost of Terrorism', *Financial Times – Survey of Insurance*, 27 March 1996.

17. For details of the bombing, see: Rebecca Grant, 'Khobar Towers', *Air Force Magazine*, June 1998. For information on the construction of the Prince Sultan Air Base, see: Bill Gertz, 'Miracle in the Desert', *Air Force Magazine*, January 1997 and William H McMichael, 'Desert Stronghold', *Air Force Magazine*, February 1999.
18. Theresa Hitchens, 'Wargame Finds US Short in Biowar', *Defense News*, 28 August 1995.

Chapter 7

1. Malcom Dando, *Biological Warfare in the Early Twenty-first Century* (London: Brassey's 1996); Malcolm Dando, *New Biological Weapons* (Boulder, Colorado: Lynne Reiner, 2000).
2. Steven Schofield, 'Militarism, the UK Economy and Conversion Policies in the North', in Geoff Tansey, Kath Tansey and Paul Rogers (eds), *The World Divided: Militarism and Development After the Cold War* (New York: St Martin's Press, 1994).
3. Because of the side-lining of UNCTAD, the acronym has been said to represent 'Under No Circumstances Take Any Decisions'. For an account of the UNCTAD experience in the context of the linkages between Third World trade and development, see Nassau Adams, *A World Divided*.
4. Any process of providing aid for sustainable development requires efficiency and good governance. In practice, the existence of corruption and malpractice is frequently put forward as a reason for limiting development assistance. This tends to ignore two aspects of the problem. One is that much of the corruption and malpractice is made possible by the willing involvement of Western-based finance houses, and is enhanced by the business practices of leading trans-national corporations, especially, but by no means only, those involved in the production and sale of armaments. The other is that corruption and malpractice are also part of the culture of Northern states. Much of it, such as 'pork barrel' politics (dividing up federal US budgets across political constituencies), is accepted with little question but occasionally, as with the Christian Democrat Party in Germany in 1999–2000, it assumes a seriousness that exceeds acceptable norms.
5. Robin Round, 'Time for Tobin', *New Internationalist*, January/February 2000. See also a succinct analysis of global financial problems as they relate to Third World states: David Woodward, *Contagion and Cure: Tackling the Crisis in Global Finance* (London: Catholic Institute for International Relations, 2000). An analysis relating particularly to the activities of the International Monetary Fund and the World Bank is: David Woodward, *Drowning by Numbers: the IMF, the World Bank and North-South Financial Flows* (London: The Bretton Woods Project, 1988).
6. Woodward, *Contagion and Cure*.
7. Within the increasingly rich literature on sustainable resource use in industrialised states, one of the most interesting is: Ernst von Wezsacker, Amory Lovins and L. Hunter Lovins, *Factor Four – Doubling Wealth, Halving Resource Use* (London: Earthscan, 1997).
8. The OSCE/NATO contrast has been made, in particular, by Scilla Elworthy of the Oxford Research Group.

Chapter 8

1. Details of the Project for the New American Century are at:
2. These issues are discussed, in the context of transatlantic relations, in: Paul Rogers and Scilla Elworthy, 'The United States, Europe and the Majority World After 11 September', *Briefing Paper, October 2001*, Oxford Research Group, Oxford.
3. Charles Krauthammer, 'The Bush Doctrine: ABM, Kyoto and the New American Unilateralism', *Weekly Standard*, 4 June 2001, Washington DC.
4. Carl Conetta, 'Strange Victory: A Critical Appraisal of Operation Enduring Freedom and the Afghanistan War', *Research Monograph No. 6*, Project on Defense Alternatives, Boston, Mass., 30 January 2002.
5. Walter Pincus, 'Al Qaeda to survive bin Laden, Panel told', *Washington Post*, 19 December 2001.
6. Walden Bello, *Endless War?*, Focus on the Global South, Manila, September 2001. This, and other analyses, is available at <www.focusweb.org>.
7. 'Autumn 2001: A Watershed in North–South Relations?', *South Letter*, Volumes 3 and 4, 2001, The South Centre, Geneva.

Chapter 9

1. President George W. Bush, State of the Union Address, January 2002, <www.whitehouse.gov/stateoftheunion/2002/>; accessed 18 May 2007.
2. Ibid.
3. President George W. Bush, Graduation Speech at US Military Academy, West Point, 1 June 2002, <www.whitehouse.gov/news/releases/2002/06/2002601-3.html>; accessed 18 May 2007.
4. Ibid.
5. Ibid.
6. For a comprehensive analysis of the development of the movement, see: Jason Burke, *Al-Qaeda: The True Story of Radical Islam* (London: Penguin Books, 2007).
7. The early development of al-Qaida is to be found in Bruce Lawrence's introduction to the speeches and statements of Osama bin Laden: Bruce Lawrence (ed.), *Messages to the World: The Statements of Osama bin Laden* (London and New York: Verso, 2005).
8. This aspect is explored in: Bruce Riedell, *The Search for Al Qaeda: Its Leadership, Ideology and Future* (Washington DC: Brookings Institution Press, 2008).
9. See *USA Today*, 8 November 2001, for these results from a CNN/Gallup poll.
10. Paul Rogers, *A War on Terror: Afghanistan and After* (London and Sterling Virginia: Pluto Press, 2004), p. 33.
11. *Washington Post*, 6 March 2002. For a more detailed account of the conflict see: <www.arlingtoncemetery.net/macommons.htm>; accessed 14 May 2009.
12. Rogers, *A War on Terror*, p. 181.
13. Stratfor, 28 August 2002: <www.no-war.1accesshost.com/stratfor1.html>; accessed 15 May 2009.
14. For a fuller discussion, see: Chapter 3, 'Oil and the War on Terror', in: Paul Rogers, *Why We're Losing the War on Terror* (Cambridge: Polity, 2008). See

also: Michael Klare, *Blood and Oil* (London and New York: Hamish Hamilton, 2004), and Michael Klare, *Rising Powers, Shrinking Planet: How Scarce Energy is Creating a New World Order* (Oxford: Oneworld, 2008).

15. Nick Ritchie and Paul Rogers, *The Political Road to War with Iraq* (London and New York: Routledge, 2007).

16. An independent assessment of casualties in Iraq has been maintained by the Iraq Body Count group: <www.iraqbodycount.org>.

17. The BJP went on to lose the 2004 election to a coalition formed by the Congress Party.

18. See: Paul Rogers, 'Aftermath: Afghan Lessons, Iraqi Futures', *Open Democracy*, 11 April 2003.

19. Pamela Constable, 'A Wrong Turn, Chaos and a Rescue', *Washington Post*, 15 April 2004.

20. Madelyn Hsiao-Rei Hicks et al., 'The Weapons That Kill Civilians – Deaths of Children and Noncombatants in Iraq, 2003–2008', *New England Journal of Medicine*, 16 April 2009.

21. Barbara Opall-Rome, 'Israeli Arms, Gear Aid US Troops', *Defense News*, Washington DC, 30 March 2004.

22. Ibid.

23. Barbara Opall-Rome, 'A Fake, Flexible City Rises in the Negev', *Defense News*, Washington DC, 11 June 2006.

Chapter 10

1. In addition to long-term supply and oil-field development agreements with Iran and Saudi Arabia, China has also succeeded in making an agreement with the Iraqi government on oil-field development, the first major foreign oil contract to be let after the 2003 war. See: Gina Chon, 'China reaches $3 billion deal to develop oil field in Iraq', *Wall Street Journal*, 29 August 2008.

2. A thoughtful and wide-ranging discussion of climate security is: Nick Mabey, 'Delivering Climate Security: International Security Responses to a Climate Changed World', *Whitehall Papers 69*, Royal United Services Institute, London, 2008.

3. Donella H. Meadows, Dennis L. Meadows, Jorgen Randers and William W. Behrens III, *Limits to Growth* (London: Earth Island, 1972).

4. Ian Sample, 'World faces "perfect storm" of problems by 2030, chief scientist warns', *Guardian*, 18 March 2009.

5. James Davis, Susanna Sandstrom, Anthony Shorrocks and Edward N. Wolff, 'The World Distribution of Household Wealth', *WIDER Angle*, No. 2, 2006, World Institute for Development Economics Research, Helsinki. For an extensive analysis of inequality and its impact, see: Richard Wilkinson and Kate Pickett, *The Spirit Level: Why More Equal Societies Almost Always Do Better* (London: Allen Lane, 2009).

6. Jane Macartney 'China creates crack units to crush poverty protests', *The Times*, London, 20 June 2005.

7. Clifford Coonan, 'China prepares to clamp down on workers' protests', *Independent*, London, 22 February 2009.

8. P. V. Ramana, 'Red Storm Rising', *Jane's Intelligence Review*, August 2008.

9. James Fontanelle-Khan, 'Retailers feel credit squeeze in India', *Financial Times*, 9 February 2009.

10. Dominique Baillard, 'The demand for grain won't stop growing', *Le Monde diplomatique*, May 2008; Michael T. Klare, 'A crisis foretold', *Le Monde diplomatique*, May 2009.

11. Mike Davis, *Planet of Slums* (London and New York: Verso, 2006).

12. *Global Monitoring Report 2009: A Development Emergency*, World Bank/IMF, Washington DC, April 2009.

13. Jim Lobe, 'Financial Crisis Pushing Key Poverty Goals Out of Reach', *Terra Viva/IPS*, New York, 27 April 2009.

14. Walden Bello, 'Capitalism's Crisis and Our Response', *Focus on the Global South*, March 2009. <www.focusweb.org/capitalism-s-crisis-and-our-response.html?Itemid=1>; accessed 23 April 2009.

15. Ibid.

16. Joseph Stiglitz and Linda Bilmes, *The Three Trillion Dollar War* (London and New York: Allen Lane, 2008).

17. Paul Rogers, *Global Security and the War on Terror: Elite Power and the Illusion of Control* (London and New York: Routledge, 2008), p. 204.

Bibliography

Nassau A. Adams, *Worlds Apart – The North–South Divide and the International System* (London: Zed Press, 1993).

Anne Aldis and Graeme P. Herd (eds), *The Ideological War on Terror* (London and New York: Routledge, 2007).

Bevin Alexander, *The Future of Warfare* (New York: W. W. Norton, 1995).

Charles Allen, *God's Terrorists: The Wahhabi Cult and the Hidden Roots of Modern Jihad* (London: Abacus, 2006).

Alternative Defence Commission, *Defence Without the Bomb* (London and New York: Taylor and Francis, 1983).

Alternative Defence Commission, *The Politics of Alternative Defence* (London: Paladin Grafton Books, 1987).

Sean Anderson and Stephen Sloane, *Historical Dictionary of Terrorism* (Metchen, NJ and London: Scarecrow Press, 1995).

Eric Arnett (ed.), *Nuclear Weapons After the Comprehensive Test Ban* (Oxford: Oxford University Press, 1996).

Edward Azar and Chung-in Moon (eds), *National Security in the Third World* (Aldershot: Edward Elgar, 1988).

Desmond Ball, *Targeting for Strategic Deterrence* (London: International Institute for Strategic Studies, 1983).

John Baylis and Robert O'Neill, *Alternative Nuclear Futures – The Role of Nuclear Weapons in the Post-Cold War World* (Oxford: Oxford University Press, 2000).

Ian F. W. Beckett, *Modern Insurgencies and Counter-Insurgencies* (London and New York: Routledge, 2001).

Peter Bergen, *The Holy War Inc.: Inside the Secret World of Osama bin Laden* (Pheonix, AZ: The Free Press, 2002).

Ken Booth, *Theory of World Security* (Cambridge: Cambridge University Press, 2007).

Ken Booth and Tim Dunne (eds), *Worlds in Collision: Terror and the Future of Global Order* (London: Palgrave, 2002).

David Brogg, *Standing with Israel* (Lake Mary, FL: Front Line, 2006).

Jason Burke, *Al-Qaeda: The True Story of Radical Islam* (London: Penguin Books, 2007).

Rajiv Chandrasekaran, *Imperial Life in the Emerald City: Inside Iraq's Green Zone* (New York: Vintage Books, 2007).

Ha-Joon Chang, *Bad Samaritans* (London: Random House Business Books, 2007).

Dan Charles, *Nuclear Planning in NATO* (Cambridge, MA: Ballinger, 1987).

Erskine Childers (ed.), *Challenges to the United Nations – Building a Safer World* (New York: St Martin's Press, 1994).

Amy Chua, *World on Fire* (London: William Heinemann, 2003).

Helena Cobban, *Re-Engage: America and the World After Bush* (Boulder and London: Paradigm Publishers, 2008).

Thomas B. Cochran, William M. Arkin and Milton M. Hoenig, *U.S. Nuclear Forces and Capabilities* (Cambridge, MA: Ballinger, 1984).

Thomas B. Cochran, William M. Arkin, Robert S. Norris and Jeffrey I. Sands, *Soviet Nuclear Weapons* (New York: Harper and Row, 1989).

Philip Connelly and Robert Perlman, *The Politics of Scarcity: Resource Conflicts in International Relations* (Oxford: Oxford University Press, 1975).

Belinda Coote, *The Trade Trap* (Oxford: Oxfam Publications, 1992).

Mark Curtis, *The Ambiguities of Power: British Foreign Policy Since 1945* (London: Pluto Press, 1995).

Malcolm Dando, *Biological Warfare in the Early Twenty-first Century* (London: Brassey's, 1996).

Malcolm Dando, *New Biological Weapons* (Boulder: Lynne Rienner, 2000).

Dilip K. Das, *International Trade Policy – A Developing Country Perspective* (London: Macmillan, 1990).

Mike Davis, *Planet of Slums* (London and New York: Verso, 2006).

Alan P. Dobson (ed.), *Deconstructing and Reconstructing the Cold War* (Aldershot: Ashgate, 1999).

Rick Fawn and Raymond Hinnebusch, *The Iraq War: Causes and Consequences* (Boulder and London: Lynne Rienner, 2006).

Lawrence Freedman, *Britain and Nuclear Weapons* (London: Macmillan, 1980).

Susan George, *A Fate Worse Than Debt* (London: Penguin, 1988).

Susan George, *The Lugano Report – On Preserving Capitalism in the Twenty-First Century* (London: Pluto Press, 1999).

Peter Gill and Mark Phythian, *Intelligence in an Insecure World* (Cambridge: Polity, 2006).

Roger Mac Ginty and Andrew Williams, *Conflict and Development* (London and New York: Routledge, 2009).

Bulent Gokay (ed.), *The Politics of Oil: A Survey* (London and New York: Routledge, 2006).

Joshua S. Goldstein, *International Relations*, 3rd edition (New York: Longman, 1999).

Shaun Gregory and Alistair Edwards, *A Handbook of Nuclear Weapons Accidents* (Bradford: University of Bradford, 1986).

William Greider, *One World Ready or Not – The Manic Logic of Global Capitalism* (London: Penguin, 1997).

Chuck Hansen, *U.S. Nuclear Weapons – The Secret History* (New York: Orion Books, 1988).

Ronald Higgins, *The Seventh Enemy* (London: Hodder and Stoughton, 1978).

Paul Hirst and Grahame Thompson, *Globalization in Question* (Cambridge: Polity, 1999).

David Holloway, *The Soviet Union and the Arms Race*, 2nd edition (New Haven and London: Yale University Press, 1984).

John Horgan, *The Psychology of Terrorism* (London and New York: Routledge, 2005).

Andrew Hurrell and Ngaire Woods (eds), *Inequality, Globalization and World Politics* (Oxford: Oxford University Press, 1999).

Ben Jackson, *Poverty and the Planet* (London: Penguin, 1990).

Aaron Karp, *Ballistic Missile Proliferation: The Politics and Technics* (Oxford: Oxford University Press, 1996).

Regina Cowen Karp (ed.), *Security With Nuclear Weapons?* (Oxford: Oxford University Press, 1991).

Regina Cowen Karp (ed.), *Security Without Nuclear Weapons?* (Oxford: Oxford University Press, 1992).

William V. Kennedy, *The Intelligence War* (London: Salamander, 1987).

Michael Klare, *Blood and Oil* (London and New York: Hamish Hamilton, 2004).

Michael Klare, *Rising Powers, Shrinking Planet: How Scarce Energy is Creating a New World Order* (Oxford: Oneworld, 2008).

Tim Lang and Colin Hines, *The New Protectionism* (London: Earthscan, 1993).

Bruce Lawrence (ed.), *Messages to the World: The Statements of Osama bin Laden* (London and New York: Verso, 2005).

Richard Ned Lebow and Janice Gross Stein, *We All Lost the Cold War* (Princeton: Princeton University Press, 1994).

Thomas Lines, *Making Poverty – A History* (London and New York: Zed Books, 2008).

Lee Marsden, *For God's Sake: The Christian Right and US Foreign Policy* (London and New York: Zed Books, 2008).

Donella H. Meadows, Dennis L. Meadows, Jorgen Randers and William W. Behrens III, *Limits to Growth* (London: Earth Island, 1972).

Zuhayr Mikdashi, *The International Politics of Natural Resources* (Ithaca and London: Cornell University Press, 1976).

Bjorn Moeller, *Dictionary of Alternative Defence* (Boulder: Lynne Rienner, 1995).

Ivan Molloy, *Rolling Back Revolution* (London and Sterling, VA: Pluto Press, 2001).

Alva Myrdal, *The Game of Disarmament* (Nottingham: Spokesman Books, 1980).

Jenny Pearce, *Under the Eagle* (London: Latin America Bureau, 1982).

Richard Peet, *Geography of Power: The Making of Global Economic Policy* (London and New York: Zed Press, 2007).

Norman Polmar, *Strategic Weapons: An Introduction* (New York: Crane Russak, 1982).

Tariq Ramadan, *Western Moslems and the Future of Islam* (Oxford: Oxford University Press, 2004).

Oliver Ramsbotham, Tom Woodhouse and Hugh Miall, *Contemporary Conflict Resolution* (Cambridge: Polity Press, 2005).

Darius Rejali, *Torture and Democracy* (Princeton and Oxford: Princeton University Press, 2007).

Bruce Riedell, *The Search for Al Qaeda: Its Leadership, Ideology and Future* (Washington, DC: Brookings Institution Press, 2008).

David Roberts, *Human Insecurity: Global Structures of Violence* (London and New York: Zed Books, 2008).

Paul Rogers, *A War Too Far: Iraq, Iran and the New American Century* (London and Ann Arbour, MI: Pluto Press, 2006).

Paul Rogers, *Global Security and the War on Terror: Elite Power and the Illusion of Control* (London and New York: Routledge, 2008).

Paul Rogers and Malcolm Dando, *A Violent Peace: Global Security After the Cold War* (London: Brassey's, 1992).

Wolfgang Sachs and Tilman Santarius (eds), *Fair Futures: Resource Conflicts, Security and Global Justice* (London and New York: Zed Books, 2005).

Scott D. Sagan, *The Limits of Safety – Organizations, Accidents and Nuclear Weapons* (Princeton, NJ: Princeton University Press, 1993).

Scott D. Sagan and Kenneth N. Waltz, *The Spread of Nuclear Weapons* (New York and London: W. W. Norton, 1995).

Trevor Salmon, *Issues in International Relations* (London and New York: Routledge, 2000).

Toby Shelley, *Oil: Politics, Poverty and the Planet* (London and New York: Zed Books, 2005).

Dan Smith and E. P. Thompson (eds), *Prospectus for a Habitable Planet* (London: Penguin, 1987).

Paul B. Stares, *Space Weapons and US Strategy* (London and Sydney: Croom Helm, 1985).

James Stephenson, *The 1994 Zapatista Rebellion in Southern Mexico – An Analysis and Assessment* (Camberley: Strategic and Combat Studies Institute, Army Staff College, 1995).

Joseph Stiglitz and Linda Bilmes, *The Three Trillion Dollar War* (London and New York: Allen Lane, 2008).

Geoff Tansey, Kath Tansey and Paul Rogers (eds), *A World Divided: Militarism and Development After the Cold War* (New York: St Martin's Press, 1994).

Geoff Tansey and Tasmin Rajotte (eds), *The Future Control of Food* (London and Sterling, VA: Earthscan, 2008).

Michael Tanzer, *The Race for Resources* (London: Heinemann, 1980).

E. P. Thompson and Dan Smith (eds), *Protest and Survive* (London: Penguin, 1980).

Anthony Vann and Paul Rogers (eds), *Human Ecology and World Development* (London and New York: Plenum Press, 1974).

Kevin Watkins, *Fixing the Rules* (London: Catholic Institute for International Relations, 1992).

Ernst von Weizacker, Amory B. Lovins and L. Hunter Lovins, *Factor Four: Doubling Wealth, Halving Resource Use* (London: Earthscan, 1997).

Arthur H. Westing, *Global Resources and International Conflict* (Oxford: Oxford University Press, 1986).

Richard Wilkinson and Kate Pickett, *The Spirit Level: Why More Equal Societies Almost Always Do Better* (London: Allen Lane, 2009).

David Woodward, *Contagion and Cure: Tackling the Crisis in Global Finance* (London: Catholic Institute for International Relations, 2000).

Index

Lightning Source UK Ltd.
Milton Keynes UK
UKHW010635081219
354962UK00001B/25/P

9 780745 329376